The Bamboo Fire

Second Edition

The Bamboo Fire

FIELD WORK WITH THE NEW GUINEA WAPE

Second Edition

William E. Mitchell
University of Vermont

WAVELAND

PRESS, INC.

Prospect Heights, Illinois

For more information about this book, write or call:

Waveland Press, Inc.
P.O. Box 400
Prospect Heights, Illinois 60070
(312) 634-0081

Cover photo: Malpul burning bamboo.

CONTENTS

ACKNOWLEDGEMENTS

To send an anthropological expedition to New Guinea – especially a family one like ours – and bring it home successfully takes the dedicated cooperation of many institutions and hundreds of people. I have expressed my gratitude to some of these institutions and individuals in other places. Here I wish to record a special note of appreciation to the National Institute of Health, whose research grant (# RO1 MH 18039 SSR) made our field work with the Wape people possible; the University of Vermont, administrator of the grant and my academic home; and Joyce Slayton Mitchell who shared the field work experience with me and encouraged the writing of this book.

I am grateful to Waveland Press for publishing this second edition which gives me the opportunity to correct errors that crept into the 1978 edition and to add an introductory chapter on anthropological field work and Wape society as well as an epilogue on my return to Wapeland in 1982 and some final thoughts about the field work enterprise. For their help in the preparation of this edition, I wish to thank Laurent A. Daloz, Aileen R.F. McGregor, Ned Mitchell and, especially, Annette Weiner.

The photographs in the book are mine with the exception of those by Joyce Slayton Mitchell on pages 132 top, 133, 134 bottom, 136, 144, 145, 146, and 147 top.

This edition is dedicated to the children, women and men of Taute village who so openly shared their lives with me. The following message in Melanesian Pidgin is for them:

> 'Mi Bil i laik tenkim olgera man, meri nau pikinini bilong Taute long lukautim nau skulim mipela long ol pasin bilong Taute long taim mipela stap insait long yupela. Long dispela buk mi yet wokim sampela lik lik stori long dispela taim. Mi tenkyu tru. Em tasol.'

ABOUT THE AUTHOR

*William E. Mitchell is Professor of Anthropology at the
University of Vermont. As an undergraduate, he studied
psychology at Wichita State University then attended
Columbia University where he received a master's degree in
philosophy and in 1969, his doctorate in anthropology. He
has done field work in Papua New Guinea among the Wape,
Lujere and Iatmul people of the Sepik River area and in New
York City he has studied a children's psychiatric ward, Chinese
students from mainland China and Jewish families of Eastern
European background. He has published extensively in the
fields of family and kinship, and psychological and medical
anthropology. His publications include,* Mishpokhe: A
Study of New York City Jewish Family Clubs; Kinship
and Casework: Family Networks and Social Interven-
tion *(with Hope Jensen Leichter);* The Living, Dead and
Dying: Music of the New Guinea Wape, *an lp recording;
and a film,* Magical Curing.

Some mornings the fog sinks deep around our ridge, and there is no sunrise. Then Aif, or maybe Malpul, disappears into the bamboo grove and sets part of it ablaze. The fire burns hot; the bamboo explodes in loud reports. Now, my neighbors say, the fog will be driven away, the sun will shine, and we will look out over the forest and mountains into the sky again.

And so it is with field work. The anthropologist sets a blaze of inquiry to drive away his ignorance and bring the light of understanding to a culture he doesn't know. This book is about such an inquiry. It is my story of discovery living among the Wape people of New Guinea.

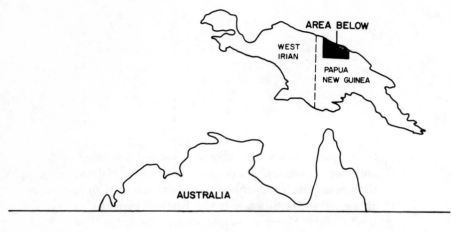

AREA BELOW

WEST
IRIAN

PAPUA
NEW GUINEA

AUSTRALIA

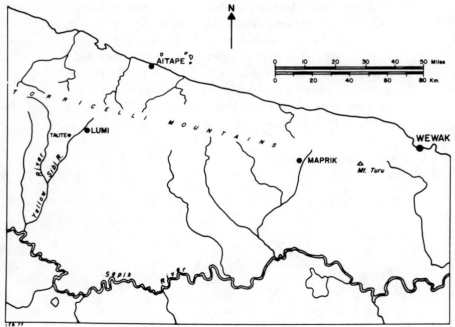

N

AITAPE

TORRICELLI MOUNTAINS

TAUTE LUMI

Yellow River

SIBIR River

MAPRIK

Mt. Turu

WEWAK

Sepik River

0   10   20   30   40   50 Miles
0   20   40   60   80 Km.

LEB 77

INTRODUCTION

The South Pacific islands long have been a favorite place for anthropologists like myself to visit to learn how indigenous peoples organize their cultural lives. Since the latter part of the 19th century, anthropologists have come to the South Pacific from all over the world to carry out their ethnographic field work studies. Today, islanders themselves trained in the method and theory of anthropology are increasingly making their own ethnographic studies and offering new perspectives on their traditional cultures and the changes induced by the impact of colonial powers who, in some cases, still occupy their lands.

The peoples of New Guinea, the largest island in the South Pacific and the second largest island in the world, have been host to over 200 cultural anthropologists since the Russian anthropologist, Mikloucho-Maclay first arrived in 1871. I made my own first field trip to New Guinea in 1967 and later returned for a two year stay with my family that extended from May 1, 1970, to April 30, 1972. It was the two most extraordinary years of my life. I have had both happier and more difficult years, but none in which my everyday life was so totally transformed or my emotional and intellectual abilities so strenuously challenged.

It is not uncommon for anthropologists to feel this way about their field work experiences. Field work is so vastly different in almost every respect from one's usual life that it is vividly framed both experientially and in one's memories from what preceded or followed it. This is not just because the locale and people are often foreign, memorable though this may be, but rather that the successful field worker must be unusually sensitive to the strange and variable events that surround and engulf him or her while, at the same time, constantly cultivating a heightened awareness of self as a perceptive recording instrument.

13

Field work, then, is not a nine to five, Monday to Friday job, but the total and unremitting emersion of the anthropologist into another way of life that must be learned. As the task is immense, the time limited, and one's abilities circumscribed, the pressure to produce understanding is unrelenting. It is this sustained affective intensity of the field work experience that makes it such a riveting experience and marks it off so distinctly from the rest of one's life.

Because anthropology is primarily a field work science, it is different from the laboratory oriented experimental sciences in a number of ways. Whereas the experimental sciences make their observations in constructed settings that permit the variables influencing the outcome of the experiment to be known and controlled, anthropology, like the science of ethology, is a field oriented science whose object of inquiry is life itself as experienced in its *natural* setting. So, instead of bringing people into the laboratory to observe their behavior in a controlled experiment, the anthropologist goes to the people and lives with them in their own setting as they go about their daily activities. To understand how people organize their lives both in thought and in action, there is no other way but to settle among them for a very long time.

The field worker's methodological goal is to observe, face-to-face, the actual on-going events of a society with a minimum of personal interference. This technique is called "participant observation" and it is the hallmark of the field work method. These direct observations are then supplemented by informant interviews recorded by tape and/or pen with various individuals who explain what was actually witnessed as well as providing information on an almost limitless number of other topics about the people and their environment. Depending upon the nature of the particular research problem, other data are carefully collected including, for example, films and photographs, census and statistical material, cultural artifacts, botanical samples, and climatological records.

Once out of the field, the anthropologist will study and analyze the information gathered to produce his or her findings in a series of research reports and ethnographic accounts that may continue for many years. In this way the findings become a part of the scientific record and available to others for generalizations about human thought and action proffering new hypotheses that, in turn, generate new excursions into the field.

Although the physical and social sciences differ considerably, today it is considered irrelevant to question whether one science is more "scientific" than the other. Each science, as Thomas Kuhn recognized in his 1962 book,

The Structure of Scientific Revolutions, is the result of a particular paradigm that demarcates what it will study, the questions asked, the methods and tools employed, and the way findings are presented. Since these paradigms are not detached from social reality but deeply rooted in historical time and cultural space, no science can be called "pure." Each science in its own way makes a valuable contribution to understanding the nature of the universe and its inhabitants. The quantitative techniques of chemistry could no more elucidate the religious beliefs of a New Guinea people than anthropology's techniques of participant observation and interviewing could elucidate the dynamics of chemical kinetics.

Anthropology however, unlike many sciences, is unusual in terms of the depth and extent of the emotional and intellectual interactions between the scientist and her or his object of inquiry. In anthropological field work a human being — the anthropologist — studies a group of other human beings. The observer and the observed both share a common humanity with the ability to speak and to listen to each other, to cry and to laugh, to hurt and to comfort. Although an objective stance permeates all the sciences, try as one might, the anthropologist cannot feel morally neutral about human behavior the way a chemist might about chemical compounds or a geologist about rocks. Whereas the calibrations on laboratory beakers can be readily standardized, the observations of anthropologists — each a separate person with a complex physiological, psychological and social background — cannot because the human world, unlike the physical, is a moral one filled with conflicting ideas about right and wrong. Indeed, it is just these kinds of value differences that are the subject matter of anthropology and contribute to its unique importance as a science.

Thus, while graduate school training may succeed in orienting anthropologists to the cannons of science and the theories and methods of modern anthropology, it does not and cannot make them "see" the same things in the field. For example, many women anthropologists — and some men too — influenced by feminist's revelations of sexism in the traditional anthropological paradigm, are looking differently at women's work and relationships and seeing new things. Although Bronislaw Malinowski's contributions to a more exacting field work methodology helped make him a towering figure in modern anthropology, it was a woman anthropologist, Annette Weiner, working in the same islands Malinowski studied some 50 years earlier, who could "see" that Trobriand women — not just men — produced wealth and that it was strategically tied to the men's wealth that Malinowski recorded.

No single anthropologist, regardless of how well trained and personally perceptive, can "see" it all. The phenomenological world of human society is too vast and too complicated and our research paradigms and individual abilities too limited for that. Regardless of the field worker's insightfulness, depth of rapport with the people studied or the extensiveness of objective measurements, (e.g., village censuses, children's size and growth, amount of different foods consumed, number of kin terms, or the use of film, photography and tape recordings to help record and verify what was seen and heard), one can only approximate a complete recording of the experience itself. From these data the anthropologist constructs a valuable *version* of what was seen and heard at one point in time and stamped with his or her personal and theoretical proclivities as shaped by interactions with the people studied. Within this research context, an anthropologist's account is a legitimate scientific finding upholding both the spirit and method of science which recognizes no specific account, judgment or experiment as final. In anthropology as in all science, old problems approached in new and imaginative ways can produce new data that may augment or correct accepted findings and stimulate new interpretations and insights.

It is one thing for anthropologists to "see" the people they study, but what about the way anthropologists "see" themselves in relationship to the products of their research? It is only recently that anthropologists have become reflective in any disciplined way about the place of the self in field work and its impact on their books, articles, films and photographs. Although the science of anthropology is dependent upon the anthropologist *qua* person in the production of knowledge, the traditional tendency was to eliminate the anthropologist's active presence when presenting the data, to consciously repudiate the self in an endeavor to mimic the prestigious experimental sciences. Often the anthropologist was purposely unseen and unfelt through an act of "objective magic" that dissolved his or her presence. At best, the anthropologist would only appear as a bona fide person in a book's preface, a footnote aside, or in an appendix on methods and, sometimes, not even then. With the subjective observer eliminated, the superficial appearance was one of objective scientific rigor. While this classical approach to the writing of ethnography has produced some marvelous books of ethnographic description, a closer look reveals an account that sometimes distorts the authenticity of the relationship between the field work experience and its products.

Today, however, there is a strong concern with the development of a reflexive attitude in anthropological writing wherein the writer is acknowledged as an observer observing him or herself observing others. Instead of the anthropologist's account focusing an analytical light only on others, that light is reflected back on the self as the creator of the analysis. The resulting account can be ethnographically richer and, with its inclusion of reflexive knowledge through the multiple focusing on the self viewing others, more scientifically authentic in its attempt to signify the natural events of the field work experience.

Some anthropologists are experimenting with writing their ethnographic accounts of the people with whom they have lived and worked in this way. Others, as I have done in this book, concentrate on describing the field work process where the field worker, by definition, cannot be excluded. In the following pages I have tried to give the reader a feeling of the reflexive nature of the field work experience itself; to demonstrate not only how the anthropologist proceeds in her or his work, but to describe the social and psychological context in which that work evolves and how the anthroplogist responds to it both within oneself and in communications with others. So in some ways, this is a very personal book. It is not so much a book about the Wape people as it is about how one anthropologist tried to understand them and the kinds of intercultural problems that were engendered in that process.

Before I begin my account of fieldwork with the Wape (pronounced "wah'pay"), a few summary notes on their country, language and customs may be helpful. Today the Wape are citizens of Papua New Guinea, an independent nation with a population of approximately two and one-half million, that occupies the eastern half of the island. The western half, Irian Jaya or West Irian, is a part of Indonesia.

At the time of my 1970-72 field work, the country was preparing for independence and profound national changes were underway. These changes, however, had little direct impact upon the residents of Taute (pronounced "tau'tay") village with whom I lived, although they were of considerable concern to the local white expatriates working in the government and in business and missionary ventures.

When I arrived in New Guinea in 1970, the country was divided into two areas, the Territory of New Guinea occupying the northern half where I worked, and the Territory of Papua, occupying the southern half. Both were under the combined administration of Australia. For a number of years the United Nations had exerted pressure upon Australia to prepare the Territories for independence as a single country. A ninety-four member

House of Assembly elected by popular vote was formed in 1964, but much of its legislation remained subject to the approval of appointed government officials. On July 1, 1971, the national name of the Territories became, "Papua New Guinea" and a national emblem and flag was adopted. Two and a half years later on December 1, 1973, the country became self governing with Australia retaining control of defense and foreign relations. Full independence was finally proclaimed in 1975. When I returned for a brief visit in 1982, I was able to access some of the changes independence has wrought and these are discussed in the Epilogue.

To assist the reader who wishes to compare the Wape to other tribal societies, the following is a brief summary of some of the important characteristics of their society. The Wape live in a mountainous tropical forest habitat, are slash and burn horticulturalists and reside in sedentary villages. Post marital residence is generally virilocal, patrilineal clans are ideally exogamous while patrilineages are strictly so. Marriage is by bridewealth and polygyny is permitted but rare. Cousin kin terms are Omaha. The society is egalitarian in terms of male status and, although the society is hierarchical in terms of sex and age differences, both women and the young enjoy higher status than in many New Guinea societies. While most Wape are nominal Christians, traditional religious beliefs and practices are of major importance. Most men also are members of curing societies that involve the population in an extensive system of culturally significant ritual exchanges.

The indigenous language of the Wape people is Olo and belongs to the Torricelli Phylum. All Olo terms in the text are italicized. The *lingua franca* of Papua New Guinea is Melanesian Pidgin (also called "Tok Pisin" or, less accurately, "Pidgin English") and these words appear in inverted commas. Pidgin, in its ancestral form, originated on the sugarcane plantations of Northeastern Australia in the mid-19th century. It was used there as an "inter-native" language by the indentured laborers who came from New Guinea and nearby islands speaking many different languages. As it spread back to New Guinea it became the major language of inter-tribal communication in a land with over 700 mutually distinct languages. With English, it is today one of the two official languages of Papua New Guinea.

1

▼▲▼▲▼▲▼▲▼▲▼▲▼▲▼

THE FIRST SPARKS

Slowly we taxied away from the black and white faces along the airstrip calling and waving good-by. The motor's roar filled my emptiness and closed my ears. Lifting gracefully toward the sun, the small plane soared in a sweeping arc, then, according to New Guinea custom, fell in a farewell salute toward our friends below. Diving earthward I watched the tiny figures grow big and warmly familiar, then slip back into a miniature world of palm trees and forest as we rejoined the sky. Sister Florianne was on her motorbike, white habit flying, scurrying back to the mission. As the other figures moved away, only Sengu, the young Wape woman who had helped care for Ned and Elizabeth during our last months in Wapeland, stood fast, gazing upward toward the disappearing plane.

I too was transfixed, choked on a monstrous lump of sadness that grabbed at my throat as a great sigh surged within me. Staring toward the window, I bit my lip with the pain of loss as when someone you have loved and fought with dies. I reached out for

Joyce's hand, but we did not look at one another or speak—we were lost in personal worlds of sorrow and relief.

Below, the forest appeared bland and impersonal, but I had walked its trails, lived with its people, watched its demons dance, and heard its ghosts call into the night. Now it was over and the finality of our good-bys cut me deeply. The excitement, the boredom, the fun, the terror, the tenderness were gone. We were going home, back to where we had started.

The snow was off the meadow, but at the edge of the woods it still lay in patches flecked with crimson buds of the swamp maple. Spring peepers soon would pipe their joyous song throughout a valley festooned with trout lilies, foam flowers, and violets. Another Vermont winter was almost over.

I sat in the milkhouse, now my study and warming hut for chilled lambs, working intently on my expedition plans. New Guinea — a tropical island of many different cultural groups that has enticed anthropologists to its enormous interior for one hundred years. One of the world's great laboratories of cultural behavior, its human communities are small enough and isolated enough to give the anthropologist a fighting chance to understand what is going on and why.

By the end of May the grant application requesting funds for the expedition was completed, and I carried it down the road and across the brook, past the lilacs and apple blossoms to the mailbox. It was my favorite time of year. Yet, as I turned back empty-handed, I felt fitful and strangely vulnerable. I had done all I could to convince the judges that my project was important and that I could successfully achieve its goals. My future was now in the hands of others, a situation guaranteed to make most men edgy and irritable.

For the next six months I lived in a nether world somewhere between New Guinea and northern Vermont. As the months ticked by on the kitchen clock, summer and autumn lingered and left. The suspense and my anxiety mounted.

The chances of getting a grant were poor. In 1969, government granting agencies and foundations began cutting back, and colleagues who knew the ins and outs of grantsmanship better than I could only further disillusion me. So Joyce and I kept our plans to ourselves as much as possible. Nothing, we agreed, is more dismal than explaining an enterprise lost. But after dinner, when the children were tucked into bed and we were alone, Joyce and I would talk about our plans. We discussed what to do with the house, the small flock of sheep, two aging cars, and Taya, whom we had raised from a pup. And with a flush of enthusiasm, we speculated about our lives in New Guinea.

From a family point of view, it was the perfect time for an extended field trip. Ned, four, and Elizabeth, three, were old enough so our world was still theirs. If that world shifted to a distant village in the forested mountains of New Guinea, we knew they would be happy as long as we were there with them.
knew they would be happy as long as we were there with them.

Two years before, I had spent the summer in New Guinea as a member of an American Museum of Natural History anthropological expedition, and I knew exactly where I wanted to return for field work—the cloud-clad Torricelli Mountains. The range stood between the sprawling malarial swamps of the fabled Sepik River and the island's north coast. It would be a gentler climate for the family than the unbearably hot and humid Sepik lowlands, swarming with Anopheles mosquitoes; a vast basin of hot swamp water through which the Sepik coils for seven hundred miles to finally spew its yellow mud and tropical debris twenty miles into the sea. I had lived in those swamps before, and the Torricelli Mountains would be a climactic paradise by comparison.

Anthropologically, the Torricelli Mountain area was unknown. Only one of the dozen or so tribal groups was studied. Gilbert Lewis, his wife, and toddler son were just returning to England from field work with the Gnau people, who lived east of the tribes in which I was most interested. His letters to me from New Guinea were filled with data on the conditions of field work, including the availability of supplies, special health problems confronting a family, and descriptive sketches of the Gnau and other peoples he had visited. I read his letters over and over with those of three local missionaries, Leo Hoy and Lyn Wark, both Australian physicians, and Don McGregor, a New Zealander, who answered in thorough detail my requests for information.

Our plan—or was it only a dream—was to spend at least two years in the field studying two tribes in as much depth as time, our energy, and wits allowed. The guiding problem for our study would be one that had continuously fascinated me since my undergraduate days and is central to much of my accomplished research. What intrigues me most about humans are their "therapeutic systems," those negative patterns of thought signaling what is wrong—not right—with people and the culturally arbitrary techniques of instruction, punishment, and healing invoked to transform the miscreant and the miserable into acceptable citizens. For it is what we are taught to abhor and fear in others and ourselves that is at the affective core of each culture. But to study what is despised and feared in a culture is also to understand what is honored and desired; for the "good" and the "bad" are polar opposites, yet, paradoxically, intimately engaged in a contrasting process that defines and determines the other. So people invent ways to remedy the bad, to correct or eradicate what threatens the good life, and to conserve the cherished concepts and customs, the organisms, and the things of which cultures are made.

In New Guinea, I wondered, what happens when the native and Western cultures, with their contrasting traditions about the good and the bad, come into continued contact? Are the therapeutic systems for changing the bad to the good—always a major cultural preoccupation—complementary or in conflict? And what is the nature of this relationship? Is it a simple and separable interface or do discordant values and actions become intermeshed in the lives of the people, and, if so, with what consequences for the individual as well as the culture?

By late November the fields were again encrusted with snow. Then, suddenly, a long-distance phone call and a friendly but businesslike voice offering congratulations. Yes, the grant is approved and funded; you are very lucky, but there are a couple of details on the budget. Could you delete one of the two Leica cameras without compromising the expedition's goals? I was pounding inside but in the disciplined fashion of the American male inhibited the extent of my joy, for Western bureaucracies are not organized to cope with affect-laden academics. The culturally rational, if personally illogical, thing to do was to discuss the camera. We do. With a politely sincere "Thank you for calling me," I hang up. Tears fill my eyes, and for a rare and delirious moment I am lifted out of myself and float skyward into the delicious Sea of Success. An exquisite sound wafts through my consciousness. I got the grant! And how do I *know* that I got the grant? Because they took a camera away from me. Of just such imponderables does ecstasy arise.

That night the old farm house glowed with happiness as Joyce and I splashed champagne and telephoned our great news to amazed family and friends. At the university I arranged for my teaching obligations to be assumed by others, and then, together, we made final plans for purchasing the expedition—our expedition—equipment and supplies. The grant began January 1, just weeks away, and our timetable was exceedingly tight. I delighted in the pressures. After months in limbo, each day was now a precious unit of accomplishment. For our gear to arrive by ship in New Guinea by May 1, it must be purchased, catalogued, packed, and sitting on a Boston dock by March 1. The children had scarcely put away their Christmas toys when I whisked out the tree and we turned our home into an expedition warehouse.

Everything we had to have for the expedition was to be purchased before we set out, for the availability of merchandise in a developing country like Papua New Guinea is, at best, unpredictable. Soon the house was jammed with an incongruous array of scientific and camping equipment and supplies. The handsome Victorian parlor looked like an Army and Navy store, and only with care did we manage to keep an open path in the kitchen between the stove and refrigerator. Ned and Elizabeth roamed among the impressive litter exclaiming; there was no doubt in their minds that we were going on a very long trip, far, far away.

As the technical equipment arrived, there was much I had to learn. To master the intricacies of the cine-sound filming equipment I went down to New York where Sander Kirsch, an extremely knowledgeable and sympathetic photographer who had helped select the equipment, and Jacques Van Vlack, an expert documentary cameraman and filmmaker, instructed me with skill and patience. Once in the field, I was on my own; there would be no one to correct my mistakes or whom I could call when the equipment broke down, as, I was told, it invariably would. With no special mechanical flair but high motivation I listened, took detailed notes, and practiced. By the time I returned home I was beginning to feel less estranged, although hardly intimate, with the equipment that initially had overwhelmed me with its intricacies.

Then, one by one, Joyce and I packed each trunk and crate, fitting the items together as carefully as a puzzle and listing the contents in a large black notebook. The weight of each container was important for, once unloaded on a mountain airstrip, it would be lashed with vines to poles and carried on the bare shoulders of men, step by step, along steep and slippery trails to a village deep in the forest. But try as we would to break up categories of items to distribute the weight evenly, the trunks containing batteries for operating the movie camera and tape recorders were always heaviest. I pitied the men who would carry them.

And then the job was done. The children laughingly climbed over and around the eleven trunks, six crates, and the three sturdy patrol boxes loaned to us by fellow anthropologist Rhoda Metraux that were veterans of her earlier New Guinea expeditions. It took several trips in the sagging station wagon to carry them all to the university's shops for addressing and banding. But we had met our deadline. By the first of March our expedition cargo was sitting on the wharves of Boston harbor.

I had watched Joyce throw herself into the packing with her usual fervor. Yet I knew it was not *her* life's ambition to live with unstudied tribes in a remote corner of the world. Even the farm was often too isolated for her tastes. And, although she knew a lot of anthropology and would be working full time on the research the first year, she had no desire to be an anthropologist. Her career was in counseling and in writing books in education. Going to New Guinea meant she must set aside work that was of immense importance to her. We talked about this before we made the decision to apply for a field-work grant. She was wholehearted in her support of the project as long as it was a family project and, as much as possible, we live together.

It was then ten years since I first told Joyce of my ardent commitment to anthropological field work. The streets of New York glistened in a cold winter rain as we traveled uptown in a taxi, talking seriously about our lives and the future. Soon we would be engaged and married. Already I had studied the subculture of a children's psychiatric ward, the adaptation of mainland Chinese students exiled in New York, and was then working on a project with other social scientists examining the kinship ties of Jewish families and how caseworkers opt to change them. But I knew, sooner or later, I would go to a faraway island and discover for myself a way of life, a culture, that was scientifically unknown.

Since that ride, Joyce knew in sometimes painful detail how I had worked and trained for this opportunity. Though we never said it, we both knew she was going to New Guinea out of allegiance to our marriage and her love for me.

The house was a shambles from the packing, but neither of us saw any relevance in restoring order. The treasures of our home already seemed less interesting, more banal and limiting, than the expedition gear now adventuring on the high seas. So we began to finish the work of going away. Ironically, the farm buildings would be safer closed and abandoned than with untried renters. The extreme severity of northern Vermont winters take considerable ingenuity and perseverance to gracefully survive. And the house itself, so very old, had many idiosyncracies that only we appreciated and understood. Who else, I asked, would slither like a lizard in dirt and cobwebs to the far corner under the kitchen to change the light bulb that kept the water pipes from freezing. I felt like moving out every time *I* had to do it. Others certainly would.

Valuables were placed in storage, the sheep and autos sold, and Taya, who accepted me like no human could, was sadly given away to a family who, like us, lived on a farm. And then there were parties with relatives and friends where we said good-by. A few thought us irresponsible for taking the children to live among a distant and unknown primitive tribe; others openly envied us for the rare opportunity to legitimately shed our everyday lives for such an adventure.

With almost perverse excitement, I covered, shuttered, and sealed the windows and doors of the house and barn. A heavy chain was set across the secluded road. The buildings, once warmly inviting, stood in silent despair like ghosts who could not see. I couldn't wait to be gone. As we drove away, I was flooded with feelings of freedom. It was April Fool's Day, 1970.

Darkness and clouds shrouded the great, rugged, lush island that lay below until we were almost on the runway. Then we saw the Owen Stanley Range, its silhouette muted in the morning mists, where the advancing Japanese were stopped in a heroic battle of World War II. Port Moresby had changed in the three years since my first visit. It had lost much of its colonial patina and was fast becoming a very modern town. The hotel was new, air-conditioned, and like thousands of others around the world. Only the carved curios for sale in the lobby were unmistakably New Guinea. There were older, more typical, and cheaper lodgings available in Moresby but I had selected this one for a gentle entry. Our color-coordinated bedroom was interchangeable with a dozen others we had stayed in from London to Manila as we moved slowly toward New Guinea to coincide our arrival more or less with our gear.

But the shipping agent in Port Moresby had no record of our trunks, nor did he seem at all concerned. After all, he intimated, this was New Guinea. All our equipment, much of it specially adapted for the research and irreplaceable, lost or misdirected! Gentlemanly insistence, I quickly grasped, was simply ignored. Then I reached back for all of the assertiveness I had perfected from twelve years of living in New York City but seldom used in Vermont, and, with aggressive badgering, numerous cables, and days of worry, I located our trunks on a dock in Sydney. They had been there for weeks; the Sydney agent had neglected to transship them on to New Guinea. Old timers told me we were lucky. Some people, they said, *never* get their gear.

Shirley Matthews, an official of the New Guinea Research Unit of Australian National University and a person of immense warmth, vitality, and resourcefulness, arranged for us to leave our high-rent hotel to occupy a house for visiting scholars and gave us the kind of detailed advice on everything we asked that saved us from weeks of floundering and frustration. Through her initiation we attended a conference on the politics of Melanesia at the new University of Papua New Guinea, where we met other scientists working in the Territory. Then, after calling on various members of the Australian officialdom, both public and private, to explain our research and enlist their help if we should later need it, we left the capital. Our destination was Wewak, the most important administrative and commercial town on the north central coast, where a youthful Margaret Mead, Reo Fortune, John Whiting, and Gregory Bateson—the Sepik's celebrated pioneering anthropologists of the late 1920s and early 1930s—had stopped to buy supplies, visit officials, and arrange for transportation up the mighty, muddy Sepik River.

Wewak is a pretty town built on a small, high peninusla thrust into the Bismarck Sea and is still the jumping-off place for the East and West Sepik Districts. Here missionaries, traders, and patrol officers living on isolated stations also come to be rejuvenated. Actually, Wewak is not especially impressive when first visited, but after three to six months in the bush, it attains the magnetism and glamor of a tropical Paris or Rome. Joyce and I were so indebted to the town that, on our return to Vermont, we named our new pup "Wewak" so we could say those marvelous syllables daily.

During World War II all of the Wewak area was held by the Japanese until finally routed in a terrible battle at the end of the war. Local men can guide you to vine-covered plane wrecks but the rusting boat hulks along the coastline are visible to all. Once, when I was waiting for a plane at Wewak's airport, a middle-aged Australian man pointed with anxious nostalgia to the hills that edge this airstrip by the sea. There he had fought the Japanese hand to hand. Now he had returned alone, so many years later, to revisit this place of youthful terror. Four hundred fifty of his countrymen and five thousand Japanese died in those hills and on the bright sandy beaches.

Wewak, unlike Port Moresby with its hundreds of automobiles thundering along palm-fringed roads, has the feel and tempo of an older New Guinea. While we played with the children in the shallow, splashy surf, farther out decorously clothed women stood breast deep in the blue-green waters, fishing with long bamboo poles. In the deep water beyond lay several ancient coastal trading boats loading cargo from even smaller craft, for in 1970 Wewak did not have a deep-water wharf. Periodically the voices of the laborers drifted in to us with the sea gulls and foam.

We stayed at the Wewak Hotel, the town's most socially important landmark. A low, insignificant, rambling building, it has a majestic location on the cliffs at the tip of the peninsula with magnificent views of the sea and the outlying islands of Muschu and Kairiru. During the Japanese occupation, Kairiru Island was the port for a tragic voyage. In 1943, a Japanese death ship, the destroyer *Akikaze*, sailed from the island for Rabaul with a cargo of war internees. After the ship stopped at Manus Island to take on other internees, there were over sixty, including twenty-one nuns and three infants. But before the ship reached Rabaul, the adults, one by one, were strung up by their hands to a gallows, shot, and cast into the wake of the ship. The three babies were tossed over alive.

Our room in the Wewak Hotel, Spartan and clean and in-

nocent of a decorator's overwrought hand, was pale green everywhere one looked. It was located in a newly completed wing and
mercifully air-conditioned, for the heat of Wewak is often extremely oppressive. Joyce, a native Vermonter who has spent the
majority of her life in a climate where twenty below is not a topic
for conversation, lay down on the bed and closed her eyes. I wondered what she was thinking. But there was no doubt what was
on the children's minds. To their surprise and shocked irritation,
I escorted them to the common toilet facilities at the end of the
units.

Frankly, I was very pleased with the room. I could recall my
first stay at the hotel in 1967, when not only was the bathroom a
community one, but I also shared the bedroom with strangers
who wandered in and out all night. That room was located just
above one of New Guinea's most raucous bars. By custom, not
law, one side of the bar is patronized by blacks, the other by
whites, but on Saturday nights they spill into each other's noisy
bastions and onto the lawns where the astringent smell of damp
salt air and the opulent fragrance of frangipani blossoms mix with
the earthy smells of beer and sweat. There, sooner or later, you
could meet every Westerner in the Sepik Districts, the traders,
prospectors, teachers, laborers, clerks, patrol officers, labor recruiters, and scientists—everyone but the most conservative
evangelical missionaries—who come to the pub for an evening of
camaraderie, gossip, and grog.

Wewak's shopping center is a block long, a short, dusty
street that terminates with the native market and the sea. The
market was over, but a few vendors, mostly women, remained
with their betel nuts, sweet potatoes, taro, sugar cane, or bananas
to entice the late shopper. We opened accounts at Tang Mows
and Burns Philp, the largest and most dependable stores, who
would send our supplies by mission or government plane to the
airstrip nearest our village. Perspiring under the intense sun, we
ate ice cream cones, poked about the small Chinese trade stores
filled with shoddy but engaging merchandise, and admired the
beauty of the young New Guineans: the men, immaculate in

their Australian-style shorts and gay shirts, and the women in flowered mini-skirts, the shortest we had seen on a trip that had taken us more than halfway around the world. The older people, by contrast, sat in faded and tattered clothes on the dry dirt in corners of shade, visiting, suckling babies, and chewing betel nut. Ned and Elizabeth viewed them without comment. They already had seen more versions of poverty than most people ever know. And there was no doubt they were sated with exotica. On the last leg of our trip, only the Living Goddess of Kathmandu, a child like themselves, seemed to stir their imagination as she stood on her courtyard balcony, a minute and exquisite figure, waving them a greeting. Patient and enthusiastic travelers, they tolerated our eccentricities about what to see as long as we occasionally visited a beach, a park, or a pool.

The small mail plane that made the one-hour flight into the Torricelli Mountains took off on schedule. The morning mists had lifted and the day was brilliantly clear. I would go alone to Lumi, the government headquarters for the Lumi Sub-District, to find temporary quarters until we established ourselves in a village. Accommodations, I assumed, would be no problem. I had written from India to the Assistant District Commissioner, the station's ranking official, about our plans, then cabled from Moresby our impending arrival.

As the plane flew west along the coast, I was completely absorbed with the landscape below. Only an occasional hamlet or garden broke the forest tapestry, and I wondered what the people were like who lived and worked there. As we approached the old German settlement of Aitape, the islands of Tumleo and Ali lay low and green in the sparkling water. On these islands in the 1890s the first permanent European settlements were made by German Catholic missionaries.

For twenty-five years the Germans actively dominated this coastline until forced to leave by Australian troops at the beginning of World War I. During the period of German rule the coast was extensively explored and mapped, mission stations were established, and large coconut plantations planted. But there is no evidence that the Torricelli Mountains that stand at Aitape's back door were penetrated. According to the mountain people, the first white men entering into their domain were adventurous Australians looking for gold, oil, and cheap plantation labor.

Flying over a long, grassy field near the beach, the pilot turned to tell me it was Tadji Air Base, now seldom used, from which American bombers had thundered north to bomb Japanese-held islands after an American landing had conquered the coast in 1944. The Japanese forces retreated along the coast and into the Torricelli Mountains, dying of starvation and sickness, especially dysentery, which spread rapidly to the native population. An unheard-of disease for which they had no cure, the terrified people fled from their villages to isolated garden huts, where they continued to die by the hundreds. Some villages simply disappeared.

The stop in Aitape was brief. Standing by the plane as the pilot unloaded the mail and heavy supplies, I looked with excited expectancy toward the Torricelli Mountains, which arose over 6,000 feet from the shallow coastal plain. The plane surged upward from the little airstrip abbreviated by swamp, skimming the towering jungle of trees and vines. High on a mountain near the crest of the range a long, slender waterfall poured out of the forest, splashing and twinkling in the bright morning sun, then plunged into the green gloom.

New Guinea planes never fly high enough for me. Instead of flying over the range, we were flying through it, and the forest's vivid tracery and intricate lace were startlingly displayed at eye level in the windows surrounding the plane. Spread out before me was a vast broken country of narrow ridges and hills that gradually descended toward the Sepik River fifty miles away. Beyond, a generous ribbon of cloud marked the mighty Thurnwald Range, named in honor of the courageous anthropologist-explorer who, in 1913, became the first Westerner to discover and ascend the headwaters of the Sepik River and the first to study a Sepik society.

Many of the ridges that lay below me were crowned with coconut palms, a sure sign of human habitation, and occasionally I caught a glimpse of the thatched roof of a village house. The area was much more heavily populated than I had supposed. Ahead and to my left, a thin tan ruler stretched the length of a low ridge. The Lumi airstrip, I was sure. Then several tin roofs flashed a dazzling welcome into the skies.

Although the airstrip was the longest and most important in the area, the Lumi houses seemed scattered and few. The wheels touched the sandy earth with expert precision and rolled down the runway to the loading bay. Everywhere people had stopped to watch the thrice-weekly mail plane while running children waved as we sped by, just as I had greeted the puffing freight trains of my Kansas childhood. I was very anxious.

My everyday strategy in field work, as it is with life, is to maintain a low profile so I can get on with my work with a minimum of fuss. Obviously, it is a strategy that can work only some of the time. Today, every Westerner on the station would know that the "American bloke" was on the plane, and, undoubtedly, I would be a diverting topic of conversation, positive or negative, for a day or two. Most importantly, their impressions of me would influence the extent of their cooperation. In their strategic positions as officials and missionaries, they controlled access to information, documents, outside communications, transportation, and supplies. They were the people who could actually make or break the expedition. Mine was an unenviable postion of dependency and powerlessness. Would they like me? Would I like them? Whoever and whatever they were, there would be no alternatives.

Even before leaving the plane, I spotted Dr. Lyn Wark in the small knot of Westerners waiting for their supplies. Only she was glancing toward the plane as if to find someone. A slender and attractive woman in her thirties, with fair skin and auburn hair, she greeted me warmly and introduced me to the other Europeans, including Roger Fairhall, the acting Assistant District Commissioner in charge of the station, and Father Gerald Walsh, who headed the local Franciscan mission. I remember nothing of those initial introductions except being struck by the relaxed cordiality. It was a very good omen. Some outstations—I had known one well—are paranoid enclaves of factionalism that radiate a paralyzing tension. Lumi, I was almost sure, was not one of these.

Outstations hold a morbid fascination for me, and my feelings about them are extremely conflicted. For one, I deplore the arrogance of Western culture that categorically defines simpler people as inferior and then, with outrageous self-righteousness and mechanical muscle, shows them what is good for themselves. Like retarded children or senile elders, they are institutionalized in their own land to be lectured, threatened, teased, and bullied—even killed—to bring their behavior into compliance with alien ideals.

Yet, I came to admire many of the men and women, idealists all, working to bring good health, modern education, and Christianity to the local people. And their personal favors for me and my family are countless. In terms of the values of Western culture, their work is courageous and important. And I find a part of myself agreeing. For industrialization has spread a network of demands and trade offs throughout the world that leaves no society, however far away, untouched. It is naïve to believe that such societies can stay unto themselves on protected reserves. Perhaps that is possible for an animal that does not possess culture, but humans live in a complex material and symbolic context that is always changing; they see and hear new things, and they want them for themselves. So, on outstations, my point of identification shifts and weaves through conflicting versions of history and cultural allegiances, swaying as a drunken reveler, a hypocrite to both the native and Western image of society.

The natives, mostly silent, stood along the edge of the loading bay watching the tiny group of privileged Westerners welcome the newcomer and receiving their goods from the pilot. An invisible line, but as fast and unyielding as a granite wall, lay between us. Two castes, the rulers and the ruled, the haves and the have-nots. That strange compulsion that animates field work pulled me toward those silent, unknown faces, and my mind tried to leap the granite wall to see what they saw, to feel what they felt, as they watched the ritual greetings of those who held them in thrall.

Even before I left the airstrip, I learned that the government's guest house was not available. Until receiving my wires from Moresby, the Lumi officials had no knowledge when I would be in Lumi and the house was already committed. My letter from India had not arrived, and it was many months more before it finally would. But I was glad when it did, for it somewhat exonerated me from a major breach of etiquette that correctly demands the station's chief administrative officer be notified well in advance of impending scientific visits and requests for cooperation and services. As far as the local government was concerned, I felt I had arrived under a cloud of presumptiveness; a stereotyped American who snaps his fingers and expects the world to jump. After all my careful planning, it was a stupid blunder not to have notified the Lumi Sub-District Office of my arrival date before leaving for New Guinea. In a country where prerogatives among groups are closely guarded, it was the local missionaries with whom I had corresponded, not the local government, who were the experts on my affairs.

But Dr. Wark had an alternative for me. Besides being the physician for the government's native hospital, she was a missionary with the evangelical Christian Brethren mission, and their guest house was empty. But she warned me it was built mainly of native materials and now completely dilapidated. It was scheduled to be demolished, and she wondered if my family would find it habitable. Dr. Wark, who I learned always spoke plainly and honestly, did not exaggerate about the house's condition. A Charles Addams horror of tropical decay, its most positive features were a comfortable roominess and a thatched roof which, in spite of its age, was still quite tight. Only in the severest of storms did it leak. To situate the house, a portion of the steep hillside had been cut away and the back windows faced a wall of dank dirt a few feet away. Rotten and sagging, the house appeared to stay upright only with the help of the great trees and spreading shrubs that completely enfolded it in an airless claustrophobia.

Inside, the woven bamboo walls were draped with cobwebs heavy with dampness. Bits of tattered curtains, incongruous in such a setting, hung limply here and there where hungry insects, sated with gingham and lace, had moved on to a more solid course of wood. The only furniture were beds and a roughly made table with four chairs apparently constructed for a family of giants. But of all the rooms, the kitchen and shower were the most deteriorated. The shower room, a black hole of mildew, and the kitchen, its moldering counters collapsing in decay, seemed almost hopeless. The outhouse standing nearby seemed hospitable by comparison.

Still, I was highly optimistic. Long ago I had made a coldwater flat in New York City into a pleasant residence, and Joyce and I had successfully remodeled an abandoned schoolhouse and a run-down back farm. Although I had never taken on anything quite as far gone as this, my imagination was challenged. I gratefully accepted the use of the house.

It was Wednesday and the family would arrive on the mail plane Friday morning; I had not a moment to lose. With the help of a mission laborer loaned from the household of Don and Aileen McGregor, also Christian Brethren missionaries who, with their three children, had worked in New Guinea for over seventeen years, I set to work. We cut back the shroud of shrubbery, pulled down the offending curtains, swept the ceilings, walls, and floors, and scrubbed the kitchen and shower. It was cleaner, but did it really look any better? And the musty smell of mildew refused to vacate, as permanent a feature of the house as its walls and windows.

What we couldn't correct, I disguised with brightly striped towels and lengths of red cloth bought from the mission's trade store across the road. The McGregors loaned me a couple of air mattresses for the children's bunks and I sunned the soggy cotton mattress that would grace our bed. Dr. Wark taught me how to start the old kerosene refrigerator that could no longer manage ice but would keep the meat and butter cool. I washed an assortment of chipped dishes and dented pots and placed a vase of red Hibiscus on the table, my work completed. But I knew it was not a success. The house was, and would remain, an unreconstructed derelict waiting for its pauper's grave. When I lived in New York, there was an old woman who took the afternoon sun on a Broadway bench near my subway stop. A battered wreck of humanity's wars, her face was splattered with powder and her lips an unfashionable cherry red. Perhaps she had been a beautiful woman just as the house once was invitingly fresh, but now no amount of gaudy distractions could hide the decrepitude.

That night, exhausted, I could not get to sleep. As I lay awake wondering, I listened to ceremonial drums booming through the night and wished I were on that distant ridge, not here.

The mail plane arrived the following morning on schedule. I have a photograph of Joyce emerging from the plane, and her expression is one of quizzical wariness. For a woman whose expressive behavior is usually direct and immediate, it is most unusual. I have seen it only once before: in a wedding photograph where, stepping from the car on her father's arm and literally, if not figuratively, unmindful of where she is stepping, she is gazing fixedly toward the church.

The station personnel welcomed Joyce and the children, then we took our few Wewak-purchased supplies down to our temporary home. Joyce could not hide her dismay and great tears filled her eyes. Dr. Wark, who lived nearby in a small but delightful house, invited us to lunch, and as we ate and visited about Lumi and our plans, the tension between Joyce and myself subsided. The children ran outside to play and found a tree to climb that they still remember with affection when the limbs of our Vermont trees seem all the wrong proportions.

The next day, Joyce and I invited Lyn—first names come quickly in New Guinea – to lunch to acknowledge her generous hospitality. Joyce felt she had mastered the collapsible Primus

stove, a rickety single-burner affair fueled by kerosene and perfect
pumping, and planned her menu. An excellent and imaginative
cook, she was not to be intimidated by the novelty of her tools or
foodstuffs and decided the single hot dish would be 'pit pit,' a
wild cane whose fruit vaguely resembles something between a
cattail and an unripe ear of corn. 'Pit pit' is usually cooked in
boiling water, but Joyce, attempting a more sophisticated version, decided a second step of sautéing in butter. First we
couldn't get the Primus started and by the time we did, Lyn arrived from the hospital on her motorbike. Joyce cursed the
Primus — and me by indirection — for providing such a lousy
setup. Finally, Joyce emerged from the kitchen with the dish,
but it looked revolting, a mass of vegetable glue. The children
refused outright to have anything to do with it, but Lyn, who
probably had seen and eaten food just as bad during her years in
New Guinea, was smilingly undaunted.

Joyce rarely acknowledges one of her rare culinary mistakes
and I prayed this time she would. But it was not until we tasted
it that she removed it from the table. Lunch was peanut butter
sandwiches. It really was a marvelous joke, and I wanted to make
cracks about "pit pit à la Joyce" or that it was a fitting specialty of
the house, but I kept my mouth closed. Joyce was not laughing.
That night she tried her 'pit pit' recipe again and it was superb.

A few days later I had a chance to fly to the Anguganak Mission airstrip near the village of Rauit where Gilbert Lewis had
worked. I very much wanted to see his village first to provide me
with some comparative data for choosing my own village, and
this was a providential opportunity. Unchivalrously I took off,
leaving Joyce and the children under Lyn's friendly and watchful
eyes.

Next morning, climbing the high and almost perpendicular
ridge on which Rauit was located, I knew exactly what Gilbert
meant when he wrote that sometimes it was almost impossible to
stay upright. But I had heeded his advice and bought a pair of
canvas golf shoes from the mission store and their metal studs
helped hinge me into the steep slippery earth. My guide, a boy

who accompanied me from the mission station at the airstrip, left me at the hamlet on top of the bluff and set me on a tiny track along the ridge toward Rauit. After the ascent, the ridge track was easy, and, feeling free and relaxed, I rejoiced in the beauty of the forest. I heard the songs of many birds, but, hidden away in the complexly variegated foliage, I never saw a one.

No dog or human saw me approach the village, and when I entered, the surprised women, naked except for a tiny seed apron, ran away exclaiming at the sight of the strange white man. The two-year residence of the Lewises apparently had not changed the Rauits much. Still acknowledged as one of the most recalcitrant and uncooperative groups in the Sub-District, in the 1950s they threatened a government patrol, which prudently retreated. Returning some months later, the patrol found the village empty and, when the people would not come in to be censused, burned down a number of their houses.

Two of the younger men, full of questions about the Lewises when I said they were my friends, escorted me through the village and someone gave me a green coconut whose cooling juice slaked my thirst. Entering the men's ceremonial house, I saw a peculiar red-and-white object suspended from a rafter. It was an inflatable Santa Claus, now innocent of air; a secular memento from the Lewis's young son.

By late afternoon I began the trek back to the mission station. Near the top of the bluff a smashing rain fell from the sky, and, no longer upright at all, I swam down the mountain. Toward the bottom I met a group of youths, stark naked, returning home from the mission station with their shorts and shirts snugly dry in plastic bags. What an excellent idea! My clothes, as cold and clinging as a reptile's skin, were saturated and I wanted to be rid of them but I was walking in the wrong direction.

That night I stayed again in the comfortable bungalow where the mission pilot, David Grace, lived with his wife. After dinner we listened to a Mozart concerto, and I guiltily worried about Joyce in her house of horrors.

For the next six weeks we lived in the mission guest house

waiting for our delinquent trunks to catch up with us, and I took advantage of the time to study the records in the Sub-District office, especially the patrol reports, and made numerous reconnaissance patrols on my own, searching for a village in which to settle. One of the tribes I was most interested in was that of the Oni speakers, who live one or two days' walk in the mountains west of Lumi. For the grant application I had even selected the Oni village of Molmo as a possible village base.

Late one Wednesday afternoon, David Grace picked me up at Lumi in his little yellow Cessna 206 and minutes later we landed at Kabori on a small airstrip nestled in the mountains and being rapidly eaten away by a rampant brook. If ever I have been to the end of the world, I felt I was there then. Even the ironic fact that I had flown there in a plane built in my home town of Wichita did nothing to dispel my initial impression of desolation.

Jerry and Betty Wunch, an American missionary couple from Michigan, had built this lonely outpost five years earlier. They welcomed me with the special warmth reserved for one's countryman when meeting far from home. As we visited during dinner, I learned that the Oni people were resistant to mission work, sometimes even hostile, and Jerry had an arrow scar on his abdomen to remind him, as if he needed to be, of the vicissitudes of a pioneering missionary's life.

I had arranged for the mission plane to return for me Friday afternoon, so Thursday morning, after a big American-style breakfast, Wes, a friend of Jerry's who would carry my backpack, and I set out for Molmo. We took a roundabout way, visiting another village and hamlets on the way. It was an all-day hike, and the country was the most rugged yet. Up and down the ridges we hiked on the narrow wet track. And it rained as it does only in the tropics, cascading through the forest with a deafening roar.

All along the track leeches waited, waving back and forth like miniature cobras. Periodically, I stopped to knock them from my shoes before they crawled inside to feast on my blood.

Wes, although a man much smaller than I and bearing the weight of my pack, seemed to have lungs of built-in oxygen, for he never hesitated as he climbed up and down the steep slopes. After the first hour my body reached some kind of accommodation, and I became more machine than man. My mind dimmed, and I found myself oddly obsessed with the memory of a university colleague, an immaculate young psychiatrist whose office was across from mine, sitting silently in his darkened, air-conditioned room as the glowing pink numerals of his electronic calculator appeared in rapid succession. How had I, a rational and intelligent person, with intentional foresight placed myself into my present situation? The sudden contrast in our lives amused and sustained me as I stumbled through the mud and swaying leeches.

Long before we reached Molmo we heard a plane. It landed at Kabori, then took off in the direction of Lumi. Strange, I thought, because there were to be no other planes until my chartered flight tomorrow. Kabori was lucky to see one plane a week; now there were to be three.

Nearing Molmo we met several men in loincloths carrying the long bow characteristic of the mountain tribes. The village was deserted, they said. The people were hunting and living in their bush houses. On the outskirts of the village, Wes gave a stylized Oni whoop to announce our arrival. It was immediately answered with another whoop, so someone at least was there.

The rains had stopped and the sun would set within the hour. The one thought I had was to get out of my cold, soaked clothes. So, while visiting with the three or four men still in the village, I hung them up to dry and examined my water-wizened feet for the inevitable blood-fat leeches. But my trail checks had paid off. Not a single leech had invaded my shoes. As I dried myself with a towel—what a comforting invention—and wondered why the natives prefer to air dry and use towels only as sarongs, a runner arrived from Kabori with a hastily scrawled message from Jerry. It was *my* plane that had come and gone! I never did learn why. But I had a momentary feeling of empathy for Joyce, "trapped" in the old mission house, and envisioned the rest of my life, probably a short one, slopping through mud and leeches, searching for a way out of this hellish land.

But Wes and I boiled some rice, opened a can of fish, and an old man brought me some pink bananas, the most beautiful and sweetest bananas I ever had eaten. I finished the meal with a boiling hot cup of instant coffee and thought I must be the luckiest man alive.

All New Guinea villages have a rest house for the occasional government official—usually a patrol officer—who visits them, and Wes thought I should sleep there while he stayed at a friend's house. But I was not about to spend the night abandoned in an abandoned village, so the invitation was extended to include me as well. That night Wes, our host Eiyevu, and I spent several hours around the embers of a fire talking about Oni culture. Throughout the day, however, Wes had been the worst kind of informant, answering my questions with replies he thought a white man would find acceptable. I was familiar with this exasperating predicament from my earlier work on the Sepik but, after all, I also don't tell a stranger things about myself I think might disgust or amuse him at my expense. And, like stigmatized people everywhere, the constant cultural put-downs by Westerners has taught the New Guinean how to expertly parry a question or artfully dissemble an answer when his self-esteem is threatened. But that night in the pleasant darkness of Eiyevu's house, our bodies warm and our bellies full, the spirit of trusting friendship prevailed and the outlines of the culture emerged as the two men, smoking and laughing over my absurd questions, instructed me in the Oni way of life. On the surface, at least, there was nothing startlingly novel about Oni culture. It fitted the general pattern of the other mountain cultures I was learning about, but that in itself was valuable information.

The next day in Kabori, Jerry tried to get through to Lumi on his ancient wireless radio in the hope of diverting a plane to pick me up. We did not know if he had succeeded or not. In the late afternoon sun we saw the yellow mission plane rise high above Lumi and head in the opposite direction. And Saturday morning he tried again, but with no luck. It would be Monday at the earliest, perhaps even later, before a plane would come for me, so I decided to make the two-day walk instead. After my hike to Molmo, I felt I was ready for anything New Guinea could throw at me. But Jerry assured me the track was a good one. Much of it he planned himself and helped to cut from the wilderness. And, most promising of all, there would be no legions of leeches lying in wait.

Seiforu, a young man from the Lumi area who looked after Jerry's handful of cattle—hopefully the beginning of a large herd—agreed to accompany me. The Wunches helped us pack a few necessities, then we were off for the morning was almost gone. Not far out of Kabori we met a young white woman while crossing a large brook. She was considerably more surprised than I, for the Wunches had told me that Kabori's missionary teacher, Dianne McEvedy, was scheduled to return that day and I might meet her on the way.

Just as Jerry had promised, the track was an excellent one. The grade was gentle, the track wide, and, being very high, the occasional forest openings provided exciting views of the surrounding mountains. As an enthusiast of waterfalls, even small ones, I had never seen so many perfectly situated ones, and I stopped to admire each one, causing Seiforu to eventually ask me if something was wrong. But it is not a simple thing to explain in Melanesian Pidgin that you are a connoisseur of falling water and he continued to throw me puzzled glances.

Our destination was the village of Inebu. Here, Jerry and Betty first settled among the Oni eighteen years ago and raised their children. Jerry had given me the key to their abandoned mission house—there seemed to be a peculiar pattern emerging here—where we would spend the night before continuing to Lumi. We passed through several villages, visited briefly, and moved on. Once we stopped by a brook for a swim. By midafternoon, it began to rain. Nothing unusual in this, of course, except there was a large creek to cross near Inebu and by the time we reached it in the late afternoon, it was swollen with the torrent of rain and impassable.

For an hour and a half we waited in a soft drizzle for it to subside. My idea of a safe crossing was for the water to be somewhere between my waist and knees, but for Seiforu it seemed to be anything below the neck. I had heard old New Guinea hands tell tales about the rapid transformations of ankle-deep brooks to drowning chutes of plunging water, but this was my first such encounter and I found the force of the foaming water awesome. My fear was that if one of us were to lose his footing on the slippery hidden bottom, he would be seized by the current and dashed unconscious against the rocks. I wanted to wait a bit longer.

Seiforu, born in the mountains, was impatient with my timidity and anxious to be across, for night would soon fall and we were not in Inebu. But I did not like the looks of things at all. The mythic movie heroes of my culture, against whom I stupidly had been taught to measure myself as a man, would have strode boldly into the surf and single-handedly burst through the tide with a grimace of toothy magnificence. I was made of something less Herculean, and the thought that I voluntarily was going to try to cross that storm-tossed creek—I, a neophyte who had yet to find his land legs and had not even considered the sport of hiking in rapids—increased my damp shiver to an observable quake.

Seiforu, cutting us each a long, strong stick, said he would cross alone with the backpack, then return to help me. Slowly, carefully feeling the way with his staff, he traversed the raging current that swirled around him. Safely across—how I envied him—he dropped the backpack on the bank and just as slowly and carefully worked his way back to me. Hoping sincerely that Jerry's departing prayer for our safe journey would be answered, I stepped into the cold foam beside Seiforu, our hands tightly gripped. Cautiously, he guided me through the rushing tide, breaking the current with his body and holding me secure when I slipped. Slowly, yet never daring to hesitate, we crossed, two men, strangers, locked together in a miniature encounter with nature. It was, I think, the longest ten minutes of my life.

Since that baptismal crossing in the high Torricellis, I have crossed many creeks and rivers in flood, but none so high and fast. It is a toss-up, I guess, as to which still alarms me the most: breaking the seething tide itself or tottering far above it on a single rotting log bridge with vertigo imminent.

It was night, a black starless night, when we reached Inebu. The houses were shut fast, secured against the elements, witches, and demons. A dog yapped listlessly as we passed through a desolate hamlet and made our way to the high ground where the old mission stood. Finding our way with lantern and flashlight, Seiforu whispered that the mission was built on ground belonging to a local demon. He did not know its name, but his fear was as audible as mine at the creek was visible. In that strange symbiosis of shifting dependencies that characterize human relationships, Seiforu fell back as I led the way up the hill.

It was impossible to make out the outlines of a house, but the path led directly to its door. I unlocked the door, pushed it creakily open, and we went inside. Wet and cold, we ate a miserable dinner. The old house groaned as the winds came up and the lantern cast ominous shadows in the empty corners. As we made up our pallets, Seiforu placed his close to mine, explaining that in Inebu there are 'sanguma,' the Pidgin word for the terrible male witches whose unsuspecting attack is fatal. If we leave the lantern burning all night, he said, they might not harm us. For him, the lantern would drive them away, but to me it was a beacon signaling every witch and demon from Kabori to Lumi to come and dance on Inebu mountain. I would have preferred the anonymity of darkness.

As I huddled into the hardness of my bed, I assured Seiforu that 'sanguma' never attack white people and would not dare come near the house. But such bravado from a man who couldn't even face a river alone was not convincing. Quietly, he picked up the Pidgin Bible Jerry had given him and began to read and pray by the flickering light. As I shut my heavy eyes, his earnest young face lingered in my mind and I wondered about the complexity of the fears and comforts of humankind.

I awakened with the sun; the mists had dissolved and I discovered that the house was spectacularly situated. I was sure that I could catch a glimpse of the sea far to the north. When we set out, I felt my body moving with a relaxed syncopation. I was learning to walk in the bush.

We walked steadily and by lunchtime were in the vicinity of Seiforu's village. Entering a neighboring hamlet, relatives welcomed us into a house and fed us boiled 'tulip' leaves and fresh sago baked in bamboo tubes. Much of the afternoon we walked in a small—and tranquil—deeply shaded river. As we climbed up from the river, I sighted Lumi, its silver roofs glistening in the sun, a jungle metropolis. Joyce and the children greeted me with hugs and kisses and poured us glasses of tart lemonade. Then Seiforu said good-by, and I never saw him again.

2

▼▲▼▲▼▲▼▲▼▲▼▲▼▲▼

THE SEARCH

Even as I was visiting different tribes, I think I already knew I
would work among the Wape. They had fascinated me since that
first night in Lumi when, lying awake worrying about Joyce's arrival, I listened to the great ceremonial drums booming through
the night from Otei village, a ridge away. Don McGregor, the
Christian Brethren missionary from New Zealand and in charge
of the pastoral work of the Lumi mission, was intensely interested
in and knowledgeable about Wape culture and explained to me
about the drumming. The Oteis, he said, were in the midst of an
extended curing festival that would climax in a few weeks' time.
It was the most important ceremonial cycle of the Wape tribe, involving surrounding villages and a variety of ritual exchanges as
well.

One evening Don took me to Otei village on his motorbike
to watch the festival. It was the final day and hundreds of people,
their bodies vividly decorated with paints and powder, bright
leaves and delicate ferns, had converged on the village to dance all

night among the magnificent Fish Spirit masks. Shimmering and shaking in towering grandeur, the masks, aflutter with bird-of-paradise feathers and flags of fur, were like Calder mobiles magically gone wild. I was captivated by the marathon dancing, the incessant drumming, and hypnotic chanting. The soaring masks, agleam in the fire of bamboo torches like iridescent fish swimming in ethereal majesty above an undertow of churning humanity, sent shocks of excitement through me. I had never seen anything like it before in my life.

Who were these Wape, I wondered, and why was ritual curing so important in their cultural life? That the Wape centered their religious ceremonies on curing instead of on male initiation rites or on elaborate one-upmanship feasts as many New Guinea tribes do was a fact that greatly impressed me. Wasn't I here to study just such events? The coincidence that I happened to choose the Lumi area, the center of Wapeland, for my research seemed too fortuitous, almost too neat. Margaret Mead, I remembered, had expressed similar surprise when she happened to study the Tchambuli, the third of three Sepik cultures that almost perfectly completed her tripartite paradigm on human sex and temperament. For when an anthropologist takes a specific problem into an unknown area, he must expect disappointment and be prepared to abandon the topic for a problem that emanates from the culture itself. But I was lucky, for surging about me in boisterous disarray were a people who could help me understand some of the complexities of therapeutic systems.

As I stood intrigued with this seething spectacle, I gradually became aware that the dancers were not an indiscriminate hodgepodge but arranged in clearly bounded groups, although at times groups might pass through one another so any observational sense of boundedness was ephemeral. The dancers flashed by, adorned with feathers and ferns, pig tusks and leaves. It seemed as if the forest itself and its myriad creatures had entered the village to merge with the people in an exuberant testimony of the transcendency of culture over nature.

The ethnographer's unconscious takes delight in the inscrutable, and mine already was at work, for my eyes, even as they roamed over this multimedia pageant of light, movement, and sound, returned repeatedly to one of the women chanters until I noticed I was following her every movement. Why was I staring at her? There *was* something unusual about her but nothing I could pinpoint. Suddenly I realized that she was a man; a Wape male in ceremonial drag. I asked a bystander, who, with a laugh, confirmed my hypothesis. I felt good about that. It was the sort of behavioral insight that makes field work as much an art as a science, and I was pleased that my unconscious could still make contact with events and lead me to conscious knowledge. People differ greatly to the extent they are able to discern behavior in strange cultural contexts, and the ability to do so is mandatory for good field work. Although my field-work skills were weak in other ways—for example, new languages come only with difficulty—I relied on my strong observational talent to pick up cultural nuances left unsaid.

As I watched this dancing and chanting man disguised as a woman, I was reminded of the transvestite rituals of the mother's brother among the Iatmul people with whom I lived briefly in 1967 and immortalized in Gregory Bateson's brilliant classic of structuralist explanation, *Naven*. The discovery of ritual transvestism among the Wape pleased me. Not because I was the first Westerner to observe it, a shallow accomplishment at best, but because any group that invents symbolic reversals are, from my point of view, exciting to work with. I am amused when symbols and signs are purposefully twisted and turned and stimulated by the problems of meaning they set up.

While I was a young graduate student at Columbia, I worked for a time as a psychiatric aide among disturbed children who, calling themselves the "Baby Disturbers," had evolved a contraculture of winning perversity to harass the adult world that had harassed them to madness. Inverting the fastidious categories of adult propriety, they collected their feces in paper cups to worship as "the greatest good," built miniature altars to enshrine tiny winged penises made of clay, and effectively taunted the hos-

pital staff by smacking their lips over cups of urine "lemonade."
The Baby Disturbers were geniuses of inventive polarity, and the
Wape, of course, could not match such felicitous perverseness—
no adult culture could.

But moving among the spectators ringing the dance ground
were several small groups who seemed to be performing humorous skits, jesters providing comic relief from the ceremonial
dancing. Two youths in skirts, their phony breasts bouncing
under old blouses and their faces obscured with oddly peaked
handkerchiefs, sang and sobbed in high, silly falsetto voices as
they mimicked the tearful laments of women grieving the loss of
their husbands gone to work on faraway island plantations. Shuffling their feet to and fro in exaggerated caricature of a woman's
dance step, the young men were funny. But from my personal
perspective, their satire was too biting, its object of ridicule too
defenseless and emotionally genuine, for where is the humor in a
lonely mother and her children left without a hunter to provide
them with meat? Lyn had told me that in villages where the men
were away at plantations, malnutrition was often a severe problem. Fathers might return after a two or three years absence to
find only an infant's grave. Sometime later I watched men, their
eyes filled with tears, climb clumsily into an unfamiliar airplane
to be flown away to an unknown plantation while their families
stood in tragic silence, afraid to cry openly because the labor
recruiter, busily loading his new laborers, did not like parting
scenes. But when the women returned to their villages, they
openly expressed their loss, not just of a protein provider but the
loss of the man who was a sexual partner, comforter, and co-
worker in the care of the children, for Wape marriages are usually
close and long-lasting.

In yet another skit I watched a costumed youth burlesque
the status of motherhood. Singing a lullaby in a cracked voice
while tenderly cradling a rubber doll in his arms, he fed rocks to
the baby then, with monstrous deceit, cooed he was feeding it
sago. What was going on here? Why were women and babies
picked out for humorous ridicule? I had no answers for I knew

next to nothing about the culture, but any culture that can joke blackly about mothers—not mothers-in-law—promised to be full of surprises.

Here was a culture so complex I could never master it, one that would keep me hard at work—and entertained—for as long as I studied it. Not that any one human can ever actually "master" a culture, but there are degrees of cultural complexity, and the Wape, for all the simple appearance of their villages and sparseness of technology, seemed to have an elaborate, and in some ways unusual, social and ritual life.

There were simpler cultures to study in the Lumi Sub-District, for I had visited some of them. But I am usually enticed by the challenge of things just a bit beyond my grasp, for it is the act of intellectually and emotionally stretching myself to reach a difficult or unattainable goal that invigorates me with a satisfying feeling of life and vibrancy. But the Wape, I would learn, stretched me in unpredictable ways that, while temporarily invigorating, left me weary from the strains.

During the weeks in Lumi, I cornered Don or Lyn from their busy schedules as often as possible to ask them about the various Wape villages. Both were avid patrolers, and although Don's present responsibilities restricted his patroling to those villages where he had parishioners, Lyn visited a wide range of Wape villages on her medical patrols. There was no village she could not describe in detail, including the conditions of tracks and rest house, degree of acculturation, whether the pigs were friendly, and the attitude of the people toward Westerners.

When I told Lyn I was definitely interested in work among the Wape, she answered that she knew the perfect village. Standing in front of my large wall map, a treasured gift from an army officer I met in Wewak, she pointed to the village of Wilkili. It was located across the Sibi River on a ridge about three hours' walk south of Lumi. But, she added, it would be impossible for us to work there for reasons of health. Wilkili had an unusually high incidence of leprosy with thirty identified but arrested cases. Because the etiology of leprosy is still unknown and sometimes lies dormant within the victim for years before lesions appear, Lyn insisted it would be a risk we dare not take with Ned's and Elizabeth's health. As it was, we were subjecting them to enough serious diseases. But without lifting her finger from the map, Lyn pointed to another very traditional village also across the Sibi and not far from Wilkili. It was named Tauwitei on the map but known as Taute by the villagers and the Lumi Sub-District office.

In some ways, Lyn said, Taute was even more traditional and conservative than Wilkili, which sent a group of boys to the Lumi grade school while Taute sent but a single child. Especially intriguing was the incident of recent deaths and counterdeaths by alleged sorcery and witchcraft involving the Tautes and Lyn's medical orderlies, most of whom were also Wape.

It all began, Lyn said, when a medical orderly just returned from a Taute medical patrol was found collapsed in his house. She was away at the time but a visiting physician examined the stricken orderly, could not make a diagnosis, and transferred him to the Wewak hospital where he died. The gossip among the hospital orderlies was that the Tautes had killed their workmate by sorcery.

In New Guinea, one death almost always deserves another, so a short time later when a vigorous Taute man died suddenly, the villagers believed the Lumi orderlies had arranged his death. His widow was pregnant at the time of his death and when the baby was born it was very sick; Lyn worked hard to save its life, not only because that was the way she always worked, but because she knew that the hospital personnel would be blamed if it died. But the baby recovered and was dismissed from the hospital with its mother. One day word came to the hospital that the infant was dead, and the medical orderly who had given the baby its last injection was accused of killing it. Then, in retaliation for the death of the Taute father and his child, the Tautes allegedly went down the Sibi River to the village of Kamnum to hire a famous male witch to kill the orderly.

At this point the Lumi government officials called the Taute men into the station for a reprimand. They listened in sober silence, protested their innocence and returned to the village. But that very night Lyn received a message from one of the orderlies that his baby was very sick. Knowing the explanation on everyone's lips if the baby died, Lyn hurried to the orderly's house, but found the baby with only a mild fever—something its father would usually have considered a minor illness and treated himself.

But the repercussions did not end there. The dead orderly's brother was also an orderly and refused to go on medical patrols to the Taute area. Eventually he managed a transfer to the coast to protect himself and family.

This series of interlocking events is a beautiful example of the impact of supernatural explanations upon everyday behavior. Like pebbles cast into a great sago swamp, the ripples of explanation circle outward and onward, sometimes overlapping and touching everything in their path. Even a year later one of those ripples would wash against me.

But the real importance of the case for my research was its clue about the nature of the relationship between the local culture and the introduced system of Western medicine. In this instance, the Lumi hospital orderlies and the Taute villagers, all Wape, were not relating in a trusting therapist-patient relationship so characteristic of Western therapeutic systems, but as suspicious enemies. But what else should I expect? After all, the Wape orderlies came from villages north of the Sibi River, which considered the southern villages especially prone to sorcery and witchcraft. In return, the Tautes were cheerless visitors to Lumi, coming to the polyglot station only on specific business, ever on guard against the black practices of their northern neighbors.

When I first visited the Lumi hospital I had no intimation of the potential mutual fears between a Wape orderly and his patients. I saw only a uniformed New Guinean caring for other New Guineans. Although the setting was strange, for bush hospitals have a decided primitive appearance, the nursing techniques were familiar and, without thought, I assumed that the relationship between the orderly and his patients was completely

secular, highly professionalized, and above narrow partisan interests of territoriality. And, just as it would never occur to me that
an American nurse might be perceived as giving an infant a murderous injection, neither would it have occurred to me that a
Wape orderly dedicated to the care of his sick fellows might be
similarly accused of such a diabolical act.

Of course, I was in complete error. I had committed that
most heinous of anthropological sins, ethnocentrism. Observing
the commonplace activities of taking temperatures, changing
dressings, and giving medication, I had unwittingly assumed a
host of unwarranted cultural assumptions about the Wape or-
derly-patient relationship based on my American experiences that
were not only situationally inappropriate, but distorted the truth
of the actual relationship. I had ignored the cultural background
of the observed behavior. It was a warning to be especially wary of
interpreting the obvious act or familiar stereotype—for the more
obvious and familiar the behavior, the greater is the tendency to
project one's own cultural interpretations of understanding.

Taute was a two- to three-hour walk from Lumi; the time
depending upon the condition of the track and one's strength and
motivation. We had finally received word that our gear was in the
Territory and enroute to Wewak. So, with a feeling of tremendous expectancy, I planned to visit Taute. On a clear, sunny
morning I set out alone, carrying only a notebook, a couple of
pens, and some candy bars tucked into a small flight bag I bought
at the Montreal airport two months earlier at the beginning of
our journey. I was particularly pleased with the compact blue
bag, for New Guinea men seldom go visiting without a bag of
some sort slung over their shoulders to carry tobacco, newsprint
for rolling cigarettes, betel nut, lime, amulets, and money. If a
man can afford one he will carry a flight bag purchased from a
trade store, as the traditional woven bag is passé, carried only by
the old and the poor. I had carried the old-type bag on my 1967
expedition, and it was a constant source of embarrassment to the
fashionable Iatmul men who accompanied me on my reconnaissance patrols up the tributaries of the middle Sepik. But the new

flight bag would embarrass no one and was an excellent conversation opener as strangers admired its compactness, strong straps, and bright color.

For one reason or another, none of the Wape villages I previously had visited met my criteria for a research station. There were, it is true, a number of factors to be considered. A foremost concern was that the village be within easy reach of Lumi in case Ned or Elizabeth suffered a severe illness or injury. Both were very genuine possibilities for the terrain was difficult and Western children are very susceptible to high fevers from a variety of tropical diseases. Taute was convenient to Lumi and Lyn's medical care except when the Sibi River was in flood. Unfortunately, it rained almost every day and the river might be unpassable for hours at a time and, occasionally, for a day or more. But it was the river that also helped partially isolate Taute from the influence of Lumi, a desirable consideration. So the river worked both for and against me.

A related consideration was that the chosen population be a comparatively healthy one. Taute, to be sure, had several cases of leprosy, but Lyn knew the individuals well. Acknowledging that from a strictly health point of view, *no* village is a desirable place of residence, Taute was no better, or worse, than many others.

From a research perspective, it also was important that the village not be depopulated of men working away at plantations, for ceremonial life, usually a male responsibility, then becomes moribund and village life fades to a colorless routine. Taute, I knew, had thirteen men away out of its total population of around two hundred people. While the number was higher than I would wish, it was lower than a number of other villages I visited with only a handful of men at home and no ceremonial life until the majority returned.

Walking along the broad road leaving Lumi, its damp surface already baked and cracked from the morning sun, I pondered the problems of selecting a research village and was pleased that Taute met my criteria so well. Yet I was ignorant and anxious about two considerations. The single most crucial question of all—would the Tautes want us to live with them?—was not answered. A crucial question, because it is unethical to settle in a village unless the villagers genuinely want you to live among them. And there were some very practical points to be considered as well. I was not just a lone ethnographer, but we were a family of four; our needs to survive in the midst of the forest would be considerable, and most would have to be met by the skill and labor of the villagers. Would they be willing to take us on and, once having assumed the responsibility, maintain it? Just then I had no idea. But I did know that field work is exceedingly difficult on every conceivable level. Even the best of initial field situations become fraught with unanticipated problems, misunderstandings, and nerve-wracking tensions. If the villagers were not enthusiastic about our coming—and there was no special reason why they should be, for the responsibility of caring for a Western family more than matched the prestige and wages involved—I would simply have to start over again, a discouraging thought.

But if the Tautes did want us, there was still the task of finding a pleasant, yet socially strategic location for our house, for no local house, small structures at best, would accommodate our many needs, and we would have to build a new one. Joyce and I already had worked on a house plan, designing it so we could maintain easy access to the people while maintaining a certain amount of family privacy. The two goals, access and privacy, are always in conflict, for while one learns nothing about the culture when hidden away, the tremendous personal demands of field work make it mandatory to occasionally disappear to read a novel or mystery, listen to a favorite tape recording, or just daydream about the more delightful aspects of Western civilization.

So many things in this "land of contrasts" seemed to be in contradiction, even the road on which I was walking. It was wide and smooth but unprotected from the glaring sun. I felt I was being cooked alive. Yet, while the forest tracks were mercifully protected by multiple layers of leaves, the trails were so narrow, muddy, and root-strewn, that one did not walk in the usual sense, but tripped and stumbled along. I longed for some happy mediums.

Nor was there any real purpose for this very wide road. It went nowhere. The New Guinea Army had constructed it as a community project while on maneuvers in the Lumi area. When they left, the road stopped. But Territorians have no corner on foolish enterprises. The year before we left for New Guinea, town officials replaced our farm bridge, old but efficient, by a giant culvert that shot downstream whenever it rained hard or the ice went out of the brook. Only with great expense and labor was it hauled back to its restless position and anchored with tons of new gravel to await its next excursion. The primitive boulevard that lay beneath my perspiring feet seemed the height of astute road building in comparison.

At the top of the rise I was slowly ascending stood a small thatched shelter perched atop the bank from which the road was cut. It was a perfect place to escape from the sun and recover my breath. I eyed it covetously, but as I approached the hut, I saw it was too crowded with other hot travelers for a stranger to enter. As I stopped momentarily to rest, I glanced up toward the hut to smile a greeting when a young man jumped gaily down the bank toward me, dazzling my eyes with the reflected glare of his new white shirt. It had to be new for most Wape can't afford the luxury of soap, and all clothes, regardless of their original color, soon fade to a dingy grey. Sizing me up with his direct bright eyes— the brightest eyes I had encountered in Wapeland—he smiled engagingly and greeted me with the enthusiasm of a man meeting an old drinking buddy at their favorite bar.

" 'Moning masta,' " shaking my hand. " 'Yu go we?' "

" 'Mi go long Taute,' " I replied simply, rather overwhelmed by his cheerful openness on such a hot, sultry morning. Graciously reaching for my flight bag, he slung it over his shoulder, exclaiming that he was from Taute and would show me the way to the village. Just ahead, he explained, the trail to Taute entered the forest leading down to the Sibi River and there were several crossing trails and I might get lost. I thanked him for his offer to show me the way, and, with several Taute women bringing up the rear, we set off.

His name was Kumoi. Of medium build, he was just five feet tall, rather short even for the diminutive Wape. In his late twenties, Kumoi not only spoke Pidgin with unusual clarity, but could read and write it as well. And, like most Wape men, he had spent his young manhood away at plantations where, among other tasks, he had cooked for a Western bachelor. With no living parents or adult siblings, he had saved his money and with the help of his lineage mates, made the necessary gift of bride-wealth for his young wife from a neighboring village. Their first child was yet to be born. I imagined, though I did not know, he was a bit bored with village life, and my visit today promised a change in the daily routine.

The track leading to the Sibi was as miserable as most forest tracks, but there were no leeches. At the river, our little party stopped to smoke cigarettes made of native tobacco rolled in newsprint or chew some revitalizing betel nut. The river was wide, very low, and we easily waded across. Unlike the people living on the Sepik or in its swamps, the Wape construct neither canoes nor log bridges, but I noticed a long vine stretched across the river where, in higher water, a person could still cross by gripping its precarious stability.

Across the Sibi we again entered the forest and began the long ascent to the Taute ridge. It was immediately evident that Taute was seldom visited by officials, for part of the track passed through the huge, straggling branches of a long-fallen tree. It was the kind of ecological adaptation by the locals that might bring a curse to a patrol officer's lips and an order to build a new section of trail or go to jail, for there are three things a patrol officer is especially sensitive about: the condition of the trail he walks, the condition of the village rest house in which he sleeps, and the number and depth of native latrines.

Kumoi and the women climbed through the tree as easily as they slipped through the ankle-deep mud. But I, unaccustomed to walking along and through the branches of a steeply sloping tree, proceeded awkwardly and wondered, if this is Taute's main road to Lumi, what, indeed, must the village look like?

After passing through a section of black palm forest, where much of the track was along slippery logs that replaced the trail washed away by cascading rains, the trail suddenly rose straight upward in front of me like a great brown snake reaching for the sky. I sighed to myself; this wasn't a trail for travel, but a jungle steeple chase designed for someone's—not mine—challenge and entertainment. Using both my hands and my feet, digging into and clutching anything at hand, I was climbing a ladder of mud, up, up, up. Panting with fatigue and every muscle aching, I reached the top of the ridge. Too proud to lie on the ground in front of my new companions, I stood exhausted, probably weaving a bit, and thought scornfully how could Lyn have recommended such a place. No wonder the Tautes were considered relatively "untouched"—who could reach them?

We hiked along the wide ridge, steep on the river's side but sloping more modestly on the other, through a series of small unfenced gardens and open spaces fringed with forest. It was pleasant and parklike, but my body continued to ache and my breathing was not recovered, probably because I was so anxious about this trip and in only minutes would know the outcome. Just ahead was a series of steps cut into the red earth and entwined by the roots of a mammoth tree. The trail was ascending again and, trudging upward, my light clothing saturated with sweat, I had not felt so wiped out since my Molmo hike with Wes.

On top I rested for a moment, gratefully noting the gentle slope of the next section of trail, when Kumoi, his shirt and shorts still impeccably clean, turned toward me and, smiling with satisfaction, pointed skyward. "Taute, i stap." On a towering forested pinnacle just ahead, I saw the graceful turrets of coconut palms and the deep brown thatch of house roofs.

A Westerner entering a mountain village is always a ridiculous figure. Even the most rugged of patrol officers enters at a social disadvantage. His body dripping with sweat and his lungs heaving like the bellows of a pipe organ, Her Majesty's official enters without fanfare, his customary bravado and magesterial authority momentarily dissolved by the climb and in no mood to give orders until he collects himself.

It was obvious to any observer that I had no special authority to lose, but I had lost my breath and Kumoi took me to his house where I drank the cooling juice of a green coconut and Kumoi answered the questions of the throng of villagers collected around us. Kumoi lucidly explained that I was looking for a village in which to live with my family for a year or so; that I was not a missionary, government employee, or trader, but sent by my school in America to learn about the Wape way of life.

I was tremendously impressed by Kumoi's quick grasp of my purpose as explained to him on our walk from Lumi. And I appreciated the gracious way he interceded for me with the villagers while I was still collecting myself from the walk. Kumoi rapidly was making himself indispensable. We had but just met, yet already we were engaged in a close relationship, and it was clear to everyone, including myself, that just then I belonged to Kumoi. He had seen me, claimed me, and brought me home.

The men, for they were the only ones to speak to me, were enthusiastic about my settling in the village. With a large noisy entourage, we toured the village's three hamlets, as the virtues of the village were extolled and many rash seductive promises made; there was no service for which my family would lack that was within their power to perform. The only condition they would exact from me was to employ only Taute villagers. It was a congenial requirement since it fit my plans as well. While from their point of view the "Taute only" policy kept wages exclusively within the village, from my research perspective it established an initial network of personal contacts with villagers based on ties of mutual dependency. In other words, the more people that worked for me within the village, the greater my network for securing information about village life. It was a simple but well-substantiated point I had learned from Margaret Mead.

Since I was now virtually certain this was the village in

which we would settle, I toured the hamlets with the principle purpose of finding a house site for our new home. The main requirement for an anthropologist's house is that it be in the thick of things; the more central its location, the more he can see and hear what is going on. He then places the data of what he has personally *observed* about the culture against the data his informants have *told* him about their culture. Sometimes the two types of data coincide, sometimes they diverge; then he must push his inquiry further to try to understand the nature of the discrepancy.

Mifu, the hamlet I had first entered and where Kumoi lived, was out of the question. Perched on its pinnacle, the houses were crowded together around the dance ground; there was simply no place to build the size house we needed. But the Mifus offered me a building site just below the hamlet where the Franciscan's catechist school stood. It was a simple structure built on the ground with open sides and a thatched roof and they would be pleased to tear it down and build me a house there. I quickly vetoed the scheme. I did not wish to antagonize the Franciscan missionaries and the site itself was too isolated. Furthermore, I had just learned that all but two of the men away at plantations were from Mifu.

Just beyond the catechist school were the seven houses that comprised Obuenga hamlet. Once a flourishing hamlet, it was now considered a satellite of Mifu. Most of the adults were old; only two of the families had young children. Nothing much of social importance, I surmised, would be happening here.

Kafiere, the third hamlet, was almost a mile further along the ridge. From Obuenga to Kafiere the ridge was narrow for much of it had fallen away in landslides caused by the heavy rains. And in 1935, a tremendous earthquake racked this area of New Guinea, slicing away a section of the ridge where a fourth hamlet, Tipiowa, stood. Throughout the mountains, villages were smashed to the ground, and rivers dammed by the landslides created great lakes only to break sweeping away gardens and houses. Keith McCarthy, then a young officer stationed in Aitape and later Director of Native Affairs, reports in his book *Pa-*

trol into Yesterday that the shock of the quake was so strong that he was knocked to his knees while bathing in the sea, then watched the water quietly recede to return in a tidal wave of breakers that flooded the low-lying coast.

The Tautes remember the earthquake with equal vividness. A man recalled how, as a child, his father swooped him up from play when the quake struck and, clutching him to his chest, ran into the quaking forest resounding with the crash of falling trees. There was no safe place to hide. But the death toll in Taute was low compared to many other villages; only Siwau's young wife and baby were killed, struck by the toppled beams of their home. Stopping, Kumoi pointed to a deep gash across the ridge ripped open by the quake and filled in only where our path traversed it. After twenty-five years of rapid jungle growth the scar was still visible.

A short way farther along the ridge I climbed a steep embankment and stepped into a beautiful hamlet. It was Kafiere. Like all Wape houses, these were made of sago thatch roofing with walls of sturdy sago palm leaf stems. Most were built on the ground in the traditional fashion and scattered along the spacious ridge amid coconut palms, Hibiscus shrubs bursting with red and pink flowers, and giant Poinsettias. After the "urban" compactness of Mifu, Kafiere had all the relaxed charm of a New England village. I immediately liked the place. As I strolled through the hamlet greeting the smiling people, I saw at least two perfect locations for a house. There was even a good spring on the ridge so water would not have to be laboriously hauled up from the Sibi for our inordinately heavy needs. Unlike Westerners, the Wape use little water; their dishes are disposable leaves and they bathe in the river and streams.

Sensing my pleasure with the hamlet, Kumoi and the others began immediately to plan where we should live and to arrange carrying our cargo to the village. I told them, however, before I could make any decision, Joyce and I would return together. It was always possible, I thought, their initial concern was only a passing enthusiasm that enlivened a quiet day. Before coming to

live with them, I must be sure they fully understood the needs of
our camp and were capable and willing to assume the responsibility for meeting them.

We walked back to Mifu where I announced I would return
to Lumi via Lau'um and Boru'um, the other two villages on the
ridge. Both were heavily recruited so I was not seriously interested in either village but only wanted to visit them for compari-
sons to Taute. When I asked if there was anyone who would show
me the way, the men volunteered the services of a young man
named Yawo. He did not want to go at first but the men prevailed until he accepted. So with vigorous handshakes all round
and my solemn promise to return with my wife, the villagers
gaily waved us off.

It was an hour's comfortable walk along the ridge to
Lau'um. When we arrived the village was virtually deserted. An
old couple smiled at us from their house but since neither spoke
Pidgin and I could not speak Wape, conversation was impossible.
I did not even attempt to have Yawo interpret because he had
quickly proved to be a very odd young man. On our way to
Lau'um he had alternately talked peculiarly or seemed deeply
preoccupied.

Leaving Lau'um, we passed through an opening in the multiple trunks of a mammoth banyan tree, a rare memento of pre-
contact days when villages were barricaded against attack. With
pacification, the gate trees were destroyed, bamboo barricades
pulled down, and the handsome black fight shields typical of the
Wape burned in great fires on the order of the Australian patrols.
It was the end of village sovereignty, for until then, each village
was a miniature nation settling its internal disputes and arranging ties with other villages through marriage. Boru'um too was
almost deserted except for a lone woman from whom I bought a
green coconut for a final drink before beginning the last leg of the
trip back to Lumi.

By this time I realized that there was something definitely
wrong with my companion. Occasionally he would look at me intently, his large eyes seeming to pop from his head, and grimace

strangely. Then with a buoyant giggle he would speak, but it made no sense though I understood the separate words. Yawo's unpredictable behavior was making me very uneasy. Also, after all of the human excitement in Taute, the emptiness of Lau'um and Boru'um seemed sinister. I was tired and anxious to be home.

From Boru'um the track dropped from the sheer cliff into the forest below, and I knew I would never find my way across the Sibi and back to Lumi before nightfall by myself. As much as I wanted to return alone, I was stuck with Yawo. Plunging into the darkness of the forest, for it was now late afternoon, Yawo insisted that I precede him. Following almost on my heels he whispered hoarsely in a curious jumble and, as usual, the meaning eluded me. He repeatedly spoke about a "wildman," and every few phrases he spoke the Pidgin verb 'killim,' to kill.

Finally unable to tolerate Yawo's unseen but very audible presence, I demanded he walk on the path in front of me although he strenuously objected. Why, when he was ostensibly my guide, did he object to leading the way? The bush became thicker, the light dimmer, the mud deeper. On another patrol I had heard talk of a "wildman" in the Lumi area, a man without a home who raided the gardens and terrorized solitary travelers by shooting his arrows at them. I had discounted the tale as just another extension of the fear the Wape have of the forest, filled as it is with an eerie caste of murderous witches, ghosts, and demons. Now I wondered, was the story true or wasn't it? Should I be concerned or was I behaving like a frightened fool? Or was Yawo himself the "wildman"?

Stopping and standing in the deep shadows of the trail, Yawo turned and approached me. Raising his arms jerkily, he seemed to want to touch me. Or would he grab me? In my most matter-of-fact and authoritarian voice I told Yawo to turn around and get moving. We had no time to stand around visiting in a swamp.

I was aware that my focus on the afternoon's activities was blurring and I found myself conjuring up a panoply of violent fantasies in which I was either being assaulted by a madman or shot full of arrows by a marauding wildman. The unfamiliar has a way of stretching one's imagination that transforms the most bizarre idea to an inevitable, commonplace act.

Yawo was obviously deranged, but I had no clues, as I would have in my own culture, as to the nature of his madness. Nor had I any way of predicting what he might do next. Perhaps he was completely harmless. Why, I wondered, had the Tautes sent this obviously unbalanced young man to escort me? Did they really want me to come and live with them or was Yawo to frighten me away? As we pushed ahead, it was now I who became the obsessive talker, encouraging Yawo to keep moving along. I only wanted to get out of that dark sago swamp and back to the army's magnificent highway where I was sure to meet other travelers.

One of the very unsettling aspects of living within a strange culture is that in the beginning one has no absolute knowledge of what is happening, absolute in the sense that one understands the background of behavior and can accurately grasp its full meaning and predict subsequent actions. Sloshing through the swamp with Yawo, I was bewildered by the events surrounding me, and my response was one of fear and frustration. I didn't know what was true or what was right. Anthropologists recognize this as "culture shock," an occupational hazard of the profession. In fact, without experiencing culture shock, I doubt if an anthropologist would learn much of significance about a culture at all, for it is from these points of confusion that he begins to ask the questions that sort out his new experiences and, gradually, arranges them into a comprehensible pattern. If he has unstintingly subjected himself to the rigors of culture shock and been thorough in the kinds of questions asked to clarify his bewilderment, he will emerge from the ordeal of field work with a formalized version of the culture rooted in the genuineness of his experiences with his hosts. That is both the method and goal of good ethnography.

Even before Yawo and I reached the army's road, I heard the welcomed voices of men laughing and talking in the distance. We already had crossed the Sibi River, and from there on the trail was well marked. So Yawo returned to Taute and I continued to Lumi, greeting each fellow traveler with a renewed sense of fellowship. The world was beginning to make sense again.

It was some time before I discovered the cause of Yawo's peculiar behavior. A few years before I met Yawo he was visiting his mother's family in Boru'um, the very village he and I visited together, when he suffered an accident. An intelligent and courageous youth, he had climbed one of his maternal uncle's tall palm trees to collect coconuts and, somehow losing his grip, had fallen crashing to the ground. Unconscious, his relatives had carried him to the Lumi hospital where he was transferred by plane to the modern hospital in Wewak. There he had undergone surgery, and a plate was sewn into his head to replace a section of his shattered skull. When he finally emerged from his lengthy coma, he saw with wonder the sea for the first time. But his brain was permanently damaged. He would never be a normal Wape man.

Returning to the village, Yawo was a figure of ridicule, a youth who talked and acted silly. At first the children teased him, but when he raged at them they learned to leave him alone. A solitary figure wandering through the village and bush, he had been saved by modern medicine for a fragmentary life.

In Lumi, Joyce and I finally received word from Wewak that our expedition cargo had arrived. Everything had successfully passed through customs except a confiscated deck of playing cards outlawed by the House of Assembly, Papua New Guinea's legislative body, and two trunks containing foodstuffs placed in quarantine. The next message from Wewak notified us that the freeze-dried hamburger and steaks, luxury items we had brought for special occasions, had been dumped into the Bismark Sea. U.S. meat products, we sorrowfully learned, were prohibited entry into the Territory, although with chauvinistic pique I noticed the Lumi trade stores were filled with canned meats, some almost unedible, from other nations.

Two weeks after my first visit to Taute, I returned with Joyce. We were royally welcomed, the villagers' enthusiasm for our coming to live with them was undimmed, and Joyce was as pleased with the village as I. But when, as we started to leave, the men offered to find us a guide to the Sibi River, I declined. I knew all about their concept of a guide. And besides, we had just walked over the track and it seemed impossible we could lose our way. But we did. Eventually we reached the river where two startled Taute men, supposing us far away by now, offered their aid. Ifau, a friendly and serious man and the father of the only child in the Lumi school, escorted us up the river to the Lumi trail while lecturing us on the folly of hiking in the forest without first learning the proper trails. Comfortingly clutching his bow and arrows, he gave us a final ominous warning about the "wild-man" then bid us good-by.

So it was settled. Taute would be our new home. In a parley with the Taute men we agreed to employ only Taute villagers, and in return they agreed to take care of all our work needs including carrying our cargo, building a house, camp chores, and, of course, teaching us about their way of life.

From the first the villagers were also insistent that I open a small trade store in Taute to save them the long walk into Lumi. No amount of explaining ever convinced them that it was impossible for me to do so. Even if I had been interested in running a small store—which I emphatically wasn't—it was not possible. Our entry permits to the Territory were exclusively for research, and we were expressly forbidden from engaging in any kind of formal trade. But the villagers were never sincerely convinced that a white person—any white person—couldn't get a license to run a store if he wished. Both of Lumi's missions, all whites, and its single recruiter, a white man, ran trade stores. To the Wape it was the one useful service Westerners provided. I know it struck the Tautes as selfish and mean-spirited that I would not open a store when I obviously had the training to keep the books and the money to buy the supplies. Not yet a resident of the village, already I had let them down. The long process of disenchantment had begun.

3

A HOME IN THE FOREST

I hurriedly finished my breakfast as Kumoi and a score of Taute men came into our yard. Today we would begin the move to the village, and the Tautes were as excited as Joyce and I. Our plan was that I would go with the cargo today, set up camp, then return in a day or two for Joyce and the children. The odd thing, however, was neither the Tautes nor I had broached the crucial topic of who exactly was to carry the cargo and exactly how much money they would be paid. In my euphoria in finding a village and in their euphoria in finding a Western family, we were avoiding the crass monetary aspect of our relationship. Apparently, our ties to each other were still too tenuous to risk money talk.

Still, it was my cargo and my responsibility, not theirs, to designate the carriers and their wages. Yet I had not done so. I was so single-mindedly intent in getting the cargo moved to the village and beginning my work after the long delay, that I was clearly evading any decisions I might blunder. Since the villagers seemed perfectly willing to move the cargo to Taute according to their own plans, I certainly wasn't going to interfere. I even rationalized that my being less authoritarian than other white men might help to lessen the terrifying cultural gap between myself and the villagers. For one thing was certain, I did not want to be a Great White Master; by muddling along I might avoid imprinting our initial relations with the invidious master-servant colonial stamp. But it was obvious, even to me, that I was creating a Day of Reckoning. Yet I had no idea that my strategy, or lack of it, would precipitate the first major crisis in my field work.

Roger Fairhall had kindly volunteered the use of the government's tractor, trailer, and driver to take the cargo to the end of the army road. The men wanted to be off before the heat of the day, so I marked the trunks in order of priority and they began loading them onto the trailer. After the fifth one they stopped. When I asked about the others, Kumoi explained they were taking only five trunks today. They would carry them in two-man relays with a team of four to a trunk.

This was certainly a departure from established custom; New Guinea carriers usually transport trunks and patrol boxes in two-man teams resting as necessary to cover the day's walk. With the tractor's help, this march at the most would be about two hours. But I said nothing. The time was past when I could express my views about the carrying. Kumoi and the men had assumed the responsibility and their plan was to complete an extremely difficult task with a minimum of discomfort. Who could blame them for that? Still, when the tractor pulled away from Lumi with only a handful of trunks and a load of laughing men, I couldn't help but feel a bit disgruntled.

At the end of the army road, the men unloaded the trunks and deftly lashed them to poles with long vines. Entering the dark forest, they moved nimbly along the muddy track, trunks swaying, toward the Sibi River below. At the river we stopped for a rest. Wape men are not particularly robust and some of the older carriers were feeling the strain. To counteract their aches, they whipped their backs and shoulders with stinging nettles, substituting one kind of pain for another. Others bathed in the river. But I was surprised at their polite modesty. Although their fathers and grandfathers wore no clothing or pubic covering, the bathers carefully shielded their genitals from view. I assumed their modesty was because of my presence, but I was wrong. White men, civilized men, do not walk naked through life, and the assuming of clothes and genital shame, I would learn, helped the Tautes to identify themselves as modern men. Although their ancestors may have been "naked savages," they proudly were not.

Now began the formidable climb to the Taute ridge. The weighted poles bit into the men's shoulder bones as they waved an arm to maintain balance and keep the swinging trunks from crashing to the ground. Finally, with stinging nettles flailing the skin, we entered Kafiere hamlet, and the trunks were gratefully dropped in front of the government rest house where we would live while our house was built. An excited and smiling group of women and children had gathered to watch the arrival of their *moli,* the Wape word for a white person, and a number of old men repairing the rest house proudly stepped forward and shook my hand. It was a warming welcome. I made a brief speech expressing my gratitude to the villagers for inviting my family to come and live with them and emphasized again I was not a government officer, missionary, or trader. I was a teacher sent by my country, America, from far across the sea to learn about their way of life. But here, I said, I was the student and they must teach me.

I ended my speech noting that eventually my family and I must return to our relatives in America, just as they must return to their families in Taute from the copra plantations. I was deliberately vague as to the length of our stay. When I had lived with the Iatmul on the Sepik, I made the mistake of telling the villagers exactly how long I would live among them. From my first day in that village to the last, the conversation opener was to sorrowfully tell me specifically how much longer I had to stay.

The trunks were carried into the house with the people following for I had decided to open them publicly. If enough individuals saw what they actually contained, it might counter the false rumors that undoubtedly were circulating. The entire village seemed to be crammed into the small house with me and it shook and creaked with the multitude of busy bare brown feet. I worried that it might collapse, for rest houses are seldom-used structures and notorious for being poorly built and maintained. On patrol in 1967 on a tributary of the Sepik River my companion, a medical assistant, stepped through the floor and broke his leg. But Kumoi only laughed at my fears. This house would not break, he assured me, and it didn't.

Unlocking each trunk, I marveled at the precision with which Joyce and I had packed them. Producing a series of exotic items from a trunk such as Ned's big brown Teddy bear, a florescent lamp or tape recorder, I held them aloft to the delight of all and explained what they were. Never had Taute been host to such a strange cargo. Then closing the last trunk to the regret of my audience, I went outside to admire the beautiful view of the Sibi twisting through the forest far below and the green Torricellis lifting upward to the hot, white clouds. But for the villagers the show was over. Like theatergoers after a spectacular play, they filed out of the house talking about the wondrous things they had seen.

Sometime during that eventful and unforgettable first day in the village, Kumoi announced he would be my 'monki masta,' or houseman and cook, and Witauwa, a strongly built but moody older man designated himself as my 'bosboi' to supervise the house building, while Maiana, a gracefully built young man of pensive temperament, volunteered his services as 'wasboi' or laundry man. I accepted their services but provisionally until Joyce had moved to the village.

Kumoi and I went to work setting up the camp, but it was almost dark before we finished. In New Guinea the sun sets precisely at seven o'clock every day of the year. It never lingers on the horizon as in temperate zones but, like a titanic golden ball, bounces into darkness and is lost. I hung up a kerosene lantern, the only one in the village, and some of the Kafiere men came to sit with me on the porch while we visited easily about the day's activities and the village. They recalled for me the terrifying earthquake that shattered the Taute ridge and remembered the names and personalities of the various Franciscan fathers who had served the village. And someone told me about the mystifying visit two years earlier of two white men and a little boy who landed their helicopter in the center of the hamlet to dig up some earth before whirling away. They wondered why they had come. But I too, like the helicopter men, would be with them only for a while and then gone. I must remember to be perfectly explicit about my work and various technical procedures to minimize the conceptual confusion I might introduce into their orderly lives.

When the men returned to their houses that night I went to bed, tired and extremely happy. I was in my village. I had begun my work, and a thrill ran through my weary body.

The next morning was bright and clear. The open dance ground that served as the center for public activities was occupied by a scattering of villagers sitting with their naked backs to the rising sun. They nodded and dozed as the luxurious warmth of the sun baked into their skin chilled by a long night of cool damp air. Only two toddlers playing with a giant leaf of a bread fruit tree seemed alive. As I ate my breakfast a flock of screeching cockatoos flew hurriedly down the Sibi River and a parrot, a vivid blur of color, dashed by on another errand. Sipping my coffee I planned my census of the hamlet's houses, for until I learned who lived where and their relationships to one another, I would remain a stranger to the complex patterns of life around me.

Several of the men accompanied me as I went from house to house, making a rough sketch map of the hamlet and collecting the census data. I worked slowly, for the men were good informants; they quickly understood the value of what I was doing and rounded out the bare-bones data with amusing anecdotes and stories about some of the people as we worked. Approaching the ceremonial house, I sketched its location then asked to go inside, although I knew no one lived there. Religious buildings always interest me, and I was intensely curious about this one.

The large single room with its dirt floor was windowless like all Wape houses. It was also disappointingly devoid of any ritual objects or masks. Then in the far corner I noticed a screen set into the ground to conceal something. It was, the men said, where the *fongoal* was kept. I, as a man, could see it without harm, but if a woman or girl looked at it, the men of the village would become sick, perhaps some might die. It was the kind of gentle reversal I came to expect of the Wape. Where another New Guinean culture might say the woman who saw it would die or be killed by the men for spying, the Wape characteristically reversed the phrasing to name her husband as the victim instead. But I was also told that while I might look at it, I dare not touch it. Only Wamala and his young stepson Miembel, to whom it actually belonged as an inheritance from his dead father, could hold it without danger.

With the excitement that surrounds all dangerous activities, I looked behind the screen and saw a strange rustic altar. It was constructed of an upright tree limb buried in the ground with several short branches arching out at chest level and encircled with several narrow strips of cane. Once it had been decorated with bright colored leaves and lacy ferns, but they now hung about it with the wispy dryness of a mummy's hair. Gently cradled in the branches was a smooth, oval, black stone about six inches long and flecked with the fragile flakes of dried blood. It was the *fongoal,* a Wape word for stone. But this was no ordinary stone. In a lowered voice I learned its true identity. I was looking straight into the heart of the *mani* demon.

Sometimes in field work it is not wise to immediately pursue a new revelation, especially if it concerns something that is sacred, forbidden, or deviant. I was gratified that this first small, but important, bit of sacred data was offered with such candor, but I dared not push my luck. In the past, the missionaries had taken strong repressive measures to eliminate Wape religion but had failed. As a consequence, work on supernatural beliefs might be resisted and difficult. I left the ceremonial house to continue the census, but I could not shake the demon's black heart from my mind.

Finishing the Kafiere census I counted eighteen family households and two bachelor dwellings that housed the young unmarried men. In all, there were eighty-six people living in the hamlet. Later, Kumoi and I sat down together and began work on the Wape language. He was, as I knew he would be, an excellent teacher, patiently instructing me in the parts of the body and correcting my pronunciation with professional diligence. Occasionally, a series of exuberant yelps drifted up to us from the forest below. It was the carriers buoying up their sagging spirits as they brought five more trunks to the village.

That night the men again joined me on the porch to visit, and I asked about their clans and lineages. It was essential information if I were to understand the organization of the village. But Pidgin vocabulary and idiomatic phrases vary throughout the Territory, and the Pidgin terms I had used successfully elsewhere to discuss family groupings produced only quizzical looks. The more I rephrased my questions, the more frustrated and confused we all became. Finally the conversation turned to the large wooden slit gongs that thunder messages across the valleys and ridges to surrounding villages. Wamala, a homely, middle-aged man of great gentleness, tapped out on a piece of wood almost a dozen different signals giving me the name for each in both Wape and Pidgin. But further questioning about the meaning of the signals were again frustratingly nonproductive, although the men were valiantly trying to grasp what I was trying to ask.

The only signal I could relate back to the culture was one called *mani;* obviously it was somehow related to the demon whose heart lay in the ceremonial house across the dance ground. The men, with exaggerated smiles reserved for a person of severely limited capacities, were pleased I had learned something. It was many months before I understood that the other signals Wamala had given me identified each of the major village patrilineages. Somehow, he had intuited what I was trying to ask and gave me an answer, but, in my ignorance, it completely passed me by. Even today, when playing a tape recorded Wape interview I am sometimes stunned by a clearly made point that, at the time, I completely failed to take in.

In the morning I returned with the carriers to Lumi where five more trunks were lashed to the sagging poles. As the men worked they were joined by twenty-odd Taute women and girls who had come to Lumi at dawn for the twice weekly market. Bringing coconuts, tomatoes, tobacco, betel nut, and other small amounts of produce, some had made a few shillings selling to the New Guineans and Westerners working for the government and the missions. Now they were mostly empty-handed, and the men loaded them with a motley array of our loose camp gear and supplies accumulated since our arrival in Lumi.

In a long, broken line that stretched completely across the station and airstrip, the Tautes began the trek back to the village. But as I watched them leave, I noticed some women carrying cases of heavy canned goods while others carried only a broom or a kerosene lamp. How, I wondered, were Kumoi and Witauwa going to decide who would be paid what amount. What criterion would they use? Also, originally I assumed the men would bring the cargo to the village, but now everyone was getting into the act. I feared the sum set aside for the move, although generous by Territory standards, would be so widely dispersed there would be dissatisfaction. I began to dread the Day of Reckoning, a day very soon, when the villagers would line up to receive their pay and regretted I ever relinquished my control over the carrying.

That evening Lyn gave us a farewell dinner, and the next day the Tautes—this time only the men—returned for more trunks and to escort us to our new home. Although Joyce had become fond of Lumi with good friends in both missions and the government's compound, she was as ready as I to be on our way. The children might have felt differently if asked. As far as they were concerned, we were settled and they seemed perfectly content with life in Lumi. They delighted in running errands to the trade store or, hearing the mail plane roar overhead, dash up to the airstrip to watch it land and unload. Nothing that exciting ever happened at home on the farm.

But walking with my family out of Lumi and into the forest, I had some disquieting thoughts. It was the first time I seriously wondered if this was the right thing for them. Although I was sure the children would find village life interesting, there was the genuine problem of their health. And I was concerned about the cultural isolation Taute would impose upon Joyce. Accustomed to an active involvement with her own work and friends, she now would be constricted to a husband preoccupied with his work, two preschool children, and villagers who could neither appreciate or understand her primary interests. And in terms of my family's happiness, I worried what life with the Tautes would be like. Everything was pleasant just now, but this honeymoon, like all honeymoons, would come to an end.

And end it did! It happened the day we paid the carriers. All my premonitions came true.

After the villagers had assembled on the dance ground, I brought out thirty dollars of small Australian coins and gave them to Kumoi and Witauwa. Both had agreed it was a fair sum for the carrying, but neither had discussed with me who was to be paid or how much. Kumoi acted as master of ceremonies calling for each group of payees to step forward while Witauwa counted out the money and Maiana handed it the villager. First, Kumoi called for the twenty-nine men who had carried all of the heavy trunks and crates to line up. Standing in rigid formation, each man to Joyce's and my horror and shame, stepped forward and was given forty cents. We could not believe it. These men had carried all of the cargo except odds and ends, and they weren't even to receive half of the money. I searched their faces for evidence of dissatisfaction but saw only stoicism. Or was the stoical expression itself evidence of anger? I didn't then know Wape facial expressions well enough to judge.

Then the men and boys who had carried lighter cargo, some of them only a single time, were lined and each was given thirty cents. .Comparatively speaking, this was all out of proportion, and I was beginning to feel embarrassed, angry, and guilty. The women who had carried things for us after the Lumi market were also each given thirty cents. And then, to my complete surprise, the women and girls who had cooked for the twenty-nine men on the days they had carried cargo were lined and each paid twenty cents. By this time I was quite overwhelmed and noticed that some of the male carriers, especially several of the strongest young men who had carried so much, were beginning to ignore the proceedings and talk actively among themselves.

There was still money left and I hoped Kumoi and Witauwa, who could certainly sense the antagonism more acutely than I, would distribute it to the twenty-nine men as a small bonus. I was just about to make such a suggestion, gladly adding more money if necessary, when Kumoi called for the old men who had prepared the rest house—a job that in my mind was completely unrelated to the cargo—to step forward and each received twenty cents. The distribution of the money was completed.

Several of the mature men came toward the house and spoke strongly in Wape to Kumoi. I didn't need a translation to know they were registering their rage. What a splendid way to begin my field work! I had succeeded in alienating the most important group of potential informants—the men who would organize all of the village's important social and ceremonial activities. But there was nothing I could do about it now. I had relinquished my authority on the matter and to interfere now, even if I knew what to do, which I didn't, would be humiliating to Kumoi and Witauwa, upon whom I was now dependent for resolving the conflict.

The men's indignation had grown to mutinous proportions, and I wouldn't have blamed them if they had rushed the house and chucked us all over the cliff into the Sibi. But Kumoi, polished and cool, was more than equal to the occasion. Stepping toward the crowd in his gleaming white shirt, a transcultural symbol of righteousness, he shouted, " 'Fasen maus!' " then

vigorously lectured the assemblage in his voluble Pidgin for
about five minutes. Before Bill came to Taute, he said, there was
no money here—no money at all! Thirty dollars is big money for
bringing his cargo to Taute. There were many men in other
villages who wanted to carry the cargo but Bill said, "No!" only
Taute could carry. And besides, he is a newcomer to New
Guinea; he doesn't yet know how to do things properly. You just
can't stand there and complain, you must think about these
things!

I had to hand it to Kumoi. Although my pride was hurt
when I heard it shouted across the dance ground and into the
forest that I was a greenhorn, the crowd dispersed. But the men
were not yet finished with this affair. They gathered in front of
the men's ceremonial house deep in conference. Kumoi and
Maiana, I noticed, were also there. Something was being decided, and I was anxious to know what it was.

It was a suspenseful hour before the conference ended and
Kumoi, with a delegation of the men, returned to the house to
speak to me. What would they say? I was expecting the worst, for
the men looked exceedingly grave. Kumoi spoke.

"Bill," he said, "the carrying is finished and paid for. We
cannot change that. But for the house, only the men you designate to build it will be paid just like at the white man's copra
plantations. There will be no group of women to feed the men;
each must get his food from his wife or mother in the usual way."

Surprised and relieved at this graceful conclusion, I publicly
acknowledged my satisfaction. Since the men who were to build
the house would be the same ones who carried the bulk of the
cargo, they could recoup some of the losses they suffered today.
So the Day of Reckoning was over. But that night, for the first
time since moving to the village, no one came to sit with me and
visit.

Margaret Mead used to tell us in her field-methods seminar
at Columbia that "everything is grist for the anthropologist's
mill," indicating that human experience, however formal or informal, planned or fortuitous, harmonious or discordant, can

teach us something about a culture and its people. Well, what had I learned from this blundering encounter?

For one, I learned that in the long run I might have saved myself and the villagers considerable anguish if I had followed the Western tradition of individually hiring and paying the carriers a prearranged sum. After all, it was the way modern business was transacted in the Territory. Perhaps I had allowed my anticolonialism and eagerness to get moved to the village to obscure the simple practical solution. But I also had learned in an intensely dramatic fashion that Taute was an egalitarian society. When Kumoi and Witauwa assumed responsibility for getting the cargo to Taute, they felt constrained to parcel out the money to as many categories of people as possible. This wasn't because they were nice guys, but because they knew that within the framework of Wape culture they had to. Distinctions between men and women or the young and the old, for example, were not drawn to exclude one group or another from having a direct share in the money. Only the children too small to participate were excluded as a class.

This information was extremely revealing about the culture. In fact, so egalitarian was Taute that, like other Wape villages, it did not have an indigenous headman with political status or influence. The Wape, I was discovering, were not only egalitarian, but fiercely so. Every man was his own king, every woman her own queen, with concessions given only to kinship obligations and the realities of Australian domination and power. At least it seemed this way. So accustomed was I to hierarchically organized societies, both aboriginal and civilized, that for months I continued to search for a covert political leader that was running the show. But the Tautes never took me to their leader, nor did I ever find him. He didn't exist.

During those first few days of tension after the carrying fiasco, Ned and Elizabeth were our ambassadors of good will. The Wape are loving and patient parents, and the villagers quickly adopted Ned and Elizabeth as their own. The old men even built a fence along the cliff near our house to keep them from tumbling off. Their own children, they explained, never fall off but, then, they were born in the forest.

Wherever Ned and Elizabeth went, flocks of children joined them to play. They drew pictures in the sand together and danced the simple dances of the great curing festivals. Ned and his playmates donned improvised masks and proudly pranced across the dance ground while Elizabeth joined the little girls, hand in hand, to laughingly circle the miniature priests. And when they tired of play, the village children would ask for another look at Ned's squeaky Teddy bear and Elizabeth's crying doll. Sitting on the house ladder, Ned and Elizabeth would put on a show with "Teddy" and "Baby-By-By" to the ringing laughter of children and adults alike. The only point of annoyance to Ned and Elizabeth was that their fine golden hair seemed irresistible to touch. Mothers even brought their babies to feel their locks. But when their own playmates, so intrigued with these pink and golden children who now belonged to them, tried the same, they were rebuffed in fluent Pidgin. Although they enjoyed their celebrity status, they weren't about to sacrifice their sense of autonomy to maintain it.

The work on the new house was moving along smoothly. Before leaving Lumi, Don McGregor gave me wise advice on how to brace the structure, which trees were the strongest for the supporting poles and timbers, and, in general, how to proceed. But except for a few important details like spacing the posts to fit my house plan, the Tautes seemed to know just what to do. They assured me they were using only the strongest and best bush materials because they wanted the house to last. We would be so comfortable in Taute, they insisted, we would never want to leave. Then someone quietly added, I think it was Wamala, that they wanted to bury me in Taute. Just as they irrevocably belonged to Taute, so should I.

Since I spent much of my day with the men gathering bush materials for the house and asking about and photographing their building techniques, we came to know each other and my contacts with some of them began to pass from one of acquaintanceship to that of friendship. Of course, my comparative wealth and Western status was, and would remain, an unknown factor influencing our relationships as was my zeal to understand their culture. Except in my role as an anthropologist, it was highly inconceivable that I would ever have reason to be in Taute. But now that we were living and working together, our lives were becoming increasingly intermeshed, and our mutual dependencies moved us closer and closer to one another. Already the villagers had stopped calling me 'masta' and addressed me as "beal," their closest approximation to my nickname, "Bill." Only the older men who could well remember when a native was beaten for failing to call a white man 'masta' still used the term occasionally to my chagrin. When they came to know and trust me, even they dropped the elitist term.

What I most admired about the Taute men was the tranquil closeness with which they worked together. I never had seen such harmonious cooperation before. And their organization for constructing the house was intelligent as well as efficient. First they discussed with me the kind of house we wanted, then sensibly divided the tasks among themselves according to each man's physical strength and abilities. That much done, they cheerfully went to work. Although Witauwa was ostensibly the 'bosboi,' his only function seemed to be blowing the conch shell in the morning and afternoon to announce the beginning and ending of the work day. Compared to the Western concept of a boss, this was a shallow parody. But no one was going to boss another Taute man in his own village, and Witauwa knew it. So with no one to boss, he did nothing but watch the rest of us work. His idle presence began to irritate me.

In fact, I had noticed that many things, often small things, were irritating me. It was, I knew, from the stress of adapting to an alien culture. Besides, our crowded living arrangements in the rest house were daily accentuating the strains. Joyce and I both were alarmingly short-tempered and impatient. In a more assertive and turbulent culture, we might have survived those first few months more easily. But knowing that we dare not lash out at our even-tempered neighbors and trying, not always successfully, to spare the children our irritability, we flashed cold anger toward one another. To the calm and collected Tautes, we must have appeared as a tempestuous caricature of all they despised in human relationships.

Only twice in those trying months did I direct my barbed hostility to the Tautes. The first time was a day or two after Joyce and the children moved to Taute. A crowd of children and women in hopes of seeing Ned and Elizabeth swooped up on the porch filling it with claustrophobic closeness, and I ordered them off. Impatiently, yes, but not with rage. But Ifau, the man who had shown us the path when Joyce and I were lost, was again to show me the way. As the blank-faced children hurried away, he turned and looked directly into my eyes with an expression of unbelieving hurt. " 'Masta,' " he said imploring, " 'tok isi!' " His words hit my face with the shock of ice water. For an instant I did not even know what I had done, then I realized the extent of my rudeness and my face burned with shame. It was the first time Joyce and I were completely aware of how much we would have to alter our behavior to live successfully with the Wape.

The second incident occurred when the house was almost finished and we were moving in. The house was magnificent, both to us and the Tautes. There was a large combination living and bedroom for Joyce and me, two smaller rooms for the children, a long pantry, a shower room, and large dining porch. The cook house was separate, and next to it sat our water storage drum, a precious present from Sisters Florianne, Kiernan, and Mary Magdalin of the Lumi Catholic mission. The outhouse was cleverly placed away from the dining porch near the top of the steep forested slope that met the Sibi far below. Although convenient to the house, it was completely hidden behind numerous large ornamental and flowering shrubs. As outhouses go, its location was perfect. Leaving the new house, Joyce glanced away for a refreshing view of the mountains and saw instead the outhouse, ostentatiously naked, glaring at her. To improve our view of the mountains, one of the men had innocently, but systematically, cut every towering shrub to reveal instead the outhouse for our dining pleasure.

Appalled, Joyce turned her open fury upon me for allowing the mistake, and I, like a put-upon husband in an old-fashioned farce, turned and berated the men. It was the kind of outrageous performance the Iatmuls would have loved, but the Taute men never looked up. They silently walked away to leave me yelling in the wind.

The Wape tolerate such angry outbursts, but they neither respect or reward them. They have a standard response to verbal aggression. No response. A toddler is allowed to lie kicking and screaming in the sand until he is exhausted, but no one goes near him. So by the time a child is six or seven, an uncontrolled temper tantrum or fighting is rare. Ned and Elizabeth seldom quarreled, but if they did, villagers clucked their tongues in disapproval. Even Witauwa, easily the most irascible and fiery man in the village, once rebuked them for hitting each other.

When a Wape feels wronged, when he simply has to express his hostile feelings or explode, he lectures. Solo'oke, angered when his child was accidentally injured by a playmate's knife, stalked over to the child's house and harangued the silent parents hidden inside about the carelessness of their child raising. Or old Wila, furious about her piglets killed by Wamala's dog, railed away at his quiet house until she was hoarse and exhausted.

Such hostile tirades are highly controlled and seldom frightening to others. What is frightening is the anger of a white person. It is the unpredictableness of the explosive outbursts that terrify. I was an old resident of the village before I heard about the special rituals to tame a white man's tendency to rage. Wild ginger is bespelled and secretly placed under his house ladder where, passing over it, his violent nature is becalmed. A person so charmed smiles with approval and kindness on those around him. But there must have been weeks of discouragement before they observed the effect of the magic on Joyce and me.

Again it was payday. Our house with its separate outhouse and cook house was finished and, just across from it on the other side of the main village path, a platform and roof had been built for my "office" screen tent where I stored my research equipment, worked with informants, and typed up my notes. From the tent I had a clear view in all four directions, and could keep track of village activities even as I worked.

Joyce and I were determined that this payday would end more happily than the last one. We spent the morning making bonus packets for each of the workers containing sheets of newspaper, prized for rolling cigarettes, and coveted twists of flavorful trade tobacco. This time the men knew exactly how much they would receive and stepping forward, each took his pay and bonus with my thanks. Afterward, Waiape, the government's former headman for Taute (a post he had held in name only), made a warm little speech about their pleasure with the wages and our coming to live in Taute. At last, we had pleased the men.

Now we were comfortably settled, but Joyce already had discovered that she could tolerate the isolation of the village only by getting away to Lumi every week or two. Finishing breakfast, she would take off at such an amazing walking speed that the villagers nicknamed her "motor bike." It was the fastest land machine they had seen. Once she slipped on the treacherous descent to the Sibi where the path had washed away and slashed her arm. As usual, she was alone for the man that carried her rucksack was far behind. Rather than return to Taute to dress her cut, she removed a band-aid from a tropical ulcer, slapped it across her bleeding gash, and proceeded to Lumi where Lyn, who fortunately was at the hospital and not on patrol, sewed it up.

While in Lumi, Joyce saw her friends, followed up Taute villagers in the hospital, and sometimes helped Lyn when she was shorthanded. The following afternoon she would head back for Taute, momentarily rejuvenated and resigned to another week or two in the bush. During the days she was away, Kumoi and his main assistant, Kuruwai, an attractive and personable young man who was the "Jack Armstrong" of Kafiere, helped me look after the children. While I was on my research errands among the Taute hamlets, the children stayed with one of the men at home, but if for any reason I had to go to the gardens or into the forest, they always came with me, carried jauntily on the shoulders of a couple of the teenage boys.

Once they were forced to spend the entire day in a hunting camp deep in the bush. I had received word in the morning that some Taute hunters had killed not only a big python, but also a wild pig and a cassowary. This was a momentous occasion and one I could not miss. Any wild game is scarce in Wapeland and to bag three large animals in a single hunt was unprecedented in recent times. I especially wanted to witness and film in the open some of the hunting rituals, for the ones I had seen were performed in the darkness of the ceremonial house. After curing rites, hunting ritual and magic seemed to be the most important area of Wape ceremonial life, partly, I imagine, because game was so scarce and they needed all the help they could get.

We arrived at the camp just as the pig and the cassowary were carried in. But the "dead" python had disappeared, spirited away by occult forces about which there was considerable speculation. As I stood in the sun filming the butchering and accompanying rituals, the sweat flies crawled over my body and into my ears and nose like ants swarming over a dead carcass. My white wet skin seemed a major lure. Although the flies also were pestering the other men, only I was covered with them. Mercifully, Ned and Elizabeth had remained in the shade of the camp shelter and, while undoubtedly annoyed by an occasional fly, were not complaining. Nevertheless, I thought it best for Kumoi to take them back to the house. But Kumoi shook his head. Neither he nor I could leave the camp until the butchering rituals were completed and the meat divided. If any of the men present in the camp were to leave, it would ruin all future hunting. It was, he added, a law of their ancestors that never was broken.

So the children stayed, bored and disgusted that they had followed me to this tedious hunting camp. They had seen pigs butchered before, watched the blood gush into bamboo tubes, and smelled the stench from cleaning the endless entrails, for they too were eaten; only the pig's genitals were thrown away.

But they did show some interest in the cassowary, the big ostrich-type bird that can rip a man apart with its strong legs and fierce claws. One of the cassowary rituals was particularly entertaining. Several of the boys built a small teepee of palm branches around a branch stuck into the ground. Only a brotherless man could go inside. Why a "brotherless" man, no one could say, but there he stood receiving through a small hole, one by one, the scraps of cassowary meat remaining from the butchering. Eventually he emerged, carrying the branch aloft decorated with the bits of meat suspended like baubles on a Christmas tree. The magic of the ceremony had insured enough "leftovers" so each man in the camp might have a share of them.

When we returned to the village in the late afternoon, the men were laden with meat to the joyous anticipation of the women and children, for in Wapeland a meal with meat is an exception. But besides feasting there was a rite of thanksgiving in the ceremonial house. The *mani* had answered their prayers for game and his hungry heart was bathed in the blood of the kill.

When Joyce was in the village, the children's schedule was more predictable. Each morning for about an hour, Ned did his first-grade correspondence-school work with Joyce while Elizabeth came to my tent for "nursery" school, where she quietly drew and colored as I worked with an informant. The tent, became a popular meeting place. There anyone could come to lounge outside on the low Wape-style benches while inside I interviewed one or another of the men. Women, men, and children from Taute and occasionally nearby villages regularly stopped to watch the activities. We were such an engaging attraction that I thought of the tent as the Taute zoo, where the exotic "beal" zipped into his nylon screen cage performed a wide variety of entertaining antics with his strange collection of toys and props. It was a performance they never tired of. And it assured me of responsive companionship as well as a group I could query about puzzling data or fill in the details of gossip on the latest village happenings.

During the beginning phase of my field work in Taute, I

found my attempts to integrate the myriad bits and pieces of data I was accumulating extremely frustrating. With only a fraction of the necessary pieces, the Three-Dimensional Wape Puzzle was infinitely scattered through the pages of my notebooks and mind like negatively charged ions. A person couldn't be an anthropologist if he or she didn't delight in this kind of intellectual challenge, but how each copes when the pieces won't fit must certainly vary. While I continued to flounder vainly with my data, I unwittingly found something I could put together with consummate closure — Lego.

As a substitute for the toys we could not bring to New Guinea for the children, we brought instead a large box of the versatile little cubes. So after lunch and dinner, to the admiring joy of Ned and Elizabeth, I played with their blocks. In masterly control of the hundreds of pieces, I aggressively built an enormous Gothic cathedral, a sprawling chateau, a fantastic restaurant and a complete Bavarian village. It was marvelous therapy. But it was difficult to explain to the children why, after such lavish play with the tiny blocks, I gradually put them aside as my initial frustration with the pieces of Wape culture subsided.

4

A TIME BEFORE

I may have been the first white man to live in Taute, but I certainly wasn't the first one to visit. That honor went to an Australian labor recruiter. Was it to keep me in line that they so often told me how they had frightened him away?

It happened at dawn several years before the disastrous 1935 earthquake. A few of the villagers in Mifu had risen to stir up the embers of their dying fires when they heard a commotion outside the hamlet's bamboo barricade. The cry went out that the men from nearby Lau'um, Taute's traditional enemy, were raiding them. The signal drums thundered, women screamed, children cried, and sleepy-eyed men reached for their bows and arrows. Clambering over the barricades came a group of native men, but they were not from Lau'um. They were the armed escort of a recruiter in search of cheap labor for the copra plantations of New Ireland and New Britain. In the noisy skirmish that followed, one of the recruiter's men was fatally shot with an arrow and the arm of a Mifu man, Wia, was shattered by gunfire. Wia lived, but his arm hung limp and useless the rest of his life.

That was the heroic part of the story. Then with scornful laughter the men who witnessed the event told of the cowardly flight of the recruiter. Waiting outside the barricade, he fled when the fighting began. Inevitably, someone would burlesque his terrified, bumbling flight through the forest.

The Tautes prized that encounter and the image of a spine-less white man running away from them in fear. It was an endur-ing symbol of their integrity and power as a village and as a peo-ple. Reaching back for the memory of the frightened recruiter, it helped sustain them through the successive humiliations their new white masters would impose upon them. For it was not long after the Mifu skirmish, perhaps in response to the recruiter's report of an "attack," that an Australian patrol officer and a long line of native policemen came to Taute for the first time. Exactly when they arrived probably never will be known. The govern-ment records of the visit were lost when the Japanese captured the Aitape coast during the war. But from that time on, Taute free-dom would never be the same. Although it was not until the 1950s that Taute was regularly patrolled every year or so, the law of the white man's government in Aitape had reached them. If a patrol officer ordered new houses to be built, a hamlet moved, la-trine pits dug, his cargo carried, or a sick person taken to Aitape, they disobeyed his commands at the risk of floggings, imprison-ment, and fines.

Although the first recruiter to visit Taute failed to sign up any men, a group of Taute men already had trekked over the Tor-ricellis to Aitape to offer their services to Charlie Gough, the most colorful and irascible recruiter on the Aitape coast. One of his native contact men had enticed the Tautes to sign up with promises of steel and money. Of that first group of thirteen men who boldly left their forest homes to work for the unpredictable white man, three were still alive. Tongol, Talie, and Fiyu were old but very active men.

Old Tongol, his fine white hair frizzed into a delicate Afro of his own invention and his little eyes dancing, recalled that historic trek to the coast. Naked, the men climbed high into the cold Torricellis, following the ancient footpath leading over the pass and onto the coastal plains below. Tongol stopped his story to laugh. Approaching Aitape, each man picked up a giant breadfruit leaf to hide his genitals from the one or two white women who lived on the station. The women, they were told, would be offended if they saw their genitalia. With a new sense of bodily shame, they walked through the station to Charlie Gough's quarters where their big leaves were exchanged for bits of cloth. Then they were examined by the government's Medical Assistant and, their contract forms completed, loaded onto a ship with other recruits to sail into a wet world devoid of ground and trees.

Tongol worked on a copra plantation in New Ireland for four years. Sometimes, as he did his monotonous work, he recalled the tears of his two young sons and their cry of desperation, "Papa, Papa, you're leaving us!" Now his two sons were mature men with sons of their own. But one thing had not changed. Just as Tongol had gone away to work on the copra plantations, so would his grandsons. There were no other paying jobs. Although the Taute men did not like the plantation work or the long absences from home, it was the only work available to mountain men who were both geographically isolated and illiterate.

Charlie Gough's own recruiting career came to a sudden end not many years after he had signed on his first Tautes. It was 1936, and Gough had gone far to the east of Wapeland to the Abelam people to recruit new laborers. The demand for cheap labor to work the newly discovered gold fields was almost insatiable, and Gough received £10 for each healthy native he delivered. Gough, like most other recruiters, did not always heed the government's regulations regarding the native population. In these early days, a recruiter was almost a law unto himself as he traveled with his armed escort through the primitive villages and into the uncontrolled areas where his presence was prohibited. But who was to know? The government consisted of only two or three men stationed in Aitape with thousands of square miles, most of it unexplored, to supervise.

Then one day Charlie Gough took a chance that cost him his life. When a young fourteen-year-old recruit from Lehinga village ran away from Charlie's camp after his father demanded that he return, he carried with him the axe and knife Charlie had given him to seal the bargain. The rugged and wily recruiter was indignant and angry. No 'kanaka' would get the best of him! Entering the forbidden, uncontrolled territory where Lehinga lay, Gough ignored the taboo signs set upon the trail that warned him and his men that they proceeded on the peril of death. Heedlessly storming into the village, Charlie Gough demanded the return of his stolen possessions. The father's spear shot through Gough's neck. No white man was going to steal his son from him! As an accompanying volley of spears wracked his body, Charlie Gough died. His body was buried near the great ceremonial house in whose shadow he was killed.

Although the Tautes never killed a white man, they killed their share of other Wape during the hundreds of years they have defended their ridge. Their last killing feud, however, was not with a Wape village but with Kamnum village, an Autu-speaking group located a two hours' walk down the Sibi River to the south. There were still six old men alive in Taute who had taken part in the wars with Lau'um and Kamnum. As young warriors, they had decorated their bodies with paint and bright leaves to strike fear into their victims. Setting out on an ambush or raid, they carried long black bows, viciously barbed arrows that ripped into an enemy's body, and large black carved shields to crouch behind when an arrow came their way. In their armbands were cassowary-bone daggers for hand-to-hand combat.

Four of these old warriors lived in our hamlet, and I thought how easy it was going to be to learn about Taute warfare. But I was mistaken. None of the old men took any delight in teaching me anything. They would quietly answer my questions but rarely expanded a topic the way a really good teacher must. Then one late afternoon while I was typing up notes in my screen tent, old

Siwau came to watch. Bilu, my neighbor, was already there, and, as the three of us chatted lazily above the din of the cicadas and my typing, I suddenly realized our desultory talk had become a vibrant interview on the Taute wars. I left the tent to join the two men, and for two hours I wrote at top speed until the sun fell into the Border Mountains and I could no longer see my notebook.

Siwau was especially detailed about the Kamnum raids because he remembered them firsthand. And although Bilu was too young yet to fight, he too had vivid memories of the events. In a mixture of Wape and Melanesian Pidgin, the story of the murderous feud with Kamnum unfolded.

It all began a few years before the great earthquake, while Tongol and the other Taute men were still making copra for their white employers on New Ireland. Siwau's father-in-law, the father of his wife who was to be killed in the quake, was murdered in his bush while climbing a tree—probably to gather nuts or hunt birds—by a poaching Kamnum man who stood unseen with his bow and arrows on the ridge above. Struck by the arrow, Yuno fell from the tree, dead. Yuno himself was not from Taute but from nearby Wilkili village. However, the villages are so closely interrelated that even today Tautes refer to Wilkili as "our little place."

Sometime later Kafiere was celebrating a *wenil* curing festival, and a number of Kamnum people with marriage ties to Kafiere had come for the festivities. The Wilkilis saw it as the perfect opportunity for their revenge. In broad daylight and with great stealth, they crept up to the hamlet. Leaping from the forest with a shout, they blocked the exits, and, as the terrified celebrants fled in disarray, Publo, a Kamnum man, was shot. Having revenged the killing of Yuno, the Wilkili men fled in turn. As the Kamnum people carried the wounded Publo in angry retreat to their village, he died.

Although the Tautes declare they were not involved in Publo's murder, Kamnum's hostility was extended to them and relations between the two villages were suspended. One, two, three suspenseful years passed, and still the murder of Publo was not revenged. Suddenly a group of Kamnum men in fierce battle array ran into Kafiere hamlet. As a little girl ran screaming across the dance ground to her grandfather, the long barbed arrows from the Kamnum bows flew toward her. The first arrow went through her lower back and out the pubic region. The second entered her back and the third her side. Tobtai fell onto the sandy ground and died. It was the same ground where Ned and Elizabeth now romped and played, oblivious, as the Taute children weren't, of Tobtai's death.

Now it was Kamnum's turn to live in suspenseful dread of a whizzing barbed arrow. When a group of Taute plantation laborers returned to the village, it was decided that the day for revenge was at hand. But the Kamnums intercepted the attack party at the river below their village ridge. While the two groups exchanged insults and arrows, three Taute men slipped away and, moving cautiously through the forest, climbed up to the ridge where the unsuspecting women and children, secure in their village, listened to the yelling between the warring men below. Entering the unprotected village, the Taute men shot and killed the first human they saw. It was a little boy. Returning victorious to their village, the Tautes beat their signal drums in triumph and danced through the night while the Kamnum women wailed the death of Wuruwe's small son.

It was almost ten years since Yuno's murder. Now three others, one man and two children, were dead. But there is no evidence that any of the murders were reported to Aitape. The Tautes' attitude, as it is now, was to keep the government out of their affairs. The white man did not understand their customs, and in imposing his solutions to village problems, he only perpetuated further injustices. Then the war came to New Guinea and the Aitape coast and something happened, something terrible, that helped to bring peace between Taute and Kamnum. It was the dysentary epidemic of 1944.

As the Tautes continued to bury their dead, one after the other, they knew what was killing them. It was Publo's vengeful ghost. Murdered in their village, he was having his personal revenge. It mattered little to him that his kinsmen already had killed a Taute child to avenge his death. Publo's ghost was not satisfied and vindictively and indiscriminately was killing Taute men, women, and children; one had only to look around at the silent dead and the dying to prove it was so.

When the war ended and normal times returned to Wapeland, Taute and Kamnum celebrated a friendship feast to end the strife between them. The Kamnums came up the river, climbed the steep trail to Kafiere, and were given bamboo tubes of sago flour and the flesh of a butchered pig. They ate only a token bit in Kafiere, then returned to Kamnum with their gifts. As they walked out of the hamlet, Publo's kinsmen called to his ghost to come with them and leave the Tautes in peace. Later the Tautes went to Kamnum for their return gifts of sago and pig to seal the peace between them. Taute's centuries of warfare came to an end.

For those New Guinea tribes that center their ceremonial life on warfare and the taking of heads or cannibalism, peace means a drastic change in the organization of their cultural life. In Taute, where warfare was not a cultural end in itself but a necessity for continuing life, the changes were less profound, but still important. In the old days an armed man always accompanied the women into the forest to work sago or gather food. And at sunset, each family went into a barricaded house to pass the long night alone in wait of the rising mists and soft morning sun. If an attack were suspected, shivering men would keep watch through the cold, damp night for a predawn raid.

Today women and children go through the forest unescorted while men laze in the village tending the infants and toddlers. On moonlit nights, families sit in front of their houses around a fire to visit and laugh with relatives and friends far into the night. They like the new, easy ways and have no wish to return to the fears of the 'taim bilong fait.' And in the forest there are still the ghosts, witches, and demons who are worry enough. But their attacks are invisible and without the terrible terror of facing a warrior's bow and loosened arrow.

All of these people in Taute, from where had they come?

They hadn't always lived on this towering ridge. Although the Wape people around Lumi had an origin myth, the Tautes did not. Their beginnings, they said, were in many places and accounted for their nine different patrilineal clans. The "Taute" clan was the first on the ridge; others migrated in as the circumstances of family quarrels, wars, disease, and hunger pushed people to find refuge outside of their natal village. If a man stayed and prospered in Taute, his male progeny called it home and brought their wives to live there too. Through the years, clans waxed, waned, and even disappeared as they continue to do today. Taolefe, the last male survivor of the ancient Taute clan, died during our field work. A sickly and taciturn recluse, he avoided me. If by chance we met on a forest path, he never spoke but acknowledged my presence by pursing his lips. Whatever he knew about the history of the Taute clan died with him.

What I did not learn about Taolefe's clan, Kumoi made it up to me with stories about his own. He belonged to Koropa, one of the larger clans, and my favorite story was about the clan's founder, the little orphan boy, Punu. It was a story of pathos and avuncular piety. Although a boy and his mother's brother, his *faf,* belong to different clans, they have a close relationship that is reinforced by a set of continuing ritual and economic obligations between them. A *faf* is expected to offer food and protection to his sister's son, his *lulem,* when he is in trouble. The story of Punu, as it has come down nine generations to Kumoi, demonstrates this tradition. But here is Punu's story.

Punu's mother was born into Taute clan, and, according to custom, when she married Punu's father, she joined him in his village near Kamnum. Punu's parents visited his mother's village to see her brother, Tublufu who, in turn, came to visit them as well. The Tublufu heard that their village was attacked and the few survivors had run away into the forest. Tublufu and his wife went in search of his sister's family, but they were nowhere to be found. Everyone, he was told, had been killed. Finally they arrived at the devastated village. They searched through the ruins, but found no signs of life. Then they noticed a tiny path swept clean of debris leading to a small opening in one of the remaining houses. Something lived there, but what was it? A dog? A person? A ghost?

While Tublufu stood guarding the little exit, his wife opened the main door and looked into the black interior. Something moved. "Are you a ghost or a person?" she cried.

"I'm a person," answered a small voice. "I'm all alone and have no food or fire."

She called for him to come outside, and, stepping into the sunlight, she recognized little Punu, starved and filthy. He told his aunt and uncle about the massacre and how he had kept alive afterward by leaving his hiding place each day to search for bananas.

After they fed him, Tublufu put the boy on his shoulders and carried him down to the river where he shaved his matted hair with a bamboo knife and bathed him in the water. Then they caried him home to their village. So Koropa clan in the form of little Punu, came to Taute. As Punu grew, Tublufu gave his *lulem* lands on which to hunt, streams in which to fish, and groves of sago palms and breadfruit trees. When he became a man, Punu married and had a son, then grandsons, and the Koropa clan flourished just as Tublufu's clan gradually diminished through the years, then disappeared forever with Taolefe's death.

Kumoi finished the story with deep satisfaction. It was because of a man's affection for his sister's son that he was alive today.

5

PHASES AND FEELINGS

Taute Village
16 Sept. 1970

Dear Lorna and Tom,

It's been a long time since we sat in your handsome living room before a roaring fire drinking a farewell scotch. At that time I still couldn't quite believe that I was going to New Guinea for two years. Well, it's easy to believe that I am here now. There is a balmy breeze and the village palms are exquisitely stark against a full moon, big as only a tropical moon can be. It is 9:30 P.M. and all of the village is quiet. It is unusual for these are night people. They love to sit up late and talk around a fire. Last night, the first night of the full moon, they were up talking long after Joyce and I went to bed at eleven. . . . But the real reason that I feel the quiet is that Joyce and the children went into Lumi this morning; it is the first time the children have gone into the government station since they were carried into Taute almost three months ago. And I will go in for one night tomorrow for my first time. Joyce, our cosmopolite, walks in every week or two. It's a two- to three-hour walk on a tiny bush track over roots, through low swampy places, then ups and downs over the magnificent jungle terrain. . . . It is a beautiful world and even Joyce, who acutely misses the kind of intimate banter with friends one takes for granted at home, finds it enthralling. We really should have someone here studying us as a family as it has been a most unique experience for each of us. The environmental stresses are at the same time psychological, social, and technological and pushes one to his adaptive capacity and then just a wee bit beyond. . . .

Our village is comprised of three hamlets along a mile-long ridge. The population is just over 200. But even after three months of living right in the middle of things, I only perceive the outline of events; only occasionally do I feel that I accurately grasp the emotional tone. It is immensely frustrating work. No matter how hard I work, the data presents itself in bits and pieces. An observation here, an informant's explanation there. Sometimes they are contradictory and then you are left with the feeling that you are totally incompetent. . . . Yet the people are more cooperative than many and want to help me. But the fact that their basic premises are unknown to me and, somehow, I must discover them is a boggling experience. It's like having 200 psychoanalytic patients on the couch at once! One is dealing with personalities involved in a complex set of kinship and cultural structures. The lovely thing is that I don't have to change anything. If I can just figure out what they are up to, that is enough.

Psychologically speaking, it is an interesting culture. It seems that the Women's Liberation Movement must have originated here and moved on to America. More than any culture that I know about, the men here are intimately involved in child raising. It struck me the first time I visited. Men were standing around with tiny babies on their hips in slings. I had never seen such a thing before. But it isn't that the men are emasculated or that there is a reversal of sex roles. No, it is more simple than that. Here the men have an equal share in child tending. The women go to the bush to make sago flour, the basic food of the area, and the men stay in the village to care for the babies. If the mother isn't too far away, he will carry the infant out to her when it cries to nurse. During the day my work is mostly with men with babies slung around their waists and toddlers around their knees. The situation, I find, still irritates me for it violates my concept of a man's role vis-à-vis me as an inquiring anthropologist. I must stop my questioning while a baby is allowed to urinate or is soothed while crying. Always, but always, the baby's needs are put first. They really care about their children.

From the moment of birth until it can walk, the baby is always in contact with a human body; mother, father, or sibling but usually the parents. Even after a child can walk, he is carried about and comforted; some nurse until they are three or four. At night he sleeps in the arms of a parent, or, when the tending parent takes a nap during the day, the baby naps, too. This is symbiosis with a big S. Yet the children are remarkably free and independent. They also, just as the adults, seldom display aggression. . . . When the adults do have a point of contention, as they did the other night when a man's dog killed another man's piglets, the villagers [meet] together and rationally discuss the situation. Many of the men carry babies or children even though their wives are there and the babies asleep. What I can't decide is whether they are truly peace-loving or afraid of aggression and violence. I am beginning to favor the latter hypothesis. The holding of babies at night, strictly at their own option, and during a time of tension, indicates to me they are unwittingly using the presence of babies to keep a tense situation disarmed.

Their respect for women is remarkable in New Guinea. Men and women use the same paths, the same doors, and sleep in the same houses. Even menstruating women sleep in the house with their husbands. Women are told some of the secret names of the demons that cause sickness and can exorcise the sick just as the men. They are, however, excluded from the more elaborate healing rituals but this is to protect them, not to scare them, as is the custom on the Sepik River. Fortunately, for my study they are tremendously involved with problems of health and sickness. All of their major rituals are related to healing and some of them are spectacular. . . .

My kerosene lamp is running out of fuel and that brings me to a question. Did I see in one of the camping catalogues you showed me an ad for an Aladdin lamp, that is, a kerosene lamp with a mantle, not a wick, that burns very brightly? I saw it somewhere but can't remember. If you come across where I can order such a lamp would you send me the information?

Yours,
Bill

Taute Village
27 Sept. 1970

Dear Mary Jo and Dick,

Your letter about the break-in at our farmhouse arrived Friday. It is cetainly depressing to think about it but, of course, neither of us was surprised. I imagine such things are inevitable. We're just happy they didn't wreck the place but, as you say, what about the next time? As you could tell we didn't leave out anything valuable, that is, things we really consider irreplaceable. We replaced them with second-rate things from the barn so if someone did break in they might have the "satisfaction" of taking something and not wreck the place in reprisal. But who knows what goes through the heads of people that break into houses? I certainly don't. . . .

Our work is going right along . . . and the phase where we were absolutely stupid about *every*thing is past. Now we are just stupid about some things but at least we know the overall outline of the culture and that makes it easier to fit all of the behavioral trivia together in a more meaningful way. But we have one "problem in living" that rural folks in Vermont don't have with their preschoolers. Everyone here from infants on up chews betel nut and our children, especially Ned, think they should not be the exception! Today Ned and Elizabeth appeared for lunch with blood red mouths and tongues. They had been "chewing" again. Believe me, it's not easy to be a parent these days even in a jungle! . . .

Yours,
Bill

Taute
26 Sept. 1970

Dear Natalie,

Our whole family has had another surge of settling in these past two weeks. Bill had a breakthrough in collecting data, a lot of it resulting from having his informants draw and color their Fish Spirit designs for their big 'sing-sings' (these are their curing festivals that are by far the biggest thing in their lives). As they draw they tell him new stories about the masks that he has never heard and he is thrilled about it all.

I have settled in now that I am out of the village at least two days a week. And everyone is happy about it. Bill wanted a semi-contacted village (Taute) with a hospital nearby (Lumi) for a comparative study. So I have started on a project that I call, "Medicine in Transition." I am looking at all the government-sponsored medicine in the villages (e.g., maternal and child health clinics, aide posts, malaria patrols, leprosy patrols) and all the village medicine in the native hospital (e.g., charms, medicine men, nettles, food taboos, sing-sings). I also am getting the background of medicine for the district, services offered, number of cases, kinds of cases, age, sex, and village of patients, etc.). What it all means to me is that I get into Lumi once a week. I get the long trek that I really love, and it is the only time that I get away from full responsibility for the children all week. I never have had the children as much in my life. I always had someone in four or five hours a day while I worked at home. In fact, for a while, I didn't think I would find a solution and I practically fell apart with the itch!

We have been here three months and to think we have seven times that more to go is really too much! I do like more variety than I am getting. But, when I get to Lumi I hit the Catholic mission first. I like Father Gerald very much and the Sisters are great. So I have coffee or a cold drink with them right off, get caught up on the gossip, watch the planes go in and out, and see all of their school children. Then I go by the Admin. Office and see the acting District Commissioner's wife and arrange to meet her later for a cold beer. Then I go to Lyn's house and play her records *loud,* shower, and go up to the hospital, where I either work on hospital records, interviw patients, or go out on a medical patrol. I usually stay overnight although sometimes I go to Lumi with the market women at four A.M. and come back the same day.

It is working out well and I would probably have lost my mind by now if I didn't have Lumi to go to. In the meantime, Bill is happier with the work I am doing than any since I came here; Elizabeth loves to be the hostess for her Daddy at the table when I am gone, and Bill says both children are better to be with than when I am there. Needless to say, my feelings are NOT hurt!

Bill is *very* happy that I am in New Guinea during this Woman's Liberation Movement and not running around Vermont spreading the word! But, I hope you do get Kate Millet's book, *Sexual Politics,* and, after you read it, send it to me!! I am dying to read it and was wondering from whom I could borrow it when you wrote you were getting it. . . .

I have started Ned on an Australian correspondence course, about an hour a day, and he loves it. Really what he needed and I needed the structured time to give to him, too. He has a teacher in Sydney that writes all kinds of helpful little messages and I am seeing his first formal learning, step by step! Of course, little Miss Elizabeth wants to be in on it too, so she takes her books and papers and goes to Bill's office and works at the same time. She is completely comfortable now for the first time since we arrived. She cleans her room with such enthusiasm and she tells people she wants to be a nurse but her mommy said she can't be a nurse, secretary, or teacher! Oh, yes, our first lesson for Ned showed a picture of a mommy knitting, a daddy reading, and children playing. I was to ask him what each person was doing. Ned said, "The mommy is stapling a book together!" Bill said they will be liberated even if I'm not!!

I am looking forward to next week. Instead of a trip to Lumi, I am meeting Lyn in a village near here for a medical survey and will be out three days. One part of the trip will be ten miles down our beautiful Sibi River. I wish you could see this jungle; when I look out over it from the window, I wouldn't believe you could go walking through it. We will have carriers but eat with the village people and I haven't had an overnight out quite like that before.

We just got our first bottle of dry Vermouth yesterday, so tonight we will have a real martini. Bill and I have had the best Saturday nights here we have ever had anywhere. Wish you could join us for this one!

Love,
Joyce

WM NOTES
8 Oct. 1970

NIGHT THOUGHTS ON WHERE I AM

I now have been in Taute about three and one half months. I still have not completed the work on the genealogies and the tie up of the men in the different lineages. It is a *priority* job but, somehow, I don't get to it. I have been working mostly on supernatural data and taping a lot of stories and information on the curing rites in considerable detail. But little, if any, of it is written up. This means that I have only "heard" it and don't have the data organized in my thinking—much of it is just swimming around.

One bad habit I have assumed during the past week is not carrying my notebook with me *everywhere* I go. I want to seem more informal and, quite frankly, just want to talk with people. But whenever I do, an important tidbit comes up and I hear it but I don't get it written down and, within a short time, the names fade away. Much time is then wasted finding the informant and getting the data again.

This, of course, is warranted when, for example, I haven't comprehended the event or events described to me. For example, Weti told me this evening that Wese's wife had stolen his dog and taken it to Parisko village and a man named Pusi had brought it back to him. Although I usually get the names of people involved in an incident, it is often difficult to ascertain their exact relationship to one another in terms of kinship without doing some convoluted interviewing. Sometimes people don't mind my doing that but other times they find it a bore or else I don't have the energy to do it in front of a bunch of onlookers to come off as a horse's ass for the 100th time during the day. So tonight I got hung up on Weti's phrase, 'Pusi karim em' and I thought he was saying that a cat had given birth to this little puppy {in Melanesian Pidgin 'pusi' means "cat" and 'karim' means both "to bring" and "to beget"} and I knew I either was on to something big or that one of us was not seeing things as they are. Finally, I discovered that Pusi was the name of a man, not a cat, and everyone had a howling laugh. After that I just didn't have it in me to go on and find out just how Pusi was related to Weti.

But this is no excuse for not sitting down and getting more facts into the notebook each day as I go along! I can't remember everything I am told and I can't type up everything in the notebook, but if I write it down, I at least have a record of my observations that will be useful years from now.

I am working more formally with informants which means that I am more restricted to the "office" and that is getting to me. I seldom leave the hamlet. I must make a point of getting out a great deal more with the people when they go into the bush.

I miss not having Kumoi around this week; he will be off work for three more weeks as well. He is really my best informant. Weti is also good but more fragmentary and I sometimes miss the point of what is happening or to whom it is happening. This is sometimes true even with Kumoi and is, in part, because Wape Pidgin speakers have a habit of not making the subject of a sentence explicit. When relating an incident or telling a myth, their presentation is very histrionic. They play all of the parts complete with gestures (I must film Kumoi telling a story), slap their thighs for emphasis and change their voices slightly as they change character. But I don't always know who the new character is or if the declamatory sequence is over and they are simply now describing what is happening. They also speak so quickly it would be impossible for me to write it down. In fact they don't like to have me write. Every informant I have tape recorded gets distracted when he sees me begin to write. It's really unusual for, at other times, they don't mind my writing although they do always drop their eyes to my notebook when I write. It reminds me of suspicious Western informants I have interviewed who want to see what you are putting down. Although the act of watching me write is similar, I think the motivation is very different. They aren't at all suspicious but it seems to have something to do with having the attention of the one to whom you speak. When I begin to write, they act as if I am suddenly talking with someone else; as if I am no longer interacting with them. . . .

When I am taping, I try only to write down the name of the people in the myth or incident and then just brief notes tracing the action so that the tapes will be easier to review. Even then, I often get lost in the trees and by the time the story is over, I can't even imagine what in hell the whole thing is about. Kumoi is the only one who appears completely accepting of my writing as I tape and that is probably because we have worked together so much.

So they really want my eyes although they actually don't interact with them a lot. But as actors they are doing a lot of "mugging" that would not be very effective if they were looking directly at me most of the time. They are very much the performers and I the audience. . . .

So where am I? Far behind on the genealogy data that I must complete or, at least for now, get the big picture more clearly. Maybe next week! Formal ritual data coming nicely. But I am not keeping track of individual illnesses as closely as I should. I've thought of keeping all illnesses in a separate book, but I'm afraid I wouldn't do it. Also thought of a card index file to keep minimal data regarding illnesses, but would I do that? Might be worth a try. The movie camera is still not out of its case but I feel that it is on its way. That's something. The idea of introducing yet another method of data collection and keeping it catalogued and typed up gives me a stomach ache. But I will.

Taute Village
21 Nov. 1970

Dear Natalie and Don,
Wow, Saturday night in the bush! And all alone. Ned and Elizabeth are sound asleep. Joyce is in Wewak, our outpost on the coast. It's
her first time out since she flew in here six months ago. It's pouring
down rain and all the local swingers have gone up to Mifu hamlet for a
wild night of 'satu,' a lightning fast gambling game played with three
dice chucked out of a tin cup onto a board, then swished up so fast I still
don't know what it is about. Even when they try to show me in slow
motion, I don't grasp the winning principles behind it all. And that is
just about the story of my life here. I'm spending weeks trying to figure
out what any slow eight year old has known for several years. Now I
know why the older generation of anthropologists never accept anyone
as a bona-fide anthropologist until they have been humbled by a "primitive" culture. It's the analog of a didactic psychoanalysis; you're never the
same again. You've been peeled, stripped, and reduced to the feeling
state of a Total Ignoramus. The level of stupidity at which I operate —
even after five months here—is absolutely appalling. And I'm not a bad
anthropologist, but the monumental shifts it takes to apprehend the
local version of reality sometimes unhinges me a bit. After all, I've
usually been able to *feel* what was going on about me even if I didn't
know the details of what was happening. Now I've been humbled on
that one, too.
Of course, I've always wanted to know everything happening
around me and maybe my standards of apprehension are higher than
some, but that sounds more like a shallow rationalization. So here I am
in Taute, stumbling along like an intellectual spastic. And it is this experience that is doing something to me. One's goals are so extensive but
one's abilities are so limited. I mean, when you know you don't know
what someone is talking about, you can't fake it. Even a seemingly non-
commital "Oh, yes" can be entirely wrong. The fact that the people
here are kind and gentle, in a funny kind of way, only isolates me further. Let me give you an example.
Weti, a married man his late twenties, returned from Lumi today
after working a week for the administration to pay off his taxes. During
our discussion of his experiences there, he mentioned a 'masta,' a European male, who has a machine with a wire that he sticks into the

ground. He puts another part to his ear and, what does he hear? It speaks to him all about whose bush belongs to whom and gives him Absolute Knowledge regarding boundaries of ownership. It also can tell him who to send to jail when the boundaries are violated. Obviously it is a wonderous machine. But, as usual, I am a bit tardy in grasping just what this machine is all about. I just want to *understand*. But my questioning is perceived as a challenge to his understanding (how could it be otherwise?), and he gets stuck in a defensive posture saying that the Admin. Office understands, all the white 'mastas' understand, in fact everyone knows what he is talking about except me!

Having unwittingly put him down, he then puts me down and we move on to a more neutral topic. But all next week I will be working that damned machine into conversations trying to figure out what in hell it is. I may not really know until I visit Lumi, which is infrequent; twice since I've been in Taute. But enough on "communications." This letter is beginning to sound like an anthropologist's soliloquy. It's not to be that.

I guess I'm resonating on Don's comment before we left that we would never be the same. To pack a family off to the jungles of New Guinea, even from rural Vermont, is a radical undertaking and it continues to affect each of us. So far it has been positive. When a family is constantly thrown back upon itself, it quickly discovers its strengths and weaknesses. But for a family to know each other so totally and unreservedly as we do, is not a part of American culture. None of us really has any place to hide as one does in a complex society. So the strains can be tremendous and agonizing. But, also, we never have known such heights of closeness and intimacy. We seem to be all or nothing, but we are never that boring gray in between. I don't mean to demean that "in between" state as that is more genuinely "me." But I have been pushed to express and accept versions of "me" I doubted existed, and Joyce, too. So if a family is looking for a new level of awareness (although we weren't) I say, go to the jungle!

Most intriguing has been the development of the children. No matter how glamorous we try to make our life in the village sound to them, there are the realities of no one who can speak our own language, no relatives to add comfort and fun to a child's life, no rides in cars, no television, no stores, in fact you begin to think, no nothing. . . .

When we first came to Taute, the four of us lived in a one-room hut while they built our house. We literally lived on top of each other.

And this was stressful. Not only were we too much for each other, but the natives, curious about who we were and what we were up to, crowded about each of us as soon as we left the house. This was our crisis period. Totally without privacy, either within the family or without, and totally unaware of what was going on about us, we were, to put it mildly, a mess. That lasted for a month. Then our handsome house was completed, the children each with their own little bedroom. And life started looking up. I was convinced even more deeply about the psychological importance of social space and how little we really know about it.

Ned's adaptation to his environment has been the most stunning. He really never withdrew like the rest of us. With surprising aggressiveness, he started learning Pidgin and bits of the local language before the rest of us knew where we were. It was extraordinary. After a week, he would stand up under a coconut tree and call out for his mother—who was in the hut—just like the local kids called to their mothers who were in the jungle finding food. And to this day, he remains deeper into the culture than any of us. Before I am even out of bed—and that is always before seven—he is up and has visited a household or two. And he goes inside the house; nothing tentative about Ned!

This morning I was awakened by the salutation, "Dad, wake up! Wamala's balls are 'solap.' He wants you to come and look at them." Ned already had checked them out and he assured me that they indeed were swollen. They were. Two to three times normal size. It's the second case of filariasis I've diagnosed in Taute. Elizabeth wasn't going to miss this either so there I was talking to old Wamala (he's my age but like my father) stretched out naked on his back by a fire (they always build a fire or lie in the sun when in pain) holding his tremendous, painful balls in his hand.

So Elizabeth is adapting too. Whereas Ned is a proficient Pidgin speaker and I listen carefully to him to pick up new idioms, Elizabeth was slow to venture into Pidgin but has done so increasingly during the past two months. And she never misses any of the village "events" as she did earlier. Last Sunday our closest neighbor, Walmaiya, who was widowed a month before we arrived here (her husband, they say, was killed by witchcraft) had what I can only call a "fit." She was calmly spending the day chewing betel nut and visiting with her women friends when, suddenly, she fell down, and became semiconscious. I went to her immediately, the children right behind me. I don't know what it was. Perhaps some kind of petit mal seizure.

When we arrived she was sitting propped up against a house post. Her eyelids fluttering, but no body trembling. Very deep breathing. Her arms were bent and fists clenched, but not rigid. I easily opened them as I could her jaw that also appeared tightly clenched. Immediately the local diagnosis was made. Walmaiya had accepted some betel nut from Naiasu, a marvelously gregarious woman, and a demon of sickness and hunting prowess called *mani* was transferred to her in the process. This is because Naiasu's husband, Auwe, is the gunsman for our hamlet and has been sleeping in the ceremonial house where the *mani* stone is kept in hope of making it "hot" so it will bring him a wild pig. Auwe, who was cooking for us that day, slapped Walmaiya all over with stinging nettles while calling out the secret name of *mani* under his breath to exorcise her.

Later in the day Walmaiya regained total consciousness but took off the following morning for her father's village with her three young sons. She was afraid the *mani* might attack her again. I can't blame her. If ever I saw a situation that looked like some peculiar power had struck, this was it. I could do nothing; I just looked on. I didn't even have the knowledge to hit her with nettles to bring her back to consciousness. When she was struck with them, she writhed around, crying out. She called her husband's name several times and finally opened staring eyes. I took a roll of film including Auwe's exorcism of her.

But the point is, these are the kind of experiences the children are having and what they are doing with them, God only knows. . . . I see that I could write on and on to you all night, but Ned and Elizabeth will be up at 6:30 regardless. Thinking about you and writing to you has made this a delightful Saturday night.

Yours,

Bill

WM NOTES

12 Nov. 1970

TELLING STORIES BY A FULL MOON

It's 9:30 P.M. and I have just returned to the office. After putting the children to bed earlier tonight, I went up to the plaza to see what might be happening. The night was glorious. A mammoth moon, full tomorrow, was moving in and out of the clouds dumping molten silver on the palms. What a sight. And the breezes were perfect, warm but refreshing.

I saw a group sitting on the ground near the cliff's edge by Witauwa's house and there were also voices and fires at Wamala's and Suwe's verandas. I decided to explore the dark group sitting on the sand. It was a group of children and young teenagers. There was Miembel, Kino, Sengu, Yamtulu, Little Yenka, Lo'obu and Apiu. A few others like Waiami and Malpul, came and went. They were telling stories and Lo'obu just had finished one. They asked me if I knew any and, jokingly, I asked them if they knew how the sun got into the sky. At Miembel's urging to tell it, I began, although I soon discovered that they all knew it better than I. When my memory began to fail with the kind of detail I knew they liked I stopped, but Miembel took it up and, with a few promptings from Yamtulu, he finished it. The ending was much more complex than Kumoi's version. . . .

Then Miembel launched into another story about a bird but I was too lazy to follow it closely. His warm and rapid speech was soothing and to grasp the content and to follow all of the shaggy-dog details was not for me. The children on the fringe of our circle visited softly and, periodically, giant fruit bats would fly over and around the palms and breadfruit trees. Then the children would grab each other and me while Malpul, jumping up with his long bow, would pose against the changing sky, alert and ready to send an arrow flying.

So while Miembel talked, I watched Malpul and the children with their delightful easiness and relaxed intimacy. So charming under a beautiful brooding moon-filled sky. Someone earlier, it was Sengu, had brought me a piece of palm stem—wonderful versatile 'pangal'—to sit upon. Then as my legs tired and I shifted my weight, an additional piece was slipped under me. They are almost always as thoughtful. No big production, just quietly meeting a perceived need. And that was my delightful evening with the young. No notebook, no questions, but just lolling in the fun and beauty of another culture.

6

THE BALLAD OF
EPILO AND PAUWIS

Epilo and Pauwis did not fit my idealized image of star-crossed lovers. Unlike Romeo and Juliet, they were neither young nor handsome. Unmarried, each seemed destined for a life of loneliness. Among the Wape there is a special poignancy about the unmarried. Without children, they ask, who will care for an aged person when he or she is too feeble or sick to hunt or make sago flour? To be old and childless in Wapeland is to die before one's time.

So I was pleased when I learned early in September about the romance between Epilo and Pauwis. I liked them both. Epilo was a quiet man with a gentle, friendly manner. During those first tense weeks in Taute, it was relaxing just to meet his even gaze and shy smile. Although we never talked together at length, I always felt that he was on my side and hoping that I would get myself together.

Pauwis, respected as a diligent worker, was handicapped by a slight disfigurement of her jaw. I thought the minor asymmetry actually enhanced her appearance, but that was not the local view. Taute men considered her ugly. Pauwis had carried the stigma from childhood into womanhood with the certain knowledge that no man would marry her. But sometimes her eyes, soft and vulnerable, seemed to be questing for something beyond her drab life. She lived with her stepfather, old Siwau, and her sister Nimse, whose feet were crippled by leprosy. It was Pauwis's lot to look after and feed the two of them. When a big curing festival was held and all the people came to dance through the night, Pauwis stayed at home with Nimse since she had no money to buy a clean skirt.

It takes money to marry in Wapeland, even if it is a woman that no other man wants. Epilo had been to the plantations a number of times and might have saved enough money for a bride. But he didn't. Generous to a fault, the monetary requests and demands of his relatives came first. And Epilo's own close relatives—Eike, his shriveled-up elder brother with two robust married sons—were not inclined to help him in return. But even if Epilo had the money to ask for Pauwis, her stepfather was opposed to the marriage. If Pauwis went off to live with Epilo, who then would care for Siwau and Nimse? So to make his position unassailable, old Siwau set the bride price for his stepdaughter inordinantly high. Some of the people laughed. It was ridiculous, they said, to set the price as if she were a young and desirable woman. But Siwau's strategy was apparent to all. Epilo would not be able to raise the money, and Pauwis would remain at home where she belonged.

In the weeks that followed there were periodic rumors that Pauwis's bride price was raised or lowered but, as far as I could tell, the marriage plans were stalemated. Then in mid-November the events took a bizarre twist, and I began to pay more attention. Pauwis ran away to Mifu hamlet to stay with a relative and while there accused Tuya, Weti's old father and one of her neighbors, of trying to seduce her. She also told the Mifu women that if she were not allowed to marry Epilo she would become a wild woman of the forest or commit suicide by drinking poison. The

latter seemed more likely, for suicide is the usual cultural response by Wape women when confronted with extreme frustration or public insults. But Siwau would have none of this talk and
brought Pauwis back home.

Tuya was indignant at Pauwis's accusations about his sexual
intentions toward her. Disrobing before some of the men, he
pointed to his genitals and, in his high, squeaky voice, asked
them if they thought his old penis was still strong enough for sexual intercourse. Among the villagers there was some disagree-
ment whether old Tuya could, or could not, still perform the sexual act. Those who favored a "dirty old man" view recalled his
shameless affair with a young single woman of his own clan when
his wife died. But that was years ago when his now mature son
Weti was yet a baby.

Then I heard that the gossiping and accusations engendered
by the Epilo-Pauwis affair was interfering with the hunting success of the village shotguns. The ancestral ghosts were expressing
their displeasure by turning the cartridges into the trees instead
of directing them to a pig or cassowary. When Taute problems
become this tangled, the inevitable solution is a meeting to
discuss the facts and straighten things out. Such a meeting, and I
attended many of them, continues until all interested parties,
whether man, woman, or child, have spoken. By that time the
topic and its issues are completely exhausted, and most are eager
to be done with it. By mutual consent a course of action is agreed
upon and the meeting breaks up with small talk about hunting,
family events, and news about relatives in other villages. The
meetings are generally low-keyed since the participants do not
want to create new antagonisms that will further anger the ancestors. I was greatly impressed with the openness and fairness of
these meetings. By comparison, a Vermont town meeting seems
like Tammany Hall.

So a meeting was called, and the villagers gradually drifted
into the dirt plaza. I stationed myself in front of the ceremonial
house, always the focal spot for a community event. True to
Wape egalitarianism, there was no leader. A series of issues were

brought up, and finally the problems centering on Epilo and Pauwis were broached and Pauwis was asked to tell her story.

Wearing only a waist cloth, Pauwis stood leaning against a front post of the ceremonial house and told her version of the events in a quiet and forthright manner. The problem with Tuya, she said, began the same day Auwe had shot, but not killed a wild pig. She was tending a relative's baby when Tuya approached her and began to visit. He asked her if her stepfather Siwau had sexual intercourse with her in the forest. She told him no. Then he offered her some meat and as she accepted it, he squeezed her hand, a cultural sign that if she took the gift he could have intercourse with her. Tuya invited her into his house to complete the transaction but Pauwis ran away carrying the baby into her brother's house. Then she told of another time when she was menstruating that Tuya invited her into his house. Of course, she didn't go.

I watched intently as Siwau stood up and walking over to Tuya, asked him if what Pauwis said was true. He denied her stories. Then when another man put the same question to him he said, "Pauwis lies." But Pauwis was not to be put down so easily and spoke out strongly saying it was not she who was lying, but Tuya.

The two old men, Siwau and Tuya were becoming increasingly irritated. But before their tempers could flare, Kumoi, always prudent and practical, spoke out. "There is nothing to be gained," he said, "by a fight between the two old men. What we better get resolved is the problem about Epilo and Pauwis's proposed marriage."

So the lovers were called before the assemblage, and each agreed that it was their desire to be married. Then Kumoi, almost as if he were seconding a motion, quickly interjected that it was the village's responsibility to abide by the couple's decision. That seemed good sense to most of the villagers, so Siwau, bowing to the mounting pressure, agreed that Pauwis and Epilo could marry.

There was no mention of Pauwis's bride price, but, later in

the day, Siwau went to Mifu to negotiate the only obstacle remaining between the lovers and marriage. In some ways the negotiation was a triumph for Epilo as Siwau agreed to accept only part of the bride price now, a major concession, and the remainder at a later date. But it was a hollow victory. Epilo's old brother and his two sons, Baiwin and Raba, stalled on making their contribution to the initial payment, and the matter dragged on and on.

It was Christmas time and Joyce and I were decorating the house for the holidays. The children were excited, but for Joyce and me a tropical Christmas in the middle of a hot, damp forest was not appealing. We completely lacked the holiday spirit but, for the children's sake, were trying to make a show of festiveness. We made some decorations for the Christmas tree, a miserable little branch of a Casuarina, stretched a magnificent paper ornament of red and green filigree we had brought from home across the room, and from the middle of it hung a mobile of golden stars that May Ebihara, a fellow anthropologist and friend, had sent to us.

The children, laughing with anticipation, placed the colorful presents sent by our friends and relatives around the tree. Even Joyce and I were beginning to feel that maybe it was Christmas after all. But our spirits sank as we crawled from under our mosquito netting the following morning. Draped across the room was a sodden dripping mass of red and green paper. How stupid to think a crepe-paper ornament that graced our snug farmhouse could survive the heavy wetness of a New Guinea night. Staining our hands and clothes with the saturated paper, we pulled it down. But May's metallic stars waved undaunted in the morning breeze. It was obvious she had spent a Christmas in the tropics before.

And then it was New Year's. Lyn invited us to Lumi for New Year's Eve, and, next morning, I began the walk back to Taute. Joyce and the children would follow me later in the day, accompanied by a young American couple, Judy and Larry Daloz. Joyce had met them in Port Moresby, where Larry was collecting data for his doctoral dissertation in education at Harvard. Now they were seeing New Guinea's back country before returning to the States.

I slowly made my way to the top of Taute ridge and was walking through Obuenga hamlet when I saw Epilo sitting on the ground and leaning against his nephew's house. He was perspiring and looked extremely ill. I knelt down beside him, felt his fevered forehead, and asked him what was wrong. "I'm better now," he said. And he told how Yukau, a native curer, had only minutes before sucked a demon's hair out of his body. "By tomorrow or the next day," he added, "I'll be all right." I had become somewhat accustomed to the extensive amount of sickness in the village and had learned to share their optimism about the local curing practices.

"That's good," I replied. "I wouldn't want you to die." It was a stock Wape expression to console the sick, and Epilo smiled wanly. Then I left him and continued along the ridge home to prepare for our guests.

The Dalozes were refreshing company, and we drank, ate, and talked long after our neighbors were asleep. The next two days sped by. We showed them the village sights and talked on and on about New Guinea and Vermont, for they owned property under an hour's drive from our farm and we were already counting them as neighbors.

After Judy and Larry left a pall fell upon us. After so much lively conversation, Joyce and I both felt a sense of loss. For a long time now our relationship had been somewhat strained as I had dug myself deeper and deeper into the culture. I acutely felt the passage of time. Each day passed was a day gone forever. What had I learned today? While my attitude made for dedicated field work, it made me a tiresome, even irritating, companion. I was obsessed with the desire to understand Wape culture. While the Dalozes were visiting, Joyce saw me open up to the outside world again, only to see my thoughts return to Taute and the problems on which I was working.

On the morning after the Dalozes returned to Lumi, Kumoi

came to me and said that Epilo was now dangerously ill. With the excitement of our visitors, I completely had forgotten about him. Unless a sick person lived in my own hamlet, it was difficult to follow each person's illness, and when I did inquire about the sick or go to Mifu to see them, invariably they were improved. But Kumoi's manner was grave. There would be a curing rite in Mifu later in the day to exorcise the demons that caused Epilo's sickness. These particular demons, Kumoi said, lived inside the Taute ridge. They were called *koyil* and had a community life similar to people. The secret entrance to their subterranean domain was somewhere in the rock ledges off the path to Lumi as it descends to the Sibi River. "If you ever meet a strange dog in that area," Kumoi advised, "be careful because it will belong to the *koyil* and they will be nearby." The *koyil*, like all Wape demons, delight in causing sickness and death to humans. The theory was that Epilo had been attacked by the *koyil* two weeks previously on his way to Lumi to meet the mail plane for me. The *koyil* are rarely seen and their attacks are painless. One can only be sure he has been attacked by a demon, ghost, or witch after he has fallen sick.

This would be the first elaborate curing ceremony performed since my arrival in Taute, so I carefully assembled my cameras and tape recorders and wrapped them in plastic covers although the sun was shining. The weather in Wapeland was just as fickle as in Vermont. Kumoi, seeing my hasty preparations to be off, assured me I had plenty of time, for the ceremony would not begin until almost dusk. Nevertheless, aware that Wape time and my time were often disjunctive, at three o'clock the family, a group of men and boys carrying the equipment, and I set off for the short walk to Mifu where Epilo lived and the ceremony was to be performed.

I had used the filming equipment only one other time just before Christmas to film a curing festival in a neighboring village, so I took my time setting up and connecting the various pieces with the appropriate wires. Then I enclosed the equipment in a circle and pronounced the area taboo. It was easy to do, for the Tautes are forever marking gardens or food trees taboo, so my intent was clearly recognized and accepted. It was the only way I could prevent the villagers from handling the equipment, especially the big, shiny zoom lens that was irresistible to touch. As we waited for the ceremony to begin, I amused myself and the villagers gathered around the impressive equipment by explaining how it operated. They shook their heads and clucked their tongues. No one seemed interested in the forthcoming curing rite; what I was going to do was far more novel and entertaining.

At around 4:30 I went into the forest to the garden house where the men were readying their costumes. But the only activity I saw was avid betel-nut chewing and visiting. Alarmed at the approaching darkness, I tried to spur them on, emphasizing my camera could not take pictures when it began to get dark. They assured me they knew all about the relationship between the performance of cameras and daylight. I was not to worry; they would come into the village before dark at the proper time.

So I returned to "the set" for the ceremony. There was nothing very complicated about it. At the edge of the hamlet where the path drops down the ridge, Epilo's clansmen had erected a screen, simple but strong, from 'pangal.' In front of it and facing the hamlet a single log was placed for Epilo to sit upon during the ceremony. I was nervously rechecking my equipment for about the tenth time when a small boy came running along the path below saying the men were on their way. I looked at my watch. It was 5:45. Then I saw Joyce start down the hill with her camera for she was to shoot the stills while I filmed the ceremony.

Creeping along the path that emerged from the forest I saw four strange creatures. They had the legs and arms of a man but apparently no head. They carried long bamboo spears in their right hands and a supply of additional spears on their left shoulders. Their bodies were covered with a fantastic array of jungle leaves, ferns, and fruits. It was the *koyil,* and their appearance was far more startling than I had anticipated. I wished that the children could see these botanical demons, but they had grown bored and hungry with the long wait and Kumoi already had started for home with them.

The *koyil*, blending almost perfectly with the surrounding forest, stood silently as I watched two men carry Epilo to his seat in front of the screen. He was too weak to sit alone and the two men held his arms to keep him from falling to the ground. While my camera ground away, one part of my mind registered the severe deterioration in Epilo's condition. The leafy demons began to creep toward the village, and I turned the camera to follow them. Without warning they gave a series of savage cries and hurled their spears, one after the other, toward the screen where they struck and stuck with a ripping thud. Then, empty-handed, they continued up the hill and surrounded Epilo. Leaning over his delirious form, they buzzed like a thousand bees and threw off their costumes.

The demons, now revealed as men, withdrew while two other men, each carrying a miniature bow and an arrow tipped with stinging nettles, crouched on either side of Epilo. Aiming at Epilo's paining chest, they let the bow string fly but held back the arrow. Each time the string twanged, they muttered the secret name of the *koyil* demons and told them to let go of Epilo. Embarrassed that they were found out, the *koyil* would run away in shame and leave their victim in peace. For the real demons had been enticed into the village by the men in the *koyil* costumes. Epilo was gently picked up by his clansmen and carried away. At six o'clock the ceremony was finished and I had filmed most of it.

Before the ceremony no one told me that Epilo was in a delirious state, and now I too greatly feared for his life. I immediately went to the house where he was carried and found him burning with fever and talking nonsense. My Western layman's diagnosis was pneumonia. Raba, his nephew, sensing my concern began a detailed résumé of his illness. At no time, however, had they considered carrying him to the Lumi hospital. To carry a person to the hospital took two teams of four men each, and only the closest relative might carry without pay. Apparently no one was willing to throw away money in paying for carriers for an old bachelor. Even my rash offer to help pay for carriers to take him to Lumi was fruitless. Raba only said, "It's useless, he is going to die." I could not be as openly frank as Raba, but I knew he was right. But why, I wondered to myself, did they go through this curing charade if they already knew he was dying? It was, I learned, to placate Epilo's vengeful ghost. They had given Epilo a curing ceremony hadn't they? What more could they do?

By the time I had packed up the equipment and started for home it was dark. I walked slowly along the ridge with my flashlight feeling guilty and depressed. What kind of a human being was I anyway? All day I was excited, even high, at the prospect of filming a ceremony that never had been seen or described by a Westerner. If I were lucky, I would record the ceremony for all time. But in doing so, my professionalism had transcended my personal concern for Epilo. Bitterly, I compared myself to the surgeon who, with august impersonality, operates on his patient without a thought of who that person is. Why hadn't I gone to see Epilo sooner instead of fiddling over and over with my equipment? It was Epilo I should have been looking after, not my Goddamned Bolex camera and Tandberg tape recorder!

The lanterns of the men carrying the equipment made the forest look terrifyingly immense. But, I argued with myself, it wasn't my responsibility as an anthropologist or as a fellow human being to take on the personal responsibility of two hundred souls with poor nutrition and sanitation. I wasn't a medical doctor! I had come here to learn how these people live and think. If I were to start caring for their health needs or to blame myself for every death, I might as well pack up and go home right now. The Tautes had lived here long before I came and they would continue here long after I was gone. I alone couldn't improve their health. And even if I did, to what purpose was it? The health services introduced by the government and missions were already raising the population even as the shotguns bought from

LIFE WITH THE WAPE:
A Photographic Essay by
William E. Mitchell

As Ned and Elizabeth played on the trunks and boxes that filled our house, there was no doubt in their minds we were going on a very long trip, far, far away.

As I watched Joyce and the children walk into the forest, I had my first disquieting thoughts about what we were doing.

On the horizon was Taute ridge, our destination and new home.

The Taute children were delighted with Ned and Elizabeth, who returned the welcome by displaying their amusing toys, Teddy and Baby-By-By.

What I most admired about the Taute men was the tranquil closeness with which they worked. With a minimum of fuss, our new house began to take shape.

We were greatly impressed with the sturdy beauty of our finished home. The villagers insisted that we would be so comfortable and happy in Taute, we never would want to leave.

The children's new playmates chewed betel nut and smoked local tobacco wrapped in newsprint.

Sometimes Ned and Elizabeth came home with betel-red mouths, and once I found Ned with a home-made cigarette stuck behind his ear, Wape fashion. Even in this remote forest, parenthood had its special problems.

After a cold, dark night, people, pigs, and puppies came to the plaza to bask in the warmth of a tropical sunrise. To the right of our house in the background is the ceremonial house where the *mani* demon's stone heart lay enshrined.

In the humid heat of a hot afternoon there was only one refreshing place to go: the Sibi River.

Outsiders often refer to the Wape people as "dour." That may be true when they visit Lumi, the government station, but in their own villages they are lively and fun. Having just skinned a possum, Malpul and Lo'obu clown in front of the ceremonial house.

Kumoi, an intelligent and inventive teacher, instructs me how to hold a bow and arrow while his companion makes a mock attack with an old adze.

Laughing and smoking, women and girls gather at a Taute house entrance to visit.

The Wape people aren't responsive to violent behavior. As Walmaiya's toddler son kicks and screams in the grass, his brother quietly watches over him while practicing his archery skills.

Wonderful, versatile 'pangal' (sago palm leaf stems) is used by the adults for house walls and bench seats, and, by the children, as building blocks.

On the sandy plaza where little Tobtai was murdered, Ned and Elizabeth now played with their new friends.

When Lyn visited Taute on her medical patrols, she gave special attention to nursing mothers and their babies.

In a corner of dusty shade, Elizabeth and Joyce join Mi-ke and Naiasu for a morning visit.

Elizabeth, Raba, and Ned watch as I set up my equipment to tape and film a Taute curing ceremony.

The Wape are one of the few
cultures in the world where
the men play a major role in
the everyday care of infants
and toddlers.

. . . but they don't do all of it!

The men of Taute have two avid passions: gambling and hunting.

Auwe, the 'sutboi' for our community-owned shotgun, cleaned and polished the weapon almost daily.

It was a highly successful hunt. A pig and a cassowary were killed but the python got away.

Back at the ceremonial house, Witauwa retells the story of the hunt.

At the 'kapti' festival for the shotgun, the women brought leafy platters of sago jelly and bowls of boiled tree leaves, the two main foods for a Wape meal.

When Walwin's infant son became seriously ill, the men created a
fantastic female demon mask then slipped a priest, the demon's son,
into its vaginal opening.

Walwin presents his terrified infant to the masked priest, who, moving his hand toward the baby's body, begins the rite of exorcism.

In the forest outside of the village the men built a shelter to construct the great conical mask symbolizing the *mani* demon.

When Walmaiya was struck down by the *mani* demon, her oldest son and neighbors assisted her while Weti, a *mani* priest, attempted to exorcise her. At left, her two young sons look on.

The *mani* mask, a magnificent tower of bright designs and waving plumes, prances joyously around the plaza.

From out of the forest came the *koyil* demons, and their appearance was far more startling than I had expected.

The *koyil* demons threw off their forest greenery in front of Epilo, now grievously ill. Then two other men aimed their miniature bows toward his paining chest.

But the curing rites were not successful. The next morning the signal
drums announced Epilo's death, and he was laid out for his relatives
to come and mourn him.

Shimmering, aflutter with bird-of-paradise feathers, the Spirit Fish masks were like Calder mobiles magically gone wild.

Parading into Otemgi village for the curing festival, the majestic masks dwarf the human celebrants.

At festival time, children stage their own festivities. Elizabeth and Ned dance in the plaza with their friends before going to bed.

As dawn breaks in Wilkili village, a Spirit Fish mask rests on the ground to await the sun and the final curing rites.

the missionaries and traders destroyed the game. They were succeeding only in making more people eat less.

As I neared Kafiere hamlet I smelled the distinctive aroma of smoke drifting through the dark damp air signaling the presence of people and human warmth. I knew my cynical mood was but a trick to protect and distract myself from feelings of personal despair, and I was glad to be almost home. An evening with Joyce would help put my world into a broader perspective. But after dinner as I stood alone on the porch looking out over the forest and into the night, I could still hear the inhuman hum of my camera as the men carried Epilo away. And I can hear it yet today.

At dawn, the thundering tones of a signal drum boomed out over the ridges of Wapeland. Epilo was dead. Pauwis's last chance for a marriage and a life of her own was gone.

When I passed Pauwis's house on my way to the wake she was nowhere to be seen. Nor did I see her throughout the day. Not yet Epilo's wife, she had no culturally recognized status toward him so her mourning would be private, not public like that of his paternal and maternal relatives.

Epilo's bachelor dormitory was built high off the ground in the coastal fashion, and I found him laid out on a bench underneath. He was dressed in his cleanest clothes and covered with a cloth from his chest to his ankles. Throughout the day his relatives from Taute and nearby villages came alone or in small groups to mourn his death. Entering the hamlet they raised their voices in a long moaning wail, a tragically beautiful sound that sent shivers down my back. Crossing the plaza they came to where he lay. Then, their crying finished, joined others for a smoke or a chew of betel nut. Some sat in somber silence, genuinely bereaved, but others appeared to switch their role from wailing mourner to gossiping communicant with disturbing alacrity. At least it bothered me at first. But no one else was concerned, for the Wape have less sham regarding death than we. In Wapeland, a decent person mourns to the extent that his kinship relationship to the dead dictates, then is free to return to his normal demeanor. While death in American society is almost a social embarrassment, watching others die is a normal part of a Wape childhood and growing up. Death *is* disruptive, but it is not hidden from the people's eyes and feelings.

What I did find offensive, however, was old Eike's constant talk about where his dead brother might have hidden his money. Epilo had become delirious, then slipped into a coma without telling his relatives where it was. It became the day's most engaging topic of conversation. Some said he probably had buried it in a jar or tin can. The question was where.

A principal mourner at all Wape wakes is the dead person's *faf*, but Epilo's still had not appeared. He lived in Talbipi on the ridge across the Sibi River, so at noon the signal drum again was beat to summon this important maternal kinsman. While Wape custom demands that the *faf* must see his dead *lulem* before burial, the government law decrees that a corpse must be buried by sundown so they were anxious for Epilo's *faf* to arrive. It was midafternoon when I noticed a tall, well-built man carrying a shotgun stride boldly into the village and up to the mourners sitting with Epilo's body. The man did not wail but spoke to Epilo's clansmen in a strong, accusing voice. It was Epilo's *faf* accusing them of not properly caring for his sister's son while he was ill. In imperious tones he demanded to be compensated for this insult. And why hadn't they taken his *lulem* to the Lumi hospital when they saw he was seriously sick? For this, he said, he could court them and send them to jail.

Turning directly to Eike's younger son, Baiwin, sitting next to the body, the *faf* slowly shook his finger and continued his wrathful denunciation of the men of Taute. As I predicted to myself, the *faf*'s anger was not met in kind. Baiwin quietly, even humbly, recounted in detail the course of Epilo's sickness and what his clansmen had done to cure the dying man. As he spoke, a gentle mist began to fall. The *faf* stood impassively, then he said a few words in a calm voice. As he sat down, the dimmest of smiles crossed his handsome face. The crisis of the *faf*'s visit was over, and the mourners returned to their gossip and dozing.

The sun flickered through the coconut palms and bathed the plaza in warmth and light. There would be no afternoon shower today, a fact certain to please everyone, especially the visitors who already were beginning to start homeward. I watched a couple of little boys open a coconut and eat its moist flesh. In honor of the dead man, no villager could eat a regular meal today; only coconuts and bananas were permitted. Someone offered me some bananas and I hungrily munched them down.

By late afternoon long shadows had slipped across the plaza. The young men who would dig the grave got up, and as they left the village to go into the forest, I joined them. In the old days Epilo would have been buried in his house as his father had been, not in the forest. And the burial would have been weeks later, not on the day he died. Funerals today were quick affairs.

Before the white man came, a dead person's body was placed in a sitting position to be smoked and dried in front of his house. While relatives kept a constant vigil, the women took turns bringing the loads of firewood. When the body was completely dried, it was buried for about a year when the grave might be opened and some of the bones exhumed. But this was done only if the dead person was a physically strong and courageous man. The retrieved bones were kept as powerful talismans against the threats of illness or personal disaster. Even today, most homes have bones of their ancestors hidden away.

When members of a family go into the forest to sleep overnight while making sago or working in a garden, a small bone, perhaps only a finger joint, of a powerful ancestor accompanies them. It is their only protection against a wrathful ghost, for the Wape know there is no fury like the ghost of a person who is recently dead. At death, the personality of the most benign person, even Epilo's, is transformed into a terrifyingly brutal ghost, shooting fire from armpits and groin. Flying recklessly through the forest, it looks for human victims, even its own children, to destroy. When a ghost attacks a victim it gouges out the eyes, mutilates the genitalia, and eats the person alive.

So when a death drum booms into the night, a father asleep

in a garden house with his family reaches for an ancestral bone and calls out to the dead ancestor to come and protect them. The children listen for a rustling in the thatch or a tap on the wall, signaling the spirit's arrival so the family may return to sleep. This faith in their ancestors to protect them is one of the reasons that Christianity in Wapeland is so superficial. There is greater assurance in calling on the spirit of a strong father or grandfather who has held you in his comforting arms than to call to the white man's God who is everyone's father and whom you never have seen.

When we returned from the forest, Epilo's body was wrapped in his blanket and placed in a coffin of palm sheaths by his clansmen and *faf*. A few coins were dropped into the coffin, a gift from Ifau, to whom Epilo always gave food from his garden or meat from a hunt. Most of the mourners were gone. There was only a handful of curious children to watch his body carried from the village to its grave. As they left, a young woman, Eike's daughter, carefully swept up the ashes of the vigil fire that smoldered near Epilo's bier throughout the day and threw them into the forest. Their removal would help ensure that Epilo's ghost would remain in the forest and not maraud the village.

Before dawn the following morning I was awakened by the muffled sound of a signal drum faraway. It was scarcely audible, but I had become as sensitive to the sound of distant drums as a mother to the breathing of her baby. Kumoi, after finishing his work the evening before, prudently had spent the night in Kafiere instead of returning to his home in Mifu. No person in his right mind would have gone abroad that night. Now he was preparing breakfast in the cook house while I shaved, but when I called to him about the drumming he answered he had not heard it. Solo'oke, one of my neighbors, was passing by and he replied it was the *maikesi* signal. It had come from Otemgi village at the far end of the Lumi airstrip and announced the preparations for a Spirit Fish curing festival.

After breakfast I joined a group of men at the ceremonial house but no one was interested in discussing the Otemgi festival. Their thoughts and their talk were on Epilo's ghost. Auwe, a friendly young man who held the government license for the Kafiere shotgun, said he had taken the gun apart yesterday and stored it in his house to prevent Epilo from damaging it. There was a sound reason for this action. A few years earlier the firing mechanism of Kafiere's first gun was irreparably broken by a rampaging ghost. Instead of hunting, Auwe planned to visit Parisko, a nearby village, to watch the final rites of their *mani* demon curing festival. And Wilkili, someone said, would begin a *mani* festival on Saturday, just two days away. I was going to continue to be exceedingly busy.

The discussion quickly returned to Epilo's ghost. There would be a seance that night to divine the cause of his death. Although I had interviewed for hours about Taute's mortuary rites, both old and new, it was the first mention of a death divination ceremony. The men, surprised I knew nothing about the custom, explained that it was performed with a long bamboo pole held in their hands but actually manipulated by the dead persons' ghost. As they described it, the technique seemed surprisingly similar to the Ouija board my sister and I used as children to predict the future and the contents of Christmas packages.

At dusk the Kafiere men and I entered Mifu and walked across the plaza to the bachelors' house where Epilo had lived. His nephews, Baiwin and Raba, were just beginning the preparations to entice Epilo's ghost back to the village for questioning about the cause of his death and, as I was to learn later, the hiding place of his money. I followed the brothers into the house and to Epilo's sleeping compartment. On his sleeping bench they placed some tobacco, betel nut, and lime, gifts no man, dead or alive, could ignore.

A small hole had been cut in the compartment's outside wall and as I watched, a section of the twenty-five-foot bamboo pole was pushed through the hole and into the room. Baiwin positioned the end of the pole just above Epilo's bed, tying to it a small packet containing a bit of hair and a finger-joint bone from Moiye, Epilo's dead brother. Epilo, Baiwin explained, was a new ghost and would need guidance in the seance. Moiye would help bring Epilo into the village and back to his bed to receive the gifts. The brothers then fastened to the pole clusters of small shells that Epilo would rattle to signal his return to his room. The men looked around them; everything was ready. We went outside, and the door to the house was secured.

A bright moon was rising into the sky spilling a silver glaze over the hamlet. Men and boys stood and sat in the center of the plaza talking quietly while the women and small children took ringside seats in front of their houses to watch the seance. The fires were extinguished—I didn't even see the glowing end of a cigarette—and as the smoke disappeared, the damp pungent smell of the forest drifted into the village. Everyone was waiting for Epilo to come. From the edge of the village, Epilo's name was called into the forest. It was a haunting cry, the syllables drawn out in a descending slur, sending a wave of sadness through me.

Then nothing. A roar of utter silence bangs at my ears. Again the lonely cry of Epilo's name rings through the night. No man stirs. Several of the men, including Baiwin and Raba, are holding the long pole, waiting, waiting, for the signal. From the house comes the dry sound of clacking shells. "He's come," Raba exclaims.

"If you're there Epilo," calls Kumoi, "move the bamboo." But nothing happens. The men decide that it was Moiye's ghost and that Epilo is still in his garden.

"Centipede!" several men cry at once and Raba jumps and turns in the air. But it scurries under the house before I can see it. Again Raba calls into the house for Epilo and this time the great bamboo pole begins to glide slowly back and forth. Epilo has come and the interrogation about his death begins.

One by one, the suspects are eliminated. It wasn't a witch or the *koyil* or any of a string of other local demons. Nor was he killed by the villages of Kamnum, Kulnem, Tabali, Senum, or Witali. And it wasn't Siwau or any of several other persons who might be angry with him. Even Pauwis's name is proposed, but she too is guiltless. Then the names of the Taute dead who might be acting for the living are called. At the name of Tulem, a relative of Siwau's, the bamboo begins to bang inside of the house. It is Tulem. Tulem killed Epilo! The men yell with excitement as the pole leaps out of the house. The remaining men run to grasp it, and it begins to dig up the ground.

From this point on the plaza was a bedlam of shouting men and I no longer could follow with precision the proceedings of the possessed pole. It raced around the plaza pulling the men along then, at their urging that I experience its tremendous power, I joined them. As the pole charged erratically, the men stumbled into each other and some fell to the ground. Duly impressed, I released my hold to return to my notebook and pen, implements over which I could exercise a degree of control.

One of the teenage boys whispers that Baiwin has instructed Epilo to show him where the money is hidden and that is the cause of the pole's surging gyrations. As the pole careens through the hamlet, the bright moon shadows of the men climb the houses and trees. Finally, it stops in front of Salbi's house and begins to dig furiously at the base of a Cordyline shrub as the exuberant yells build to a deafening crescendo. The men grip the pole with all their strength to keep it under control as silver beads slip down their faces and sides. There is, the boy whispers to me, thirty dollars down there. But several of the exhausted men release the bamboo and, gradually, it spends itself and is finally lowered to the ground.

For an hour and a half, Epilo possessed the bamboo pole before returning to the forest. The women already have gone inside and the men slowly return to their houses. The Kafiere men and I start for home, but Raba doesn't see us go. Poised over the money hole, his eager fingers dig among the roots for his dead uncle's wealth. But it never was found.

7

THE DANGEROUS
DESIRE

I was in Wilkili when the earthquake struck. The *mani* mask, a
majestic black cone extravagantly decorated with colored feathers
and fruits, had returned to its enclosure. I snapped shut the big
aluminum case after storing my cameras and glanced across the
village clearing toward the departing people. Suddenly they froze
in their tracks, and, at that instant, the ground surged upward
beneath my feet. People screamed, the houses rocked like ships at
sea, and the dogs began to howl. As parents scrambled for their
children, my thoughts leaped to Joyce, Ned, and Elizabeth in
Taute.

People swept by, fleeing from the ridge's edge toward the
forest. Kumoi grabbed his younger brother and started to run but
before they could escape, I grabbed Kumoi and the three of us ran
to the edge of the woods while shock after shock jolted the ridge.
As soon as the intensity of the tremors subsided, we were joined
by other Taute men and took a low track through a sago swamp
back to our village. As if our anxiety level hadn't peaked, some of

the men heard Epilo's ghost calling through the forest gloom. Bunched together on the narrow trail, we hurried onward.

It was dark when we entered Taute but the village was intact and our families safe. The posts of my house were shook so loose a baseball could be dropped into the post holes. The short-wave radio reported that the seismograph in Rabaul registered the quake at 8.1 on the Richter scale, one of the strongest ever recorded in Papua New Guinea. Joyce told a harrowing tale of being alone with the children on the ridge trail to Mifu only yards from the 1935 quake's gaping fissure when the first jolts struck.

The tremors continued throughout the night, and we slept hardly at all. Once we bolted out of bed after a particularly sharp jolt. Elizabeth was awake and frightened, and our neighbors called to us to leave the house. But eventually we returned to bed and I lay awake counting the tremors as I watched a dimly lit kerosene lantern sway back and forth as if caught in a wild wind.

When I returned to Wilkili the following day to film the concluding ceremony of the *mani* festival, I was told gently but firmly that I could not take the big movie camera out of its case. Woma, Wilkili's *mani* ritual expert dreamed *mani* had shook the earth with his anger at the filming of his rites. If I turned the camera toward *mani* again he would devastate both Wilkili and Taute by sliding them into the river below. Although initially astonished, I quickly apologized, and even as I did, the earth tremored slightly. But the Wilkili men took care to assure me that I was personally welcome in their village, that they would continue to teach me about their ceremonies, and that I could tape record and photograph. But after the quake and Woma's dream, I dare not bring the big camera with its long glaring eye into the village again.

So it is that the demons punish the villagers for insults and transgressions. And, while movie making may have its perils, they are nothing compared to the everyday dangers inherent in sexual intercourse. In fact, any activity related to one's sexuality is fraught with fear because of the forest demons' disapproval.

The people of Taute can't explain why the biological activity of human sexual organs so enrage the demons, but they are environmental facts about which they are as sure as the course of the sun and the moon. They have plenty of evidence to support their view.

While Kowokil, Bilu's mad brother, was exiled from the village because of his erratic behavior, his wife gave birth to a baby in their lonely forest hut. But the forest is the abode of the demons, and *kilfene* was so outraged by the bloody wastes of childbirth that he scraped his blade-encrusted back against the hillside causing landslides that ruined gardens and valuable trees. After that, the villagers decided they preferred Kowokil's madness to hunger, and the family returned to the village to begin building a house next to ours.

It was from these kinds of isolated incidents that I first began to gain a vague understanding about Taute sexual beliefs and behavior. Direct questioning about sexual matters, especially about sexual behavior, was met with embarrassed giggling or great guffaws. Even Kumoi, who rarely failed to have something enlightening to say on all matters, would break into a bemused grin and, shaking his head as he did whenever I behaved outrageously, say only, "Oh, Bill!"

What I hadn't learned was, although the Tautes sometimes publicly joke about sex, they don't like to discuss it. A young couple going to their garden might be assailed with a mocking call "We know where you're going and what you're going to do!" but no one wanted to talk with me about the positions and frequency of sexual intercourse, the function of semen or about masturbation. And it was made very evident to me that I was overstepping the bounds of propriety and friendship when I did so.

It was only by chance that I learned how to interview about Taute sexual behavior. Kuruwai and I were traveling alone together in the forest walking single file when, to my surprise, he began to interview *me* about the white's sexual practices. I not only was surprised but pleased because the people of Taute had demonstrated an almost total lack of interest in anything about our own beliefs. Even when I showed them American magazines filled with exciting and colorful pictures, they looked on with polite boredom. Or if I made a comment contrasting American and Wape customs during an interview, it was passed over as if I had coughed. But it was soon apparent that Kuruwai's questions about Western sexual practices stemmed from an immediate problem of his own.

Kuruawi and his wife, Yaoki, had one child, the cuddliest toddler in Taute, and neither wanted more children. Although Kuruwai was one of the strongest and most energetic young men in the village, the possibility of spending one's short life scrounging for food for several children did not appeal to him or his wife. He had observed that Western families usually have one or two children and the wife does not get pregnant again. "What do you do?" he asked. It was obvious to him that the magical rite the Wape women use to prevent pregnancy wasn't very effective while the Westerners seemed to have a technique that worked.

As we walked through the forest alone and one behind the other, I explained to him some of our techniques for birth control; the condom, the pill, the diaphragm, and the IUD. Occasionally we stopped while I demonstrated how a particular device operated. But our eyes never met. We could talk seriously about sexual topics only as long as we were completely alone and avoided eye contact. Eventually I turned the questioning to Wape sexual mores. So the few really valuable sexual interviews I obtained were when isolated with a man while walking in the forest or when visiting in total darkness. There was also one remarkable interview with a man who was lounging, audible but unseen under my house while I was inside.

And, eventually, I learned about the homosexual practices among the laborers segregated from women on the copra plantations. But there was no evidence that such practices were a part of Wape village life.

WM NOTES

7.12.70

PLANTATION LIFE

After dinner tonight Kumoi and I sat on the front steps talking. It was dark and Remau was high in a nearby palm cutting down coconuts. This prompted Kumoi to recall as a plantation laborer how the men would sometimes take coconuts from the 'masta's' palms. Four or five men would climb a single tree and pass the coconuts from one to another like a bucket brigade to avoid the noise of the falling nuts. Then they carried them into the bush and ate them.

About 20 men lived in a single dormitory. They went to work in the morning but never ate until noon . . . then they ate again in the afternoon. It was always the same food—rice and meat with only an occasional variant. But at Christmas the 'masta' gave them special rations. At night they would visit and sing. If there were 20 men in a house about five kerosene lamps were given to them although some places had electric lights. They went to bed about eleven or twelve P.M.

In the early days when Fiyu, Tongol, and Talie first went to the plantations on three-year contracts, there was a lot of anal intercourse among the laborers. It was simply accepted. Then the 'kiaps,' Kumoi said, tabooed this kind of behavior although some laborers still have 'fren' [sexual] relationships with each other. Around the Kokopo plantations there is a lot of homosexuality. The young men are taken by the more mature men for sexual partners and sometimes there are fights over them. . . .

During my first interview on Wape sexuality with Kuruwai I mentioned "menstruation," and he interrupted me to say that a plantation 'masta' told the black laborers that white women don't menstruate.

"Isn't that right, only black women menstruate?" he asked.

I sighed to myself in anger. It was the typical kind of condescending misinformation given to villagers that some white men think is a great, thigh-slapping joke. "No," I said, "that isn't true. Joyce menstruates, the Lumi sisters menstruate, all women, regardless of their color, menstruate." He nodded slowly and I could feel him wondering, why is it that white men lie to black men? Just then I am sure Kuruawi trusted me as completely as I trusted him. Later he may have changed his view.

While we were talking about contraceptives, I explained that Dr. Wark sometimes fitted women with IUDs, and Yaoki could ask her about it during the next Maternal and Child Health patrol to Taute. I later learned that his wife was fitted with an IUD, the first in Taute, but for some reason it was not effective. Yaoki became pregnant. Kuruwai never mentioned it to me but I knew my credibility was damaged. Did he think I was putting him on like the plantation 'masta'? Was I just one more white man that lied? I never would know.

From my interviews on Taute sex practices I learned that the periodicity of sexual intercourse should be strictly regulated. A couple can't have sex just any time. If a couple has sex in the garden they must abstain that night. Nor can they indulge in erotic pleasures the next day or even the day after. But the fourth day they may have intercourse again.

Why the widely spaced contacts? It is because a man who has sex too often will loose weight, his strength will fail, and his skin will droop in folds like an old man's. He becomes soft like an overripe banana, a deplorable state for a man who must be strong for the hunt. Semen is thought to be an "energizer" and as it pours out of the male into the female, so does his strength pour into her and, as she grows strong on his semen, he becomes weakened with its loss.

Once a man's wife is pregnant and misses her menses, the couple must abstain completely from further sexual intercourse. They must abstain not only until after the baby is born but until it has grown strong enough to walk alone. Obviously this is an ideal that not even the well-disciplined Wape can always achieve. But the consequences for breaking the taboo are severe. The couple's child will be weak. Unable to walk, it crawls instead.

In a society where malnutrition is rampant, more than one Taute man was secretly described to me as a lecher whose impatient sexual desires were responsible for his child's puniness and inability to walk. But this is no macho-phrased society where an intensified sense of maleness is sustained by the myth of the male as a tireless and fearless human stud. It is a society where a man's expression of his masculinity in the sexual act not only diminishes his physical powers but may endanger the development of his children as well.

Like so many other aspects of Wape beliefs, the cultural expression of male sexuality is defensive. The Wape male is not a sexual predator but must defend his sexuality against excesses, and just as his intrusive raids on enemy villages were widely spaced, so are his sexual encounters as well. To conserve and defend are the twin ideals of Wape culture. These are not men searching for new worlds to conquer, peoples to enslave, or harems of wives. They know that women's physical capacity for sustained sex is greater than their own and, in self-defense, act accordingly.

So a central assumption of any male version of Wape culture is that sexual desire is dangerous. The sexual act itself is no voluptuous and carefree dalliance under a tropical moon, but a furtive forest encounter, carefully rationed, with an aftermath of fear. For sexual intercourse, like childbirth and menstruation, is intimately associated with female sexuality and, therefore, ritually polluting. The sex act is a risky undertaking that drains the male and places both him and his partner in a position of demonic jeopardy.

If Wape sexuality with its twin concerns for conservation and defense is an apt metaphor for much of Wape culture, there is one important male activity where it doesn't fit. And it isn't the hunt, for the Wape style of hunting is not especially aggressive or adventuresome. Although a particular successful hunt may be glorified in story and song, there is no reckless flamboyance exhibited in the hunt itself. Extreme caution against the chance of personal injury is always foremost in any hunting strategy.

When I was first instructed in Wape hunting techniques I was told and shown, over and over, how to take my shooting stance holding the bow while balancing with one foot on the ground and the other halfway up a small but sturdy tree. The rationale is elementary. A man charged by a wild boar or even a cassowary has only to drop his bow and bound up the tree to safety. To the Wape this is not timidity but planned prudence.

No, it is only in gambling that caution is completely thrown to the winds and a vigorous all-or-nothing stance is assumed. For most Wape men the sense of high adventure is not found in sports, hunting, drinking, fighting, or womanizing, but at a 'satu' gaming board. Whether a game is announced by word of mouth or the lusty boom of a signal drum, the men of neighboring villages crowd into the host village to bet upon the dice. Held in a tin cup, the dice are slammed smartly against the board with a resounding crash, and almost before the money has changed hands, the cup is slammed down again. The bets and side bets are small, usually only a shilling, so a game lasts through the night and often far into the following day. As the loosers retire, newcomers take their places, and finally when all are exhausted the game ends. Big winners are expected to show up for the next game so the losers can recoup their losses.

The men know that gambling is illegal, and the Lumi officials and police also know there aren't many nights in a week when a game isn't being played somewhere. When the Lumi jail population becomes too low to keep the grass airstrip cut, the police have only to raid a game to fill the jail once again.

Because I could not risk losing my visa, I never gambled with the men. Yet they knew I would not report them. So for a time Kafiere became a popular gambling rendezvous. When a game got going, it always meant a poor night's sleep with banging cups, high-spirited talking, and occasional shouting. One night an argument broke out over a throw of the dice, and an angered player threw the dice over the cliff and stormed down the path past our house denouncing his fellow players in a yelling rage. So close did we live to the path that in my predawn stupor I thought the house was invaded and jumping out of bed, almost pulled down the mosquito net, frightening Joyce even more than the shouting.

The next morning I asked the men to please take the night

portion of their games elsewhere. Also, if Kafiere developed a reputation as a center for 'satu,' the government could make it difficult for all of us. The men accepted my reasoning and genially ended the all-night sessions. But this did not signal an end to my 'satu' adventures.

As I was preparing to return to Taute from one of my infrequent visits to Lumi, Assistant District Commissioner Peter Broadhurst, Lumi's top official, said he would like to make the hike with me. He had not visited Taute and was interested in seeing our camp as well. Besides, he wanted to initiate a new junior officer to the rigors of bush patrolling and also give his sedentary police sergeant some needed exercise. Frankly, I did not want to return to my unsuspecting village with this formidable official entourage. No one in Taute would like me for that, and I wouldn't blame them.

Peter was an open and friendly man, and both he and his wife Helen were our friends and had extended many kindnesses to us and the children. Taken by surprise at his invitation to accompany me, I could not think of a way to say no that would not sound insulting to him personally or his official position. It was the typical kind of completely innocent but confusing dilemma I came to associate with Lumi.

My fear (it would become an obsession before we reached Taute) was that the Tautes and their neighbors would be in a nonstop game of 'satu.' We proceeded at a moderate pace for neither the young officer or the old sergeant were in condition for the hike. My one hope was in meeting someone from Taute on the trail. There was no doubt that once they saw me approaching Taute with 'kiaps' and police they would double back to the village and give the alarm.

But where were the Tautes? I always met some of my neighbors on the trail but today, no one. As we came closer to Taute, my 'satu' fantasy became a nightmare. I imagined entering the unsuspecting village to find the biggest 'satu' game in all Wapeland. Looking up in horror, the men would see their alleged friend, Bill, leading the 'namba wan kiap,' his assistant, and the sergeant into their midst. The arrests would be made with dispatch and the men of Taute marched away to jail. End of Mitchell. End of field work.

As we climbed the mountain up to Mifu, I made sure I was in the lead and took a miserable little path that bypassed the hamlet. If they were gambling, Mifu was the more probable place. I stretched my hearing for the telltale crash of the 'satu' cup but heard nothing. Mifu was strangely quiet. I did not even hear the voices of playing children.

As we walked along the ridge toward Kafiere, my fearfulness increased. Were the Mifus in Kafiere? Was that why Mifu was so quiet? We stepped into the hamlet at the far end away from the clearing where 'satu' was played. No one was in sight. The first house was deserted. Then, as we came to the second house, I called to Tongol and he came out to welcome the prestigious party of government dignitaries. But when his grandson eyed us he gave me a look of cold panic and disappeared. Something *was* wrong, so I prolonged the conversation with Tongol although it was obvious my companions wanted only to get to my house where they could rest with a long drink of cold lemonade. We gradually made our way through the hamlet, and it was the first time I was thankful for its strung-out configuration.

When we arrived at my house, there was a very large complement of Taute men to greet us. Many were from Mifu. There was only one thing that would bring them all to Kafiere. 'Satu!'

Peter stayed for about an hour visiting with the men and was appalled at their lack of understanding of the organization and goals of the government. He then returned to Lumi with his two weary assistants. But by then I already knew.

When we entered the hamlet there was a large group of men from Taute and neighboring villages playing 'satu.' It wasn't a nightmare fantasy after all. The warning came in time for the visitors to flee the village while most of the Tautes remained to give the Lumi 'kiaps' a proper welcome.

The men and I laughed and moaned as we compared stories of our close encounter with disaster. It was a very narrow escape for us all. When the men went off to continue their game I stayed quietly at home, too unnerved by the near fiasco to venture forth again that day.

8

GUNS, GHOSTS, AND GOODNESS

From the first day I arrived in Taute, the men repeatedly made two urgent requests of me. One was to open a store in the village to save them the troublesome walk into Lumi. The other was to buy a shotgun to help them kill game more efficiently. This was the least, they seemed to indicate, a fair-minded and, in Wape terms, obviously rich neighbor should do. One of the hardest things the field anthropologist must learn is to say "no" to deserving people. It is especially difficult when those people are your friends. But we had come halfway around the world to learn about the Wape way of life, not to introduce stores and shotguns that would alter the village's established trading and hunting patterns. It seemed harsh, but that was the reality of our presence in Taute. As both responsible scientists and temporary guests, our impact on the society should be as minimal as possible. So I said "no" not once, but many times.

Eventually the villagers despaired of my uncompromising position, and Kafiere and Mifu hamlet each decided to buy a community shotgun. The investment was a sizable forty-two Australian dollars; forty dollars for the gun and two dollars for the gun permit. Each hamlet made a volunteer collection from its members and I, as a fellow villager, contributed to both guns. It was the first week of October. For me it would become the memorable "month of the guns." As things developed, my refusal to buy a personal shotgun was one of the most crucial field work decisions I would make. Otherwise I might have missed the most important ethnographic discovery of our expedition: the shotgun cult.

In Western society a shotgun is a prosaic machine. It is a utility weapon with none of the glamor and mystique associated with high-powered rifles and hand guns. The heros and villains of TV and films don't shoot it out with the slow and clumsy shotgun. But to the Wape man, whose native weapons are the bow and arrow and bone dagger, the shotgun is a marvelous technical achievement. Around this rare and expensive machine, the Wape have built an integrated system of beliefs, behaviors, and rituals focused on its hunting fortunes. So profound was the impact of the shotgun cult and so extensive its ramifications, it affected the daily lives of everyone in the village including those of my family, documenting beyond a doubt that we were now an integral part of Taute's indigenous cultural life.

I did not know any of this when the guns first arrived in the village. But as the entire repertoire of beliefs and behaviors were dramatically played out before me, I gradually realized I had discovered, and was recording on paper, film, and tape, a remarkable type of syncretic cult—a cult melding specific Wape and Western beliefs and practices into a novel whole. No similar type of cult centering on a Western weapon had been described before, and the thrill of the discovery stimulated me to push my inquiry deeper and deeper.

Especially interesting was the new precept accompanying the arrival of the guns that, henceforth, there should be *no* quarreling among the villagers. Could this be true? The well-behaved Tautes were going to be even more cooperative and virtuous?

Joyce and I could never measure up to this more stringent morality. At least we would try to understand the dynamics of the cult.
So with Joyce collecting information from the government in
Lumi while I concentrated on the village, the background of the
shotgun cult began to unfold.

When the first guns were brought into Wapeland in the late
1940s and early 1950s by missionaries, traders, and government
officials, the natives were not permitted to own them. A native
could use a gun only as an employee of a white man to shoot game
for his table, a coveted and prestigious job. Then, as confidence
in the native population grew, the government regulations were
changed in 1960 permitting natives to purchase single-barrel
shotguns. At first only a few Wape men living near the government station in Lumi and helpful to the 'kiaps' were granted gun
permits. Eventually more permits were issued with some villages
having several guns, others having none. When the already sparse
game rapidly disappeared, the government, in a vain hope of
preserving the remaining game, established a limit of one gun
permit for each one hundred people.

The shotgun, like Melanesian Pidgin, is associated by the
Wape with Westerners and modernity, and, not surprisingly,
Pidgin is favored for shotgun parlance. The man who receives a
gun permit is not only called 'sutboi' ("shootboy") but also
'loman' ("lawman"), the latter a term connoting his official tie to
Western law and government as perceived by the villagers.

When a candidate for a gun permit appears before the 'kiap'
in Lumi, he is examined orally on the use of firearms, then given
an unloaded shotgun and tested on his handling knowledge.
Under the direct and questioning gaze of the examining official,
candidates sometimes become flustered. Kumoi was the first man
to try for Mifu's gun permit, but he inadvertently aimed the gun
first toward the wife of the Assistant District Commissioner and
then toward a group of observers. His examination ended igno-
miniously on the spot.

But if the candidate passes the test and the 'kiap' approves of
his character, he is then lectured on the use of the gun: only the

man with the permit may fire it; he must willingly shoot game for his fellow villagers; the gun must be used exclusively for hunting. He is strongly warned that if any of these rules are broken or if there is trouble in the village, he will not only lose the gun and his permit but be imprisoned as well.

The candidate's friends and the inevitable audience of on-lookers witness the 'kiap's' exhortation. Here, as in many spheres of native life, the official's power is absolute, and his charge is not an idle threat. Not only does he decide who can have a gun, but guns actually have been confiscated or destroyed without reimbursement and gunmen have been jailed.

So the 'kiap's' charge to the candidate is willingly accepted. Henceforth, he will seldom leave the village without proudly carrying his gun. He is now a 'laman,' and he has the gun and permit printed entirely in English to prove it.

The 'kiap's' strong sanctions against village quarrels are motivated by his fear that the gun might be used in a village dispute. These sanctions are further upheld and emphasized by the missionaries' and catechists' sermons against quarreling and wrongdoing as they work to teach the Christian doctrine of brotherly love. The message the villagers receive is this: to keep the white man's gun they must follow the white man's rules. This the Wape do, not in servile submission, but with some pride because the presence of the gun and the public focus on morality mark the village as progressive and modern. The licensed gunman, therefore, is not only the guardian of the community gun but of the community's morality as well!

Rain or shine, he is expected to go into the forest without compensation to hunt for his fellow villagers, who give him cartridges with some personal identifying mark upon them. After a gunman makes a kill, the owner of the cartridge receives the game and distributes it according to his economic obligations to others. But the gunman, like the bow-and-arrow hunter, is forbidden to eat from the kill for to do so would jeopardize further successful hunting.

In Kafiere, the clan that contributed the most money toward the gun and whose lands held the most game appointed Auwe as gunman. Auwe was a very likeable young man, serious and soft-spoken, with the characteristic gentleness of those who have successfully survived a difficult childhood. Orphaned as a child during the dysentery epidemic, he had lived with various relatives, knew what it was to be deprived, and was deeply attuned to human suffering. Auwe's wife, Naiasu, a woman much older than he, was as lively as he was retiring. Listening to her full-throated laughter wafting through the soft night air as I typed up my notes is one of my most engaging memories of Taute.

Auwe had not chosen Naiasu for his wife. He had, in a sense, inherited her and her two small sons when her husband, Auwe's clansman, died. Although Auwe sometimes privately lamented she was not a young woman nearer his own age, he and Naiasu had a close relationship. And he was an attentive father to her sons and their own infant daughter. Just how close he was to his family I learned from a frightening accident.

I had lived in Taute only a few weeks when a child, a girl, came running into the village from the forest screaming that Naiasu was dead. She was collecting leaves high in a tree, had fallen, and was killed in her plunge to earth. Auwe, stumbling out of his house, sick with fever and a blinding headache, grasping what had happened, turned and dashed into the forest as I ran toward him. In my alarm I foolishly forgot to put on my shoes and Auwe quickly outdistanced me.

When I finally reached him, Naiasu was sitting dazed upon a rotting log in Auwe's embrace. Tenderly he massaged her breasts, belly and back with stinging nettles. Tears streamed down his face. It was a few moments before he noticed me; then, in speech both rapid and intense, he explained what a terrible thing it is when a woman with young children dies. Without a mother a child is hungry and cries because there is nothing to eat. Some children waste and die.

As he continued to massage and comfort her, several men

who had joined us made a stretcher to carry Naiasu back to the village. Miraculously she had suffered no major injuries and would recover. But before Auwe returned to the village, he angrily chopped down the homicidal tree.

When Kafiere initially proposed Auwe as their gunman, Naiasu was against it. Semer, her former husband, was Kafiere's first gunman, and she argued that the community hunting responsibilities of a 'sutboi' forced him to neglect his gardens and family obligations. So when Auwe went to Lumi to apply for his gun permit, Semer's ghost followed him and influenced the 'kiap' against Auwe, who returned to Taute empty-handed. This was the first of many stories I would hear about the relationship between ghosts and the gun. But Auwe went back to Lumi for a second try, and this time he won his permit. Kafiere now had a licensed gunman, and hunting could begin in earnest. Or so I thought. I had yet to learn about the 'kapti' ritual.

WM NOTES
14 October 1970

THE 'KAPTI' RITUAL

What a world of behavior this crazy shotgun has opened up. More actual data on ghosts than I have been able to get before and now the first full-fledged ritual feast. True, it is a meagre feast, but the first I have observed that included the entire hamlet and not just a family as did the ritual feasting in Wamala's garden at the first planting of taro. (Not really the first planting but the ritual planting *symbolizing* the first planting). Anyway, all of the following data was collected either in interview or by observation yesterday, Tuesday.

Auwe was finally successful in getting his gun permit on Monday and that night told me about a kind of "confessional" ritual that would take place the following day. Then yesterday while visiting with Kuruwai and Baiwin I asked them about the gun ritual and they took over the interview telling me what was to take place later in the day. This is a synopsis of the interview notes.

There are two parts to the 'kapti' ceremonial for a new gun. It is a new ritual introduced by the guns and does not have an exact analog with bow-and-arrow hunting. They are quite clear and emphatic that it is not a ceremony they got from their ancestors. In fact, the reason for the 'kapti' (must be from the English "a cup of tea") is to inform the ghosts of their dead relatives about the gun and to seek their help in bringing game to the new gunman. "The dead men don't understand about guns so we have a meeting so they can hear about them. Then they will send game to the gunman and he can kill it." Thus a new major hunting technique means a special ritual to inform the ancestral ghosts who are the patrons for hunting.

The usual food for a 'kapti' ceremony are 'hatwara,' 'saksak,' taro, banana, and pig. If a wild pig isn't killed then everyone contributes to buy a small domestic pig. (While I was talking with Kuruwai and Baiwin we heard that Wamala had tracked one of his small male pigs to an area not too far from the hamlet. Later the men and boys joined him to help surround it but were unsuccessful. Ned and I joined them for a while. At least we trekked into the bush and stood with young Malpul who took a stand on a log with his bow. Then we met Auwe who was having trouble with the new gun and I tried to help him with it; a problem of his not pulling the hammer back aggressively enough. Kuruwai went on with him and he later shot a bird that had to substitute for the pig at the 'kapti.')

The 'kapti' is held at the house of the man with the permit. . . . First the men and boys eat the food the women have brought, then the meeting for the ancestors follows. (They also refer to the 'kapti' as a 'pati bilong masket' [party for the gun]). The men eat just a bit of the food then the boys the rest. The food, however, is really for the ghosts who, unseen, devour its "essence." . . .

Angry arguments or fighting are antithetical to successful hunting; 'ol i mas stap gut' [everyone must behave]. If the ghosts hear an argument, they will 'bagarap' [ruin] the shotgun. Therefore husbands and wives can't fight; men can't argue with each other. When I asked if parents could strike their children as I had seen Tume strike Auti the other day, they said that was all right. The discipline of children is permissible and will not anger the ancestors. (I would hate to imagine a taboo against disciplining children; they have the run of it as it is!)

If the argument is a small one, then things can be set right by the person who is angry (It's fascinating, but as I have observed before, people here don't argue. It's always one person who is angry and the other one takes it passively) making some taro soup (scrappings and chunks of taro cooked in water until rather mushy; delicious, better than mashed potatoes). The angry person then calls for the gunman and gives him some of the soup, but not a lot, others actually eat it.

However, if the 'kros' [quarrel] is a serious one, e.g., two men fighting (could it actually happen here?), then a feast like the 'kapti' must be given by the angry person and must include meat, preferably pig.

There is also an important sanction against gossiping or 'tok tok nating' when men are hunting with either bow or gun. . . . Kuruwai, to demonstrate how it works, used the hypothetical example of Aif, a Kafiere man, on a hunt. When he returned he gave portions of the game to Tebia and Witauwa, then a smaller portion to Lamu. This angered Lamu's wife and she began to talk about it and her children, overhearing their mother's displeasure, also began to gossip about Aif's stinginess. Then Lamu's father's ghost learning of Aif's injustice to his descendants followed him into the forest on his next hunt and turned a pig away that was headed straight for his bow and arrow. The ghost can even ruin the hunting for the entire village if he wants to.

But there is a way to placate the ghost to restore good hunting and it is incumbent upon Lamu to do it. First his wife must make big sago dumplings (sago flour turned into hot water forming a big gelatinous blob and usually eaten by twisting a portion from it with bamboo tongs. The Oni and Yellow River people make theirs in small individual portions and maybe they do here sometimes but I haven't seen it yet) and these are served with boiled leaves to the men of the hamlet. After they have eaten the men gather around Lamu. First he chews some 'kawawar' [ginger root] (kawawar seems to be a part of all important rituals) then spits it over a stalk of betel nuts. He then flails the stalk against the ground and the loosened nuts roll among the standing men. They pick up the nearest nuts and begin to chew them. . . . The important thing is that the 'smel' [odor] of Lamu is transferred to the hunters signaling Lamu's father's ghost that Lamu is no longer angry with Aif and that he must stop his interference with the hunt. (This 'smel' thing is actually that; something personal like spittal usually mixed with betel or 'kawawar' is communicated to the person who needs it in the same way that the mask wearers at the curing ceremonies put their sweat on the persons who are ill.) Now, my informants tell me, the men may find pigs again. . . .

WM NOTES
15 October 1970

WITAUWA AS INFORMANT

This morning I got Witauwa to come and talk about the 'kapti' ceremony and hunting in general, both with gun and with bow. As I already had considerable data on the ceremony from Baiwin and Kuruwai, I wanted to see what he would add, or perhaps detract. But first, how about Witauwa as an informant? It's an important question for he was my principal interviewee for almost all of the first month in Taute while the house was being built. During this period the men would come to my house every night and he would be the main person to talk. Younger men like Aif, Kuruwai, Weti and Auwe would not talk if Witauwa was talking. Even when I asked them something directly they would defer to Witauwa to answer.

(During this period I was getting increasingly annoyed with Kumoi as he seemed to be taking everything over; he was 'bosboi' and 'masta' both! Joyce was extremely annoyed with him as she felt he did not listen to her household instructions. As I came to know him better, a lot of it wasn't him but an overreaction based on our own insecurity in the village situation. We obviously didn't know what was going on around us and were trying not to overdetermine the situation. We were both extremely up-tight, plus the four of us crowded into one room for all of our living. Rather nightmarish as I think back on it.)

Anyway, I now know that Witauwa is a fairly reliable informant as far as he goes. But he never tells me everything he knows. I've checked him out over and over regarding cultural motivations behind an act and he pretends he doesn't know. " 'O, mi no savi tink tink bilong em' " or "'Mi no savi long em, no gut mi giaman yu.'" ["I don't know what they are thinking" or "I don't know about them, and that's the truth."] When, of course, he knows all the magic and ritual there is to know. And now, even though he knows I know about ghosts, sorcery and demons, when I asked him what ruined Semer's gun he gave me the common-sense answer that all guns break sooner or later. Not a mention of a ghost having broken it as others had told me.

In the past I used to call him on this kind of evasion and he would smile glancing downward and say something like, "Yes, I've heard this talk." So, to evaluate him as an informant he can always be depended on to *not* tell me everything. He won't lie but he will give a commonplace explanation or say he doesn't know (which, in a way, is a kind of lying but not the kind that is distorting and extremely tricky to deal with.)

He is straight on historical events and in citing observable behavior but never the cultural reasons behind it. For this I must depend upon the younger men, e.g., Kumoi, Weti, Maiana, Baiwin, Kuruwai, and sometimes Auwe, although he hasn't been as straight as I would like regarding his stepson's sickness caused by the *malangan* demon. It was only as I became displeased with Witauwa's work as 'bosboi' that I began to avoid him and him me. Then Kuruwai was the first to begin explaining things to me and the other younger men followed. And once you get your foot into the magical thinking door, you can usually keep edging it open by telling your informant what you already know then let him go from there. But if you don't know *anything,* I suppose it's difficult for them to know where to start. And if the older men are holding back and I talk only to them, well, the younger men probably aren't going to stick out their necks.

Anyway, it is great to have the Witauwa phase over. We seem to have an easy relationship now with no big expectations on either side.

The 'kapti' for the new shotgun was a failure. In the month that followed Auwe hunted constantly, saw at least eight wild pigs, but each time they ran away before he could get off a shot. He also missed three birds, precipitating a meeting where it was decided to have another 'kapti.' But it would be more elaborate than the first. This one would include rice and canned fish as well as the traditional foods and wild game.

The villagers knew why Auwe couldn't kill a pig, and it had nothing to do with his unfamiliarity with the gun. Wamala and old Moala, who was celebrated as having killed more pigs than any man in the village except Tongol, had decided that one of Auwe's ancestral ghosts was angry because he permitted Maiana and Weti, both of the Koropa clan, to hunt with him in his bush. Auwe belonged to another clan, and his clansman Potalai had been murdered by Koropa men. So when Potalai's ghost saw Auwe bring the clansmen of his murderers into his bush to hunt, he angrily frightened the pigs away. Now they would placate

Potalai with a 'kapti' feast and, while they had him there, carefully explain to him that the gun and the shells were not Auwe's exclusive property and the Koropa men had a legitimate right to accompany him on a hunt into his bush.

It was midafternoon of the designated day when Wamala walked into the plaza and called out in Pidgin for the women to get their food ready. They would prepare native foods for themselves and the children while the men of Kerate and Koropa clans cooked rice and canned fish for a ceremonial exchange. Because my house was in the Kerate part of the hamlet, Auwe and Kuruwai suggested I give my rice to Koropa. It was the first time I had been formally considered as more closely affiliated to one clan than another and it gave me a strange kind of pleasure.

The pungent smell of smoking fires and cooking food filled the hamlet. Just as an American household is active with expectancy on Thanksgiving morning, so the entire hamlet was waiting for the coming feast. Auwe and I watched the preparations.

"I will not be able to hunt on Sundays," he said. "It is a big taboo."

"Why is that?" I asked.

"Well, Wama of Wilkili had a gun blow up just like a piece of bamboo last year when he shot at a cockatoo on a Sunday. On Sunday the gun must rest."

And he continued to explain that just as most white men rest on Sunday, so must the gun. The analogy was beautiful. It was, I think, the first time I clearly grasped their image of the gun as a primary symbol of modernity. Suddenly it seemed so obvious. The shotgun was the central symbol of what they saw as a "modernized" culture integrating the Wape past with their version of the Western present gleaned from the constraints and strictures set down by the 'kiap's' government and the church's teachings. How ironic that the supeme message of both groups— for such different reasons—animating the shotgun cult was a Western mother's plea to her children, "Don't fight!"

This 'kapti' would not be held at Auwe's house but in front

of the men's ceremonial house where a special altar, rude but effective, was being hurriedly constructed on the plaza. It was a tablelike affair with tall saplings at each corner. A bright chartreuse fringe made from shredded sago palm shoots and studded with sacred ginger, red and pink Hibiscus flowers, and highly colored leaves was gaily draped around the top of the altar. Catching the fringe, the evening breeze waved it enticingly.

Auwe placed his polished gun upright upon the altar, and others placed their cartridges around it. Twelve battered tin dishes of expensive rice and meat were placed on the altar while over a score of traditional containers with traditional foods were placed on the ground in front of the ceremonial house. Everyone in the hamlet was there.

Wamala began serving the ceremonial rice shortly after five, and the villagers fell upon the food with gusto. Witauwa, although not a member of Koropa clan, grabbed my big pot of rice and hot dogs and practically devoured the entire contents. Joyce, who already thought Witauwa the only really offensive male chauvinist in the hamlet, was disgusted with the way he hogged down our food while the other married men, in more typical Wape fashion, ate some of their rice offerings then shared the rest with their wives and children.

The feasting was over in less than thirty minutes and the meeting began. Wamala called out to his ancestors to send game, especially pigs, to Auwe's gun. Auwe soberly faced the assemblage and commanded them to behave themselves, especially when he was hunting. Then there could be absolutely no quarreling or malicious gossip. "If you will just be good," he promised, "I'll bring home meat."

Although most of the men and boys were in the plaza or in front of the ceremonial house, the women and children were watching the proceedings from their dirt porches. Witauwa, true to Joyce's perception of him, addressed his vigorous comments to the women, blaming them for many of our hunting problems because they sometimes stole food from each others bush. Railing like a Pentecostal preacher addressing a band of incorrigible thieves he shouted, "You women can't steal food!" Around me I could hear men and boys alike muttering about the perfidy of women.

Regardless of how thorough I was in collecting information about an upcoming event, I never succeeded beforehand in finding out everything I should know. Something important always occurred that took me completely by surprise. That is why the interview is never a sufficient research technique for the anthropologist. He also must witness the actual event—if he can—for direct observation remains the single greatest strength of the anthropological method.

So when Poluwa, Bilu's wife, quietly stepped forward toward Auwe and his companion hunters, Maiana, Kuruwai, and Weti, I knew I was going to see something I knew nothing about. Taking some sacred ginger, Poluwa chewed it then spat it out on the naked backs of the four men. Even before Poluwa had finished the rite, Wamla's wife Lemto had joined her in spitting more sacred ginger upon the young hunters.

It wasn't until the following day that Auwe told me what it was all about. Poluwa, he said, had suffered a spell of madness shortly before I came to live in Taute during which she had done many irresponsible things. One of them was to clap her hands behind Auwe's back, a woman's traditional curse to block a man's hunting prowess. Even Auwe confessed he was surprised when Poluwa stepped forward to remove her curse.

Lemto's involvement in the rite was motivated by another incident. One day while Auwe was tracking a pig that escaped him, Wamala asked Lemto, his wife, to go to the Lumi native market to sell some sago. When she refused to go he became insistent. So to convince her husband she would not go, she struck him on the back with a piece of firewood. Although everyone in the hamlet seemed to know about the incident except me and was laughing about it, she publicly acknowledged her part in ruining Auwe's pig hunt and the anointment of the hunters with the sacred ginger would bring them future success. There was, it seemed, no end to the entwining of the villager's lives with the fortunes of the gun.

A few moments later Auwe called to Naiasu to bring him some money. Standing with Weti and Maiana, the Koropa descendants of Potalai's murderer, Auwe shook hands with the two men while simultaneously exchanging six shillings with each of them. This would convince Potalai's irate ghost, and any suspicious Koropa ghosts too for that matter, that the hostility between the clans was settled.

Now it was Weti's turn to surprise me. Auwe already had removed his gun fom the altar and was putting the cartridges into a small bag. People were beginning to relax and visit when Weti, in a loud voice, asked me if I had anything to say to the people. I was still enthusiastically writing in my notebook when it finally sunk in that I was expected to give a little speech. An astute politician would have been overjoyed at such an opportunity, but the best I could manage was to mutter something about my hope that we could all behave ourselves. I was suddenly caught between cultures and I felt slightly hypocritical and foolish.

Weti, ostentatiously and uncharacteristically referring to me as 'masta,' repeated my comments in an authoritative voice. But at that point in the proceedings no one could have cared less what I thought. Like the gun, tin dishes, rice, and canned meat, I was but another captive symbol of Taute's modernity. It was not the villagers but the old ghosts, so unfamiliar with these new ways, that Weti was trying to impress and influence.

After the second 'kapti,' everyone's expectations were that Auwe now would certainly kill a pig. But no such thing happened. Occasionally he would bag a bird or a few giant fruit bats that flew right into the hamlet to feast on the breadfruit trees. But that was it. As more and more cartridges went astray of their mark, their owners became increasingly irritated about their economic losses. Whereas the villagers previously had kept to their own affairs, they now became embroiled in meeting after meeting, seeking out transgressions, quarrels, and wrongdoing.

As Auwe continued to have bad luck, his efforts to discover the cause became more zealous. A certain amount of polarization resulted: Auwe accused the villagers, the men accused the women, and the adults accused the young people of hiding their wrongs. And a few who had lost many cartridges wondered if Auwe was keeping the game for himself. Still, no one suggested he was an inexperienced shotgun hunter. Auwe was generally considered to be blameless; in fact, the more game he missed, the more self-righteous he became and the more miscreant the villagers.

The weeks passed. It was the day before Thanksgiving and Joyce and I were having fun planning the menu. Don Laycock, a visiting Australian linguist who had done extensive work classifying the Sepik languages, and Don McGregor and Betty Gillam, a mission nurse who worked with Lyn and whose positive good humor always cheered me, would be coming out from Lumi to help us celebrate. Foreign festivals, regardless how exotic and fascinating, lack the comforting nostalgia and predictability of one's childhood holidays. As our day-to-day lives were so dominated by Wape culture, we made a special effort to celebrate our American holidays to maintain some sense of the traditional rhythm of our lives, both for the children and ourselves.

There would be a turkey Joyce had special ordered months before from Tang Mows, her favorite Wewak store. Since our only mode of cooking was on an open fire, it would be boiled in a big pot. And there would be baked 'kau kau,' an excellent substitute for sweet potatoes. Lyn couldn't join us but she sent out a mincemeat pie—her first one and baked just for us. We had a can of American cranberry sauce ordered from an Australian catalogue and thus all the essential ingredients for a successful American Thanksgiving.

Then Kumoi brought some news that broke off our menu discussion. Auwe had shot—and killed—a pig! Not any pig but a huge wild boar deep in the Yingowam bush. He had returned to the village to recruit men to help him to butcher it and carry it home. I had just enough time to eat some lunch before setting out with them. The sky was darkening, and glancing toward the higher mountains, I saw the rain sweeping down upon us. It would not be just a shower but a severe storm, and I could already feel the cold rain pouring over my blinded face and the wretched clutching of saturated clothing. So with not a little guilt, I rationalized that I had observed the butchering of wild and domestic pigs before—it was the same procedure—and recorded the accompanying rituals. Although one of the two cartridges that killed the boar belonged to Kumoi, I was certain he would not object too strongly if I asked him to stay in the hamlet and work with me.

As the men filed out of the village, their high spirits already dampened by the impending storm, it began to rain. Somewhere in the heavens a dam had broken and the drowning torrents continued into the evening darkness. As Kumoi and I worked snug and dry through the afternoon discussing a series of photographs I had taken of a curing festival, he paused occasionally to shake his head and express concern for our friends sloshing through the swamps and mud of a submerged forest. Perhaps he felt more guilty than I.

The night was black and still raining when the men came trudging across the muddy plaza to dump their loads of pig on the ceremonial house porch. The men were cold, exhausted, and miserable. Someone started a fire, and I brought them two kerosene lanterns so they, and I, could see what they were doing. Untying their packages of pig, they began to arrange the pieces for the final cutting and distribution. For these shot-out mountains, it indeed was a trophy pig. The tusks were about two inches long and from the dismembered bloody hulks around me, it must have weighed at least three hundred pounds. Our elaborate 'kapti' finally had paid off.

The trenchant smell of pig blood was overpowering. Already the scroungy little dogs of Taute had gathered, and as they crept in to lick at the precious blood—there was no way they would ever taste the meat—the boys would shout and strike at them with sticks. Cringing only momentarily, they crept back for more invective and blows. I admired their heroic persistence. The ability of a New Guinea dog to tolerate continuing abuse must be unmatched in the animal world.

In the flickering shadows I saw Auwe go into the ceremonial house carrying a half-opened package containing the boar's head and what appeared to be some of the internal organs. Almost immediately, he returned carrying only the heart. Moala, who seemed to be supervising the arrangement of the pig sections, told me Auwe went inside to secretly separate the heart from the body. I never did discover why. I had wanted to ask, " 'Bilong wanem?' " (why?), but I could see that he and the other men were too preoccupied with their work to go into details. So I filed it away in a mind cluttered with hundreds of other bits of half knowledge and scratched a sentence in my notebook. But it was one of the many items that I never got back to again.

Most of the Kafiere men had gathered at the ceremonial house and talked rapidly in Wape about the distribution of the pig. Eventually Moala turned to me and asked what part of the pig I wanted. Because I was the single largest contributor to the purchase of the gun, they always had said that I would get a leg of the first pig killed. With meat so scarce I could never accept it, but it was mine, I knew, if I wanted it. I had heard Kumoi answer a similar question by requesting only a small piece, although one of the killing cartridges was his. So I replied similarly, adding that we had freezer meat in the refrigerator and to give me just enough so my ancestors would not become angry. It was a completely spontaneous answer and I was pleasantly amused at how assimilated I had become. At that moment, I think, I was at my apex of popularity in Taute.

As each man received his portion of the pig, he folded it carefully in banana leaves and either carried it home or sent it away with a child. Auwe and Bilu had gone inside the ceremonial house, and as soon as Moala finished the distribution, he followed them. Typically, no one had bothered to alert me but, from the way the three men had separated themselves from the group, I knew something special was going to happen.

The men seemed surprised to see me enter but I had no intention of leaving. Later I learned that the ritual I was about to witness is performed only in the presence of men who have killed a pig. If a neophyte hunter were to watch the ceremony it would permanently imperil his success. Since I owned neither a bow nor a gun, they must have assumed I had nothing to lose, so said nothing.

What I next saw was one of the most mysterious rites I would ever see in New Guinea. Auwe, still weary from the arduous hunt and chilling rains, stood in the dim light of my lantern in front of Moala. Picking up the boar's heart, Moala cut away a sliver of tissue from its tip and wound it tightly with the stem of sacred ginger. Holding the tiny bundle aloft he blew strongly on it several times; then, to my amazement, he placed it into Auwe's slightly open mouth who immediately swallowed it. Was this more Christian-Wape syncretism? A native Eucharist for Taute's gunman? No it wasn't. The ritual, I discovered, long antedated the coming of the missionaries and was traditionally performed when a man killed a wild pig.

But there was more to come, something that to my knowledge has no analogue in Christian ceremony. Again picking up the heart, Moala first blew upon it then wrapped its top with stinging nettles. As Auwe turned away from him, Moala first struck him with the nettled heart between the shoulders then, successively, on his shoulders, elbows, and the back of his knees. The stinging pain was so intense that Auwe winced, clenched his jaw, and seemed about to cry out. Facing Auwe, Moala finally struck him in the belly with the heart pulling it slowly up his body to his chin. The ritual finished, Auwe turned away to rub his red welts and dance a tormented jig. The rite, Moala said, would prevent Auwe from shaking with excitement when he next took aim at a pig. What I had seen was a ritual prophylactic against "buck fever."

The following morning Joyce began to prepare our Thanksgiving Day dinner. Since deer hunting in Vermont coincides with Thanksgiving and Joyce's father was a locally renowned hunter, it was unusual for us not to celebrate the day with both venison and turkey. But this Thanksgiving would be New Guinea style. With Betty and the two Dons as our welcome guests, we had wild boar and turkey instead.

In the months that followed, there was no letup on Taute's involvement with the shotguns. Raba had succeeded in obtaining the permit for Mifu's gun, and they too had their meetings and 'kaptis' and another problem as well.

WM NOTES

II DECEMBER 1970

RABA'S HUNTING DREAM

Yesterday morning we heard the Mifu signal drum; they were signaling for us to join them in a pig hunt, but our men were already far into the bush on their own hunt. I got the story in bits and pieces during the day, mostly from Kumoi, as new data dribbled in.

Two nights ago Raba dreamed he was in the bush and had killed a pig. He knew, of course, that his ancestral spirits had killed it and if he went hunting he would kill it in the flesh. So hunting he went. He and some companions went into the big bush near Lau'um where domestic pigs usually don't go. Raba saw a nice big pig all right, and he shot it. But it was Aipau's (Lau'um man) pig! It is the second time he has killed a domestic pig by mistake since I've been here. . . .

Most of the men hunting with him ran away when they saw what he had done as it is a shameful thing to do. So Raba, with help, had to carry the pig to its Lau'um owner and offer to buy it. Usually one gets off with buying only part of it. No extra fee is involved for the killing; you just pay what it is worth.

I had to laugh when Kumoi told me about the mistake but I think perhaps I shouldn't have. He said, "Oh, Bill!" then laughed himself. But he wouldn't joke about the incident as extensively as I did.

Frankly, I was glad that Mifu was farther along the ridge so I could not follow in total detail the affairs of their gun. As it was, I became involved deeply enough. Then an event occurred that convinced me that I was as tightly integrated into Taute society, at least on a spiritual level, as any white man could hope to be. Here is what happened.

Raba had shot a pig, but the kill was kept secret from me. It meant more pig for the Mifus as I was the only Kafiere man who owned an interest in their gun. But it is difficult to suppress such important information in a small face-to-face community, and it wasn't long until I heard all about it. What to do? I really didn't care about receiving a piece of every pig shot, but not to act within the values of the society would also, I thought, be a strategic mistake. So, partly as an experiment to see if my ancestors counted for anything in Mifu and partly because I did not want to let Raba's calculated slight go unchallenged, I, in typical Wape fashion, said nothing to Raba but quietly gossiped about his selfishness. Raba continued to hunt but with no success. When his bad luck persisted, a meeting was called to find out the reason. Mifu was often derelict in advising me about their shotgun meetings and other community events as well, but this day special care was taken that I be informed and to assure my presence.

The meeting began around 10:00 A.M., with Raba soberly documenting all of his wild shots. Some of the women were being accused of causing trouble for the gun when Lakie, a miserable-looking adolescent orphan, suffered an epileptic fit. He had fallen next to a fire and was in danger of seriously burning himself, but the assemblage pointedly ignored him. It was as if he didn't exist. Although Raba probably thought me rude for interrupting his meeting, I went to where Lakie had fallen and kicked away the fire while one of my companions pulled him out of danger. But the meeting continued without a second's hesitation. There was no doubt that the shotgun was of infinitely greater importance than the stricken Lakie.

Eventually Raba looked toward where I was sitting and, showing a long row of small betel stained teeth, smiled as he made a brief reference to my disapproval regarding the little pig he had shot. "Little" pig, that was a new one, but with some jubilation I scrawled in my notebook, "I was right, my talk is blamed!" The meeting proceeded at a leisurely pace and included a number of tangential issues ranging from disgust regarding taxes to annoyance with several domestic pigs defecating up and down the village paths. It was after eleven when Raba picked up the shotgun and, handing it to Moala, asked me to straighten things out. It was a request I couldn't refuse.

With some deliberateness I rose from the ground and, walking toward Moala, took the gun in my hands. The solemnness of the occasion impressed me and I felt an acute identification with the destiny of Taute and our guns. Glancing toward Raba I told him that I must speak in English since my ancestors did not understand Pidgin. Then, with sincere conviction, I asked them to bring game to the gun.

But it was not to be. Apparently there were still undetected problems in the village. Meetings, 'kaptis,' even the hiring of a clairvoyant from a neighboring village proved futile. As long as I lived in Taute, Raba rarely returned from the hunt with even a bird to eat.

9

MADNESS AND THE
MOTHER MONSTER

Every night when the moon was bright the little man picked up
his hand drum and slipped into the forest. There, high in the
trees, he joined a band of jovial possums to sing and dance away
the night. But at daylight the possums crawled away to their
dens, their revels over, and he returned to the village to sleep.

It sounded like the senario for a Walt Disney film, but it
was Kumoi telling me a story. Gesturing broadly and playing all
the parts from the man to his possum friends, Kumoi was a wonderful storyteller. As usual I was tape recording our interview.
Kumoi could go his own pace and I was free to give him my
complete attention, an audience of one, writing only an occasional note about the cast of characters, the development of the
plot, or a change of scene. When he finished I would have another
tale filled with amazing events, strange reversals of everyday life,
and, almost certainly, a murder to add to my growing collection
of Wape myths. Although the killing of a close relative was rare
in Wapeland—I never recorded a single case—family murders

seemed endemic to the fantasy life of Wape stories. When someone began a story I wondered who would be murdered this time: the wife? the father? a son? a sister?

As Kumoi continued his story, the emotions of humiliation and revenge took their toll. The tragedy began innocently enough. Although the neglected wife had no idea her husband was cavorting with possums—he was supposedly hunting—she had darker ideas about his nocturnal absences. She decided to teach him a lesson.

One night after her husband had gone into the forest she covered her body with a coating of mud. Then she climbed a tree near the trail and lay upon a branch to await his return. All night she waited. Finally, just before dawn broke across the sky, she heard her husband coming down the trail. Closer and closer he came. Just as he approached her lair, she leaped from the tree screaming, "I am a ghost and will eat you alive!"

The startled husband was so terrified he fell to the ground and ruined his dance decorations and broke his drum. "What kind of ghost is this," he thought, "that hides by the road to frighten me and break my drum?" But the ghostly apparition already had disappeared. She hurried back to the village, stopping only to wash the mud from her body and to gather some food.

When the distraught husband arrived home he told his wife how a terrible ghost had leaped from the forest to attack him. But she only said, "I've told you before you can't treat me this way. You never stay home and sleep with me but go hunting night after night. Now something dreadful has happened to you!"

"It's true what you say," he replied. "I was lucky not to be killed."

The husband sat down to rest and watched as his wife prepared something to eat. As she turned her arms with vigor to mix the heavy sago dumplings he suddenly noticed something; her armpits were plastered with mud: "Aha!" he thought, "that ghost was my wife." But he said nothing.

After they had eaten the husband told their two grown daughters that he and their mother were going to the forest to pick nuts from the *poril* tree. When they arrived at the tree they saw that it was bearing heavily and climbed up into its thick branches to collect the nuts. They worked steadily and when they almost had finished he called out, "Wife, where are you?"

"Here I am," she answerd. "Here, where I am shaking the leaves. See?" She said again, "I'm standing where the leaves are shaking."

"All right," he said. "I'm going to throw down my spear." And he threw it directly at her neck.

"Yeee!" she screamed, "you've speared me! Yeeee! Why did you spear me?" But before he could answer she fell dead from the tree.

The husband climbed down and dragged his wife's body to the base of the *poril* tree and covered it with brush. Then he returned home with the nuts. But when his daughters saw him returning alone they said, "Papa, Papa, where is Mama?"

"Oh," he replied, "your mother wanted to take some of the nuts to her relatives and will stay all night with them. She'll come home tomorrow."

The daughters believed their father and, after preparing and eating a meal of sago and *poril* nuts, went to bed.

All day long the two daughters waited for their mother to come home. As darkness approached they said, "Our father has lied to us. He has done something to Mama or she would be home by now."

So they followed their parents footprints into the forest to the base of the *poril* tree where they found their mother, dead. Already her body had begun to decompose and swell.

"Mama," they said, "if you are pregnant with a girl your body will decompose but if you are carrying a boy that must not happen. Then only half of you will decay and the other half will remain good so he will have milk to drink and can grow up to be a man."

The mother heard this, and, since she was pregnant with an infant male, half of her body remained that of a living person. Eventually the baby was born. Then he crawled up onto his mother's body to nurse from her breast. Every day the two sisters went into the forest to look at their mother and when they saw their new infant brother nursing they carefully tied him to his mother's body. The baby stayed at his mother's breast, and after a time he became strong and big enough to be brought to the village, where they hid him from their father.

One day the father said to his daughters, "Come, let's go work in our garden." When they reached the garden, the father said he was thirsty, and he asked his daughters to bring him some water. Dutifully they complied with his request, but the older sister placed flying insects in her water while the younger sister put centipedes in hers.

The thirsty father gulped down the water. Then, as the insects and centipdes began to bite and tear at his liver and other organs, he became deathly sick. Crying out in pain, he vomited time after time after time. Then he was silent. Their father was dead.

The two sisters ran back to the village to get their little brother then fled into the forest. But no matter where they went their father's ghost followed after them.

The little boy grew into young manhood. He had not yet shot his first pig, and one day his father's ghost overheard him say that he wished he would. So the next time his son went hunting the father's ghost went ahead of him and shot the spirit of a pig so that his son could shoot its body. After that the son went hunting many times and, each time, his father helped him kill a pig. Finally the father's ghost came and spoke to his son. "Very soon," he said, "I want you to make a *poril* curing festival."

"But," the son protested, "I don't know how to do anything like that."

"I will help you. First you must shoot a chicken or find some game. Go kill a forest rat and bring it back. Then get some limber saplings and bark planking to build the *poril* mask."

The son agreed. "After I have finished," he said, "I will tell my two sisters and send messages to all the villages so that they may come and see what I have done."

So the son made the *poril* spirit mask and extravagantly decorated it with panels of tiny embroidered shells and great ropes of glistening shell money. His father's ghost taught him the new curing rituals while his sisters cooked a feast of pig, sago, and boiled greens, and all the villagers came to sing and dance to celebrate his accomplishment. The rejoicing continued through the night until the sun announced a new day. Then before the celebrants departed, the young man told them that he was the son of the *poril* spirit.

"And that," Kumoi finished, "is how the *poril* curing festival began."

I had not seen the festival performed but wanted to very much. According to Kumoi, the festival had originated in Yebil, but other villages had bought it from them. Although it was never performed in our hamlet, both Mifu and Wilkili could give it; each had a *poril* priest who knew the sacred rites. If I stayed in Taute long enough, Kumoi assured me, I would probably see it.

Other men besides Kumoi told me their versions of the *poril* myth but they differed only in small details. However, regardless of how many questions I asked about the mask, I never could quite comprehend what it looked like. And drawings of it confused me even more. All the Wape masks and costumes I knew about were mobile. They were something that men put on or got inside of, then pranced around the village plaza. But the *poril* mask was immobile. It was built with a framework of saplings stuck into the ground and almost filled the ceremonial house. The priest, to perform his rituals, entered the mask through a hole and lay on his belly on a bed. It made no sense to me at all.

It was well after the shotguns had arrived, almost Christmas, before I saw my first and only *poril* festival. It was the strangest curing festival I studied in Wapeland; so unique is the mask and the ritual that no anthropologist in New Guinea has recorded another quite like it.

With great expectations I went to Wilkili on the designated day only to learn that the ceremony was postponed to the following day. The men were still collecting materials for the large mask. Although I had lived among the Wape long enough to know that ceremonial postponements were commonplace, they always piqued me. Try as I would, I never could assume an attitude of nonchalance when my complex plans for recording or filming were upset. It was irrational, but I always felt used or somehow tricked by a delay to which no one else in the village gave a second thought. The Western insistence on temporal precision that contributed to my accuracy as a scientist also contributed to my feelings of harassment as well. But Wonai, a native of Wilkili who manned the government medical aide post there, sensed my consternation and assured me the ceremony would begin the next day. Since he was a man I trusted and liked, I stored my recording equipment at his house and trudged back to Taute.

When I entered Wilkili the following afternoon the men were busy assembling the materials to build the *poril* mask. Then, once inside the ceremonial house, I watched with fascination as the awesome monster took form. It looked like nothing I ever had seen or imagined. If it resembled anything at all from my own world of imagery, it was a tailless and legless diplodocus dinosaur.

When the work on the mask slackened, I walked around the village visiting people I knew and photographed two delightful girls making cat's cradles. Since I would sleep at Wonai's house, Walos and Kapul, old Tongol's young bachelor grandsons from Kafiere who had accompanied me, helped put up my mosquito net and boiled some rice for dinner.

It was dusk when I returned to the ceremonial house. In the dim light the sinister monster seemed to have grown in size. It stretched over twenty feet down the middle of the ceremonial house. Its main body was almost five feet wide and its six-foot-high back, towering above the working men, sloped gracefully downward to an extremely long and slender neck that lay along the ground before curving upward to an opening in the back wall. Protruding two feet beyond was its tiny head crowned with a halo of shiny dog's teeth and blue and yellow plumes. Just inside the ceremonial house entrance was the monster's rear with a large opening where tomorrow the priest would be lifted prone and feet first into the creature and placed on a bed of bark planks. From this position the priest, or *poril ninge* [son of the *poril* spirit], would perform the curing rituals for Pobis's baby.

At last the myth and the mask were beginning to come together. The great female creature with its attenuated neck and the priest who lay inside of her were dramatic physical transformations of the woman killed by a spear through her neck and her unborn son.

I went to work setting up my tape recorder in the vacant area at the back of the house near the monster's neck. The placement of the mike was not right so I stepped over the neck to locate it more strategically. My leg was in mid-air when I heard Kapul gasp. But it was too late. How insanely stupid! I already knew enough not to step over sacred objects, but in my singlemindedness to set up the equipment I had forgotten.

"Kapul," I asked, "what are the consequences?"

"If you step over the *poril* your children will die." He was almost whispering.

I said no more but continued my work. My lantern was fluttering ominously and I must repair it since I needed the light to see.

Several groups of men were clustered around the monster, its framework now swathed in palm leaves. They carefully unpacked their elaborate shell decorations stored after the last *poril* festival to protect them against the ravages of rats. It was the first time I had seen these magnificent shell decorations.

Diamond-shaped panels meticulously crafted and encrusted with hundreds of polished pieces of shell were placed around the base of the creature. Great lengths of shell embroidered bands were unfurled and draped its entire length while multiple strings of shell beads were hung from its body and ropes of dazzling cowries slung along its side. The rear of the monster was majestically draped with strand after strand of carved shell rings—a fortune in bride wealth—and more clusters of dangling beads.

The rear opening was provocatively veiled with palm fronds. Other leaves, these lancelike and brightly colored, ran along the creature's crest from end to end.

The overall effect was one of overpowering opulence. The creamy tones of lustrous shell gleamed softly in the lamplight. No designer in the Western world with all the glittering jewels of Cartier and Tiffany at his disposal could have designed a more incredible creation.

Awed, I slowly walked around the mask as one might a Brancusi marble. Then, bursting with pride and tribal chauvinism, I wrote in my notebook, "The mask is fantastic. What a cultural gold mine are these Wape people. I'll make them famous on the Sepik—the Iatmul and Abelam tribes aren't everything!" My arrogant words are embarrassing today but, just then, I wanted to shout to those who dismissed the Wape as passive and uninteresting that they were a superbly imaginative and energetic people.

The night was starless, the sky a black void that sucked up the light from the men's bamboo torches as they converged on the ceremonial house to sing the *poril*'s sacred songs until dawn. Inside the house my two small kerosene lanterns burned steadily. While waiting for the festivities to begin I busied myself with notes on the mask, writing down in Wape the names of its various component parts. When I came to the name for the large rear opening, someone at my elbow quietly said it was called *yelme*. No one actually had told me the sex of the poril mask—I just had assumed it was female—so to make sure I asked, "Does this *yelme* belong to a male or a female?"

A great roar of laughter went up from the group. But no one answered my question. Finally an old man in a loud whisper said, "It belongs to a female," and someone else again explained how the *poril ninge* would go inside her in the morning.

I was a bit puzzled about the sudden laughter. Then I asked another question about the *yelme* and this time, even the boys joined the men with hoots of merriment. I seemed to be unusually dense this evening. *Yelme*, obviously, was a female sexual anatomical term not to be used in ordinary conversation and I had violated Wape social niceties by doing so.

The men sat on two rows of low benches on either side of the main body of the mask. They were in a relaxed mood, talking easily and joking while they smoked and chewed betel. There were over twenty men in the house, some with hand drums that they tapped absent-mindedly as they talked. As usual they sat closely together, their arms and legs in warming contact with a genial intimacy so different from the brittle boundedness of American men's bodies. Yawo, my deviant guide from Taute, was among the men, and I chided him good-naturedly about his planting some pineapples in my yard. He smiled an appealing grin but the meaning in his reply as usual escaped me.

It was almost nine o'clock. Wonai said the singing would begin soon, so I left the men and stationed myself at the tape recorder with flashlight, notebook, and pen. But I was not particularly surprised when I missed the opening notes of the singing. There was no glee-club director to raise his arms to alert me when, quite suddenly, one of the old men who looked asleep began to sing. The other men joined in, adding the syncopation of their hand drums to the resounding boom of two signal drums in front of the house. Singing in unison, the repetitive melodies surged on and on in a loose flow of intoxicating sound foreign to the tight structures of conventional Western music.

A Westerner might describe the singing and drum work as "ragged" but that is imposing a sound expectation of "cleanness" alien to Wape music. Perhaps that was why the Lumi schoolteachers found the Wape children such poor performers of Western songs. The songs themselves were untranslatable. Although I could distinguish an occasional Wape word, the men agreed the overall sounds did not always make sense. Like Yawo's idiosyncratic talk, the key to exactly translate the songs, if it ever existed, was lost.

The men were in good form and greatly enjoyed singing together. Occasionally they took a break to rest, visit, and smoke. Then they would begin again. By 10:30 I had an excellent sample of *poril* songs and, since they would be singing all night, I decided to give both the tape recorder and myself a rest. I had worked steadily since early evening recording in one form or another a tremendous sensory output and wanted to unwind a bit. Crossing the dark plaza alone I went to the veranda of an empty house where the men sometimes played 'satu.' I sat down and closed my eyes. The soothing waves of forest insect sounds flooded my consciousness washing away the compelling sights and sounds of the festival. Then I drifted into a delicious, thoughtless reverie wrapped in the security of darkness and the villager's friendship. So I was completely disarmed for the event soon to follow.

Eventually my empty meditation was broken by Walos, probably come to check on my absence, and then by Wonai who also sat down with me. Wonai was an avid conversationalist, but, feeling rather weary and closed to discourse, I asked him to tell me the Wilkili version of the *poril* story. I could listen and learn but say little.

Wonai was well into the story when I noticed a man, his face painted white, walking slowly behind a nearby house. I thought he was carrying a bow and arrows. Then he disappeared, apparently heading for the plaza and the ceremonial house. My immediate reaction was one of annoyance. His appearance and demeanor was so unusual I knew he must have something to do with the *poril* ritual, some important part that no one had bothered to tell me about.

As he stepped into the plaza I could see that he was a young man, slight but well built. He was clad in shorts and carried his bow with an arrow ready as if stalking game. But I was more puzzled than alarmed until Wonai suddenly stopped his story and focused his flashlight on the young man. "He's crazy," he said softly.

The young man did not like the blinding light in his eyes and, turning toward us, took several menacing steps as he raised his bow. Wonai turned the light away shouting that I was the 'masta bilong Taute' and that he must go away and leave us alone. But I thought the prudent thing was to get out of there first. I had no intention of being posthumously celebrated as the first Columbia University–trained anthropologist martyred in New Guinea. I stood up and walked backward as casually as I could into the doorless house.

But the mad bowman did not go away and Wonai continued to plead with him to put away his weapons and leave. Then Wonai, apparently in desperation, called for me to come back outside to show conclusively that I was the 'masta bilong Taute' and not a ghost. It was an agonizing request. I had come inside to secure my safety. To leave the relative security of the house to face an unknown armed madman was, by my logic, an even greater act of insanity than the bowman displayed. I was frightened; Wonai's plea to come out was insistent, but I did not know what to do. The *poril* celebrants were singing lustily and I cursed myself for leaving them.

Every story I had heard about Wape madmen flashed through my mind searching for a clue of how to proceed. Once Bilu had come into Kafiere hamlet with a drawn bow and everyone scrambled to safety. Everyone but Witauwa's old father who sauntered into the house just as Weti pulled shut the door. But Bilu's arrow was swift and strong. It broke through the door and pierced Weti's belly. He showed me the scar. For that very reason, I was standing toward the center of the room right now. Since my assailant was crazy there was no sensible reason for him not to shoot me if he wanted to, and if he was determined to learn if I were a ghost or a man, he undoubtedly would pursue me into the house. How close was he now? Or should I put my faith in Wonai's friendship and advice and go outside. In the open I might at least have a chance to dodge an arrow. Like a lemming leaping into the sea, I stepped out into the night.

But instead of night it was Wonai's light flashing in my face as he proclaimed my humanity to the bowman. Blinded, I could not evaluate my position. Helplessly posed in the doorway I did not know if I was making an entrance or a final exit.

Wonai dropped his beam and I saw the man whirl to one

side, his bow string aggressively arched with an arrow ready to shoot at something in the plaza. Wonai's flashlight picked out a small boy frozen in a crouched position. Yelling at the bowman, Wonai called out the name of the child and their kinship relationship. Gradually the man relaxed his bow string and, turning his back on us, proceeded silently across the plaza and down a path. The entire incident had not lasted five minutes.

Our assailant, Wonai said, was Werie, the son of Walwin, Wilkili's 'sutboi.' Sometimes after chewing betel nut he became crazy and prowled the village with his bow and arrow. He never had shot anyone but could, Wonai suggested, if a person ran away from him in fright. Then he might think the person was a threatening ghost. But Wonai's explanation did little to ease my still heavy breathing and quivering legs.

We returned to the ceremonial house where I crowded onto a bench and, safely surrounded, slowly regained my outward composure. No one else seemed much concerned by the incident. Walwin, the madman's father, was one of the lead *poril* singers and, ignoring what had happened, launched into song after song. But his son's adventure had deeply affected me and I remained apprehensive the rest of the night.

The singing was vibrant and virile. As I listened, I watched old Woma create a long, fanciful headdress for his role the next morning as the *poril ninge*. It was after two when I went down to Wonai's house for a nap. About five I was awakened by the sound of clacking shells coming from the ceremonial house and got up. As I walked alone through the dark village I hoped Werie was somewhere fast asleep.

When day broke across the sky Woma began to dress for his starring role as the son of *poril*. His face, chest, shoulders, and hands were smeared with aromatic plants and his face and arms blackened to near invisibility. He put on bracelets of possum fur, and his lower arms and wrists were wrapped in shell embroidery. Extending over his bony fingers were long, stiff, red and green leaves, and suspended from each hand was a cluster of cowrie bells. Woma, standing in front of the creature's *yelme*, was lifted

aloft and slipped inside her belly. Then the long conical headdress was fastened in place. Erupting in an explosion of fur and
feather plumes, its spectacular veil of scarlet Hibiscus flowers
tumbled down to his shoulders. In every way, he was a son
worthy of his magnificent monster mother.

The front of the ceremonial house was thrown open, and the
poril ninge slowly began to move his hands up and down as the
cowrie bells clacked. A group of early risers, women, and children, stood in silence to watch the wondrous creatures that had
come in the night. And the men again began to sing.

It was long past 10:00 A.M., and the curing ceremony for
the ill baby still had not begun. I had completed three rolls of
black-and-white photographs, one of Kodachrome, several hours
of tape recordings, and filled pages of my notebook with notes
and drawings. I had also visited Wonai's government aide post
and watched him treat a number of patients. By 11:00 I wondered if the ritual curing would ever begin.

The men stopped singing. No one mentioned that Pobis
had brought his baby into the ceremonial house, but there they
were. I ran to the front of the room. After waiting this long to
record a curing ceremony, I always become obsessed with the
necessity to observe and photograph the exact moment of exorcism, almost as if I half expected to witness and record a miracle.

Pobis held his son on outstretched hands directly under the
face of the *poril ninge*. Terrified, the baby's screams came in painful, mechanical jolts. I never before had seen such concentrated
panic in a human being. Too weak to raise its arms, the infant
gazed upward into the deep black countenance and rhythmically
shrieked while the priest rubbed its belly and anointed it with a
small amount of water. Under his breath he muttered the incan-
tation to remove the sickness. I wondered if the infant, so tiny
and weak, would die of fright before it was over. It was a great
relief to see him finally returned to his mother's breast.

By the time I packed my gear and was ready to return to
Taute, I almost had forgotten about the *poril* festival that had
brought me to Wilkili in the first place. I was thinking about my

experience with Werie the night before and the whole business of madness among the Wape. It was a peculiar kind of business because so many Wape men experienced similar aggressive episodes.

Madness in any society is often frightening and always perplexing. During my first months in Taute I was only partially successful in finding out about Wape patterns of madness. Everyone agreed that Kowokil, Bilu's brother, was mad because his behavior was *always* strange. He behaved much too childlike for a mature man who was both a husband and father. At curing festivals he would go into the plaza alone and dance a silly jig. When I first came to Taute, he brought me a gift of fat grubs neatly skewered on a twig. It was a present that would make any Wape's mouth water, but everyone else knew that Westerners did not eat them.

I also knew that the two epileptic men of Taute were considered crazy when having a seizure. A ghost temporarily had gone into their bodies making them fall down into fits of nonsensical behavior. But no one told me about the homicidal mania to which some of the other men were subject. Perhaps they thought I might not stay in Taute with my family if I knew that these men sometimes threatened their neighbors and closest relatives with knives, hatchets, and arrows. In fact, the Wape generally had done a good job of concealing the extensiveness of this form of madness from both the missionaries and the government. It was a community problem that they characteristically thought best to deal with themselves. The less outside interference the better.

Once again it was Kuruwai who opened the door of knowledge for me. A gentle evening rain was falling when Kuruwai came by the house to greet me good evening. But the rain grew more fierce and it was an hour and a half later before he decided to make a dash for his home. In the meantime we talked about madness.

I recently had learned, quite by chance, that Bilu was mad for a long period before I came to Taute. At that time he lived in the forest between Kafiere and Mifu, and so frequent were his raids on passersby that the trail was almost abandoned. Sometimes he would charge into the hamlets themselves. It was during one of these attacks that he shot Weti. Although most of the villagers still considered him to be a little crazy, he no longer terrorized the community as he once had. The treatment that finally cured him was performed by his family. His wife and daughters wrapped him securely in large sago spathes then put fire to a bundle of bamboo stalks. The sharp reports of the exploding bamboo rang out like a devil's tattoo and frightened away the resident ghost. As a form of shock therapy, it seemed both more humane and sensible than the electrical assaults of Western psychiatry. But it wasn't a total cure—Bilu still was susceptible to an occasional intrusion by a wandering ghost.

I was sitting next to Bilu one night when a ghost went into him. It was a rather low-keyed meeting about the shotgun. We men were squatting around the embers of a dying fire while Auwe, in his quiet and deliberate way, was trying to figure out what had gone wrong with his hunt that day. I was bored and inattentive, but Bilu quickly changed that. A piercing yelp rang out from him and for a split second I am sure I was in full levitation off the ground. Then, although he did not lose consciousness, his legs and arms began to tremble. Later he explained that a ghost of a certain dead man had come to tell him that if the gun wasn't straightened out, Auwe would not find game. That information was nothing new, but it was the first time he had received this kind of benign public visitation from a ghost.

There was one time, however, when a ghost did cause him to become angry and at least potentially homicidal. Kumoi had accused the Kafiere children of stealing some money from him at the cook house. As the culprits could not be positively identified, the men decided that all of the families must contribute to repay the stolen sum. The meeting was in front of the ceremonial house, and I was watching it from my veranda.

Money was always a highly sensitive subject among the villagers, and several of the men were visibly irritated about having to contribute. As the donations slowed down, Bilu became increasingly annoyed then, overtly angry, began swinging his arms wildly and yelling in a strange singsong voice, " 'Mak i kam! mak i kam!' " [bring your money!]. But to demand anything in Wapeland is always a poor strategy. The more imperative Bilu made his authoratative commands, the quieter the people became. This only accentuated his hostility until finally he was jumping around the plaza threatening to get his bow and arrows. At this the children and young people who had watched his performance with amused fascination ran off in all directions shrieking with laughter. He chased one group into the ceremonial house where they fled out the back door. Kuruwai, who happened to be with me at the time, said Bilu was crazy again. Then Bilu turned and ran down the path past my house to get his weapons. Running with a painful, awkward limp caused by a large boil on his hip, he continued to holler out threats with a wild, unfocused look in his eyes.

Kuruwai and I ran to the path to head him off while Aif came running to help us from the other direction. Running alongside of him, Kuruwai placed a strong comforting arm around Bilu's shoulders while both he and Aif talked calmly to him. Thinking a white man's face might have some shock value, I thrust my face in front of his and, following the men's example, spoke gently. Soon his run slowed to a trot then a walk, as he and I continued to his house with Aif and Kuruwai behind us. Leading the procession was Poluwa, his attentive wife, who turned around occasionally to chastise her hotheaded husband. At home he sat down. After a few moments he looked up at me saying softly, "I'm all right now."

I had learned from Kuruwai that Bilu was not the only Taute man with a tendency toward attacks of homicidal madness. By the time I left Taute at least five other men were similarly identified. That was almost 13 percent of Taute's married men. But there was only one Taute woman who, either in the past or the present, was thought to be crazy. She was Bilu's wife, Poluwa. Her madness, which Kuruwai referred to as a "sickness," ended shortly before we moved to Taute. Even as our house was being built she returned to her native village to be exorcised by her relatives, but I was not able to learn the details of the treatment or its specific rationale. As long as I knew Poluwa her actions were that of a normal Taute woman. Only as I was leaving the village at the end of my field work did she do something unusual. As I shook her hand and said good-by, her eyes filled with tears. No other Taute man or woman cried when I went away.

During her episode of madness Poluwa was not, like the men I knew, overtly aggressive. Her most hostile action was to put a curse on a man's hunting as she had done to Auwe. But she was very destructive of her own things. Sometimes at night she would get up and throw out the family's food and belongings. In the morning the villagers watched Bilu and his daughters carry what wasn't broken or ruined back into the house. Other times she would dress up for a nonexistent festival and go to the plaza alone and vigorously sing and dance. When angry, she might accuse a fellow villager of trying to kill her or perform the most insulting gestures a woman can exhibit toward another person. Holding out her two hands and clutching them upwards, she cocked her head to one side and stuck out her tongue. So erratic and unpredictable was Poluwa's behavior that a family member always followed her to prevent her from dancing off the cliff or running away into the forest.

What had provoked her madness? I never came close to finding out. So unusual was her behavior that the villagers did not have an established theory to which they could relate it. Perhaps it was a ghost, but no one knew for sure.

Most Wape women who are unhappy and miserable turn their hostility directly against themselves. Suicide, not homicidal attacks, is the culturally patterned response for unhappy women. But, unlike the man who runs amok, the woman who attempts suicide is not considered crazy. Nor are ghosts dragged in from the forest to explain these acts of self-destruction. A woman attempting suicide is considered a desperate person driven to despair by damaging gossip and personal insults. The first Wape funeral I attended was for a young woman who killed herself a few days after I landed in Lumi. She committed suicide by drinking poison made from the root of the deadly Derris vine. At that time I understood nothing about the cultural dynamics of suicide among Wape women. But I would learn. Three of the young wives of Kafiere attempted similar suicides while I lived in the village.

Interestingly, in each case the young woman lived in a household with her husband and one of his parents. A precipitating event in two of the cases was criticism from her husband for not supplying sufficient food for the family. Although I became involved in all three cases, the one I knew and understood the best was the near tragedy of Mi-ke's attempted suicide.

Mi-ke was the only child of Naiasu's first marriage. A gentle and shy person, she was one of the most attractive young women in the village. Although she and Weti had been married several years, her pregnancies always ended in miscarriages. I first met her before moving to Taute when she was recovering from a miscarriage at Lyn's hospital in Lumi. Mi-ke and Weti very much wanted a child, but I soon heard black rumors that she was doomed to childlessness because of sorcery. So it was especially poignant to see her caring for and cuddling her mother's infant as if it were her own.

Living with Mi-ke and Weti was Weti's troublesome old father, Tuya, and it was Mi-ke's job to keep house for both men. It was an incident with the two men that precipitated her suicide attempt.

Mi-ke was drinking from a long bamboo water tube when, as often happens, more poured out than she could drink. The water sloshed down her arm and onto her father-in-law, Tuya. Annoyed at her clumsiness, he exclaimed loudly. But his anger quickly moved to other areas as he chastised her for not producing more sago flour, although he knew that she still was not strong after her miscarriage. And, using the logic special to the man who has planted his own food trees, he found it incomprehensible that although she now ate from his trees she didn't prepare food in sufficient quantities for the family's needs. What was even worse, he stormed, she couldn't even provide him with a grandchild!

It was a cruel insult. Weti sided with his father. He verbally attacked his wife; then, in a final gesture of disdain, he took the bamboo tubes of sago she was cooking and flung them out the door. The incident occurred in the late afternoon. A short time later she disappeared from the village.

Weti told me he watched her go into the forest but thought she only intended to relieve herself. When she didn't return he decided she had run away to her father's mother's people in Kamnum village. But when he went to look for her foot prints on the Kamnum trail, they weren't there. He had gone to another trail to search for her when he heard a signal drum telling him to return to the village.

I was at home enthusiastically reading a batch of new mail when I heard the signal drum boom its message through the village and into the forest. What was it all about? Joyce got the news first. She was standing at the window when a passing neighbor said that Mi-ke had taken poison. I told Joyce to follow me with some soap chips for an emetic then dashed out of the house with only a flashlight. I couldn't locate my shoes on the veranda so made my way to Weti's house on a gooey track in a pair of Joyce's too-small thongs. And I had forgotten my notebook. I soon met Kufa hurrying the other way. Kufa was a hospital orderly Lyn had sent to the village to help with a flu epidemic that was finally subsiding. He was on his way to my house to get some salt to make a brew that would induce Mi-ke to vomit. The traditional emetic for a woman who has taken poison is to drink forceably her husband's urine. But Weti was not yet there so a substitute must be found.

When I arrived at Weti's house a couple of minutes later Mi-ke was sitting on the ground and leaning against the chest of her neighbor, Mehti. She was in acute discomfort and occasionally spit a clear bubbly sputum. Her head rolled about like a rag doll's, but I couldn't tell if her discomfort was primarily physical or emotional. Mehti, as he held her, was encouraging her to throw up. A group of children had gathered, but no women were present. Her pulse was regular and strong. Kuruwai was there and told me he saw her come out of the forest, then stumble and fall. He had rushed to her side then saw the empty bamboo tube that had held the poison. According to Kuruwai she apparently had not vomited since drinking the poison. From what I had heard about Derris-root poison from Westerners and villagers alike, I wondered why she wasn't already unconscious or dead.

Kufa returned with the salt but no one had a cup. It seemed like everyone was in slow motion. Even after the emetic was prepared, Mi-ke refused to drink it although Kufa repeatedly assured her it wasn't urine. By now there were five of us men trying to get her to drink the salt water. Finally I could stand the inertia no longer and, seizing Mi-ke's face in my hands, pressed strongly against her jaws forcing her mouth to open. It was the first and only time I physically hurt a villager and I felt dreadful doing it. But my anxiety about her dying was greater. I don't believe a Wape would have transgressed another person's body in this way; certainly none of the men with me just then would have. But she did drink the emetic.

Just then Naiasu came up to the house carrying her baby and leaning with one arm against the house began a ritual wail. She made no attempt to help her, and it puzzled me. The men continued to work with Mi-ke rubbing her sides and stomach, but still she didn't vomit. Joyce with Ned and Elizabeth in their nightclothes arrived with the soap and an extra lantern, but by then we had decided that either Mi-ke already had vomited the poison or hadn't really drunk it. It was another instance where I never would know the facts.

The men helped Mi-ke into the house and there I saw old Tuya lying on his bench. He raised up to look at us, then, saying nothing, lay back down. A few minutes later Weti came in and stood silently by the door. No one had to tell him what had happened. Finally, he went to his bench opposite of where Mi-ke lay and sat down. Already an inquest had begun. The principal questioner was Kufa. Each said what he knew; only Mi-ke was silent. Gradually the basic facts were established.

It was now obvious to everyone that Mi-ke was clearly out of danger, and the men began to leave. And I, too, returned home to read my letters. But Kufa, a dedicated modern practitioner of medicine, remained with Mi-ke and Weti until late that night.

In a couple of days, Mi-ke was again strolling through the village tending her mother's baby. Her suicide attempt would not be forgotten by those who were there, but little else would be said about it. There would be people living as near as Mifu hamlet who would never learn of it. Madness and suicide, like sex, were neither pleasant nor proper topics for open discussion.

A stranger walking through a tranquil Wape village would find it difficult to conjure up scenes of raging homicides and angry suicides. At first encounter, Wapeland appears to be a never-never land of quiet goodness, a simple culture of shy and complacent people, perhaps even a pacifist's paradise. But he would be dead wrong.

10

FLYING BLIND

Father Gerald took one look at Joyce and me and decided we needed a holiday. He was passing through Taute on a pastoral patrol and had stopped to say hello. A seasoned Franciscan missionary who had lived alone at remote mission stations, he was sensitive to the emotional strains of bush living. While living among the Au people, a group bordering the Wape to the east, he endured with stoic fortitude the people's gradual abandonment of him as an antiwhite cargo cult swept through the area until the bishop, fearful for his life, ordered him to leave.

Joyce and I knew we were in need of a field break and had scheduled a week's holiday in Wewak for March. But that was over a month away. Father Gerald insisted we take a holiday now! With a genial smile he added, "And I know the perfect place." It was Seleo, a tiny island paradise off the Aitape coast. The sun always shone, the beaches were beautiful, there were no mosquitoes or flies, and the Franciscan mission had a house we could use.

He would make all of the arrangements as soon as he returned to
Lumi in a couple of days.

The prospect of trading the torrential mountain rains and
the forest's gloom and mud for bright golden sunshine and the
luxury of running on a beach of white sand was exhilarating. It
was the rainy season, and the dripping forest that surrounded us
was claustrophobic. Plants, vines, and grasses grew with alarm-
ing speed; only the men's constant hacking at the lush vegetation
kept if from swallowing up the village.

On the following Monday afternoon the Franciscan mission
plane made a soft landing on the little grass airstrip—now seldom used—in the center of Seleo Island, and we unloaded our
supplies for a week's vacation. In some ways it was a strange place
for a holiday. We still would be an American family isolated from
everyday contacts with other Westerners; the only other inhabitants on the island lived in two small native hamlets. But the
great attraction of the island for us was its sunny seashore and the
chance to completely escape the daily routine of field work. I
promised Joyce I would forget my research for the week and enjoy
my family instead. And I hoped the change would clear my head,
at least momentarily, from the muddled scramble of ethnographic facts and half-facts that ordinarily dominated my
thinking.

Slowly the ocean, the sun, and the sand worked its relaxing
magic, and the Wape receded into the lavender and blue Torricellis visible across the narrow sea that separated Seleo from the
mainland. Taute village and my work lay within those mountains, but for this one week I couldn't have cared less. I read
novels, helped Joyce with the meals, and we both played and
sunned on the beach with the children. One afternoon Ned and I
walked around the little island, stopping occasionally to splash
and swim in the gentle surf or visit nonchalantly with an islander
who crossed our path.

In the evening before dinner, Joyce and I went down to the
beach with a drink and, relaxing together against a driftwood

log, watched with mute enthrallment the magnificent interplay of colored lights in the metamorphosis of clouds as the fading sun dropped below the horizon to light an oriental afternoon. But it was impossible to totally cease my obsessive habit of collecting and arranging materials. During the day I found myself exploring the beaches—not for ethnographic facts—but for shells, collecting the most minute ones I could find. Then the children and I would arrange them in different ways, perhaps by their exotic shapes, their bold patterns, or their delicate hues.

The island itself was unusual by being physically dominated by the abandoned buildings of a Catholic boys' school. The school was built at great expense after the war as a boarding school to train an elite group of young native males. Seleo Island was selected as the school's site because it gave maximum control over the boys' environment and also prevented those overcome with homesickness—always a problem at boarding schools—from fleeing home to their native villages. But the mainland boys disliked the isolated island setting. And the expense and problems of transporting food and supplies to the island—including water when the rain tanks were empty—became too great. Eventually the school was closed, and the students were sent elsewhere.

At one time, however, the now derelict school was the showplace of the Aitape coast. Then there were broad streets and walks of glistening crushed coral bordered by extravagant gardens filled with blooming shrubs and tropical flowers. There were well-appointed classrooms, dormitories, shower buildings, lavatories, numerous supply houses, and, at the very center of this impressive complex, the headmaster's imposing residence, a large two-story window-filled house.

Now long vines stretched across the walks, trying, without success, to root themselves in the coral packed tight by hundreds of strong bare feet. The gardens, overgrown and wild, were still movingly beautiful. But the buildings were decrepit and ruined. Windows were broken, doors were missing, and the floors were littered with rubble. A desultory air of catastrophe hung over the place that was sweetened only by the heavy scent of exotic flowers.

The headmaster's house was the one building in fairly good repair. It was kept locked and used as an occasional holiday house by the Franciscan missionaries who, weary from their outstation assignments in the mountains, came as we had come for a needed rest by the sea. The cluttered rooms of the big old house had the strange allure of a forsaken castle. Ned and Elizabeth ran from room to room and up and down the sturdy stairs exploring with delight this curious new home.

The school buildings were under the nominal care of Father "Dom," who lived on nearby Ali Island. Father "Dom" was a big, gregarious Tasmanian who had emigrated to that southernmost isle from British Columbia when he was eight years old. Now a resident of Ali for many years, he was regionally famous for a boat industry he started with the island men. He warmly welcomed us to Seleo, showed us around the compound, and gave us careful instructions on starting the gasoline generator that powered the school's electrical system.

That evening Joyce and I went down to the generator shed and, after some work, got the thing going. The roar was tremendous, shattering the soft cadence of the surf and the comforting night sounds of the island. The street lamps filled the complex with a blaze of light, and the ceiling bulbs inside the house, glaring harshly, reduced the contents, including us, to a clinical insignificance. There was something eerily inappropriate and hauntingly sad about the illumination that only intensified the ruin of the school. I went down to the shed, stopped the generator, and returned the island to exquisite darkness.

Returning to the house I was welcomed by the soft, romantic gleam of kerosene lanterns and a smile of relief from Joyce. When Father "Dom" joined us for dinner later in the week, we ate, to his surprise and puzzlement, by lamplight. I'm not sure he ever quite understood how an American couple isolated for months in the forest without electricity could forego such a luxury when available.

On another evening our hospitable host sent his boat to take us to Ali Island for a farewell party given by the islanders for the Aitape Assistant District Commissioner, Harry Roach, and his wife, who were being transferred to Bouganville Island in the Solomons far to the east. Several other Australian couples had come across the bay from Aitape for the celebration, and as we waited for the festivities to begin, we visited on the beach, ate, and drank beer.

The climax of the celebration for me was the dancing. Before this evening the only New Guinea dancing I had observed was by the Iatmul of the middle Sepik River and by the Wape. Both of these groups concentrate their aesthetic concerns on spectacular masks; to me their dancing was a humdrum affair of endless shuffling or trotting. By comparison, the dancing of the Ali Islanders was as intricately expressive as classical ballet. Lined on the beach were nine men and seven women in traditional dance skirts who gracefully danced the stories of their ancestral myths with sinuous gestures and telling motions. It was a beautiful performance, and, again, the complex differences among New Guinea cultures were impressed upon me.

When our plane left Seleo we were rested, tanned, and refreshed. Landing in Lumi we had lunch with Father Gerald and Brother Steve, then began the muddy trek homeward with a group from Taute who had come to welcome us. It seemed good to be back in the forest again. Even the tree roots that laced the trail and conspired again and again to trip me could not irritate me today. As we walked along, the men gave me the latest village news, and I mentally planned work I was eager to begin. So, when several weeks later it came time for our visit to Wewak, I wasn't enthusiastic to go. But there was no question of canceling it; Joyce and the children were looking forward to a week in Wewak. This time I reluctantly left the village, filled with silent guilt about the work I was leaving behind and the events I would miss while away.

In Lumi, while waiting for our plane to Wewak, we saw for the first time the beginnings of Joyce's new house that Don McGregor was building for us on mission land. It was strategically placed at the end of the ridge to take advantage of the mountain scenery, while only steps away were the homes of Lyn, the McGregors, and the other missionaries. According to the mission's building policy, we would pay for the house at cost then donate it to the mission when we returned to the States. No outsiders other than converted natives who worked for the mission were allowed to live in the mission's compound, so it was a generous act of charity that Joyce and the children were to be included. While we considered ourselves a Christian family, we certainly did not measure up to the strict criteria of the Christian Brethren.

Joyce's house would be constructed from a combination of native materials and milled timber from the mission's sawmill and, compared to our Taute house, lavishly appointed with a flush toilet, lavatory, and shower cabinet in the bathroom, and for the kitchen a new kerosene refrigerator, aluminum sink, and a two-burner propane stove. There would be a small bedroom-playroom with built-in bunks for the children and a living-sleeping room for Joyce. A section of the attic under the thatch would be floored for storing supplies with space for a folding worktable when I visited. And at one end of the house there would be a sheltered veranda where the Tautes could rest when visiting Lumi.

The completion of the house was planned to coincide with the end of our year's work in Taute village. The family would move into the new Lumi house while I would move away to study another society, still unselected, that provided some interesting contrasts to the Wape people. Joyce's spirits soared as she examined the beginnings of her new home, a tangible symbol that her isolation in Taute would soon end. But the sight of the new house precipitated in me an acute attack of field-work panic—there was so much work yet to be done in Taute and only three months remaining to do it. I had no business going off to Wewak on a holiday. Then the government mail plane landed, and we were soon in the skies on our way.

The week passed rapidly. We shopped for supplies, took a day trip out to the Abelam people famous for their soaring ceremonial houses, visited old and new friends, saw our first movie in almost a year, celebrated Ned's sixth birthday at a local restaurant, and, of course, took the children to the beaches. Just by chance I met up with two young American anthropologists, both doctoral candidates, also working in the Sepik—Peter Huber and Don Tuzin. Peter and Mary Huber were on their way home after eighteen months with the Anggor people west of the Wape near the Indonesian border, and Don and Beverly Tuzin were returning to the Ilahita Arapesh after a field break in Australia. Wewak was indeed the crossroads of the Sepik. We even saw Father Gerald, who was in Wewak on business, and we had dinner with Helen Broadhurst, Peter's wife, who had come to Wewak to have her baby.

At the week's end, Joyce and Elizabeth decided to stay a few more days in Wewak, but Ned and I went out to the airport to take the scheduled Aerial Tours mail plane back to Lumi. It was not a good day to fly. The Wewak skies were overcast and the skies to the west even darker. After the plane was loaded with cargo and mail, the only passengers, a Tolai policeman and his family stationed in Lumi and Ned and I, climbed on board. It was still morning, and I hoped by the time we got to Aitape, our only stop, the skies would have cleared.

But the Aitape airstrip was closed. It was a very short field bordered by a swamp, and water on the strip was a frequent problem. So we landed at Tadji, the old airdrome outside of Aitape built by the Americans during World War II. Ned and I got out and stretched our cramped legs while we waited for someone to motorbike out to exchange mail bags.

By now the clouds, thick and gray, had descended deep around the Torricellis. This meant the flight probably would be delayed for the weather to clear or, more likely, we would return to Wewak. Scheduled planes, unlike private mission planes, sel-

dom take chances with the weather that risk breaking the Territory's strict aeronautical regulations. Finally, the Aitape mail bag
arrived, and, tossing it into the plane, our young Australian
pilot, competent and taciturn in his white tropical uniform and
knee socks, signaled for us to come aboard. As I hesitated, the
motorbike roared away. I felt certain there was no way our plane
could get through those ominous clouds. And even if it did somehow manage the trip without scraping a mountainside, Lumi almost certainly was shrouded in clouds and fog, making a landing
almost impossible. "Gloomy Lumi" had justly earned its sullen
sobriquet.

But when I asked the pilot if he intended to return to
Wewak, he gave me a thin, reassuring smile and said we would
try for Lumi first. Sometimes, he added, the situation looks very
different aloft than from the ground. I looked out the windows,
and the idea of stranding Ned and myself at Tadji with the rusting debris of war was not appealing. I should have deplaned with
Ned then and there, but stupidity, machismo, and the desolation
of the abandoned airdrome conspired to keep us on board.

The little plane climbed higher and higher, and as we
neared the heavy clouds, I felt a shiver of fear. The pilot had
found a momentary opening in the clouds and he *was* going to try
for Lumi. The clouds moved with great rapidity and as they
swirled around us, the pilot, miraculously it seemed, worked his
way from opening to opening. But there was no way to know exactly where we, or the mountains, were. Then there were no more
openings. The clouds sat about us as thick and stationary as cotton batting.

We had apparently crossed the divide and were now over
Wapeland because the pilot began to circle the plane. Was he
trying to locate the Lumi airstrip or were we already over it? I
looked out into the thick clouds surrounding us in the hope of
seeing a tin roof or the airstrip itself, but saw nothing.

The plane's circle seemed to become smaller and smaller,
and an unpleasant sensation of nausea swept threw me, then
passed away. Why didn't the pilot say something to us? Was he

locked in this tight little coil because he simply didn't know which way to go?

On many a cloudy or stormy day I sat working in Taute, listening to a plane repeatedly circling in an attempt to find the Lumi airstrip. Regardless of how important my work, I eventually was forced to stop and await either the pilot's successful landing or the disappearing roar of his motor as he tried to find his way out to the coast. Once a plane, far off course, had circled Taute as if imagining our dance ground to be its airstrip. I wondered whose dance ground we were circling just now or if, indeed, Lumi was below and the pilot was confidently waiting for a break in the clouds to make his landing.

The only sound was the pulsating roar of the engines. I glanced back at the Tolai family, but we did not smile. Our faces expressed only the blank tension that forecasts terror. When I turned around, the pilot motioned for me to take the seat next to him and Ned climbed in with me. When he spoke, his voice was cool and even. "Do you recognize anything?"

We *were* lost! I was struck simultaneously with fury and fear. Fury at his needlessly risking our lives and at myself for allowing him to. And I felt the fear of those who are afraid to die. Our situation had all the prerequisites for the classical New Guinea plane crash—a small plane with limited instrumentation flying blind in a mountainous area. It was a tragedy that happened at least once or twice each year. I wanted to curse his arrogance, but I checked my temper. I saw the sweat of fear upon his intense young face. If I ever wanted to walk in the forest below with my son again, I must give him all the help I could.

As the circling plane continued to descend, I began to see occasional patches of forest. Then a road! "I think that's the tractor road north of Lumi," I ventured, but there was no way I could be sure. Then a village appeared and slipped from view, obscured by the clouds. Was it Wagoitei? If we were where I imagined us to be, we were north of Lumi and the surrounding mountains posed a dangerous threat. And by now we were circling very low.

"Dad," Ned said quietly, "I'm going to throw up." For

once the pilot did something right. He handed Ned an air-sickness bag just in time.

When I next looked up, we had risen high into a fanciful network of dark, billowy clouds. The pilot had given up his search for Lumi and, once again, was threading his way through the cloud-hidden Torricelli Mountains toward the coast.

Perhaps we were already across the mountains when it began to rain. It slashed at the plane in heavy torrents and with such force that the windshield was completely obscured. I don't know how we reached the coast, but we did. We had no forward vision, but it was just possible to see the murky terrain through the side windows. That was satisfying to me but hardly helpful to the pilot. Opening a small side window to the storm, he leaned far to his left to peer out the window and set his course above the seething froth of waves as the rain whipped in against his face.

And so we flew back toward Wewak while I sat plotting my revenge against this damn fool pilot. I wrote mental letters to every authority in the Territory, citing his blatant unconcern for aeronautical regulations and human life. He would be sent packing home to Australia post haste!

But I knew I would never write the letters except in my mind. I had no business living in the New Guinea hinterland if I wanted a life without crazy risks. Though I saw the pilot a number of times after our aborted flight, the incident was never mentioned. It was New Guinea's ultimate irony that it was he who flew us from Lumi to Wewak after we said our final good-bys to return home.

11

HIGH HOPES AND
BLIGHTED DREAMS

The day following our harrowing flight, Ned and I returned safely to Taute. The storm we had flown through and two others that occurred earlier while we were in Wewak had badly damaged the thatch roofs of both our house and my office. But the rains and high winds had brought an even more severe misfortune to the village. Several villagers were sick with an unidentified illness—an American might have called it flu—that was blown into the village, Kumoi said, by the great winds.

But there was good news too. On the day I returned Kuruwai shot and killed at the edge of the hamlet a wild boar who had adventurously followed a village sow homeward. Something similar, the men pointed out to me, occurred immediately after my return from Seleo Island. Then Kuruwai had killed a pig and Auwe a cassowary. It was my presence in the village, Auwe explained to me, that made the hunting successful. Not that I personally had anything to do with their good fortune, he added, but it was because my father's spirit followed protectingly after me wherever I went. When I was away from Taute, so was he, but on our return he led the game into the deadly paths of Taute arrows and shells so that I and my family would have meat to eat.

But the generosity of my father's spirit that so bountifully benefited the entire hamlet could never make up for my own contrariness. Since my initial appointment of Kumoi and Kuruwai as our housemen and principal research assistants, the village men had expressed to me in a variety of ways their extreme displeasure regarding this arrangement. I knew that the men more than simply tolerated me and that many of them genuinely liked and enjoyed my company. But they all deeply resented the way I had organized our household. To them it was wrong—unethical really—to reserve the prestigious and relatively well-paid housemen jobs for only two men. It was unethical because I was giving Kumoi and Kuruwai an economic advantage over themselves. I was blatantly violating the rule of Wape egalitarianism, the almost sacred principle that no man should profit at the expense of his fellows or raise himself economically or politically above them.

Social scientists confusingly lump together two types of status systems, calling them both "egalitarian." One type, like in American society, believes idealistically that "all men are created equal" but that each person should have the opportunity to rise and fall in a loose status hierarchy according to his ability and good fortune. The Wape also believe that all men are created equal. But they emphatically add that they should stay that way!

The profound difference between a truly egalitarian society like Wape and a society like our own that is idealistically egalitarian but actually hierarchical in structure is that in Wapeland there are no traditional superordinate political statuses to which men may competitively strive or that they receive by inheritance. In an egalitarian society each man, in a sense, is a ruler, with his wife and minor children his only subjects. Beyond this minimal family grouping he has no culturally sanctioned power. And any authority he may wield over others in the wider community is usually strictly defined by kinship statuses. A Wape man, for example, may have some authority over his sister's child, his *lulem*, in a narrowly circumscribed situation, but his own mother's brother, his *faf*, will have similar authority over him.

It is a relatively simple thing for men to maintain status equivalency among themselves in a hunting and gathering society like those of the African Bushmen or Australian aborigines. In these societies the harsh environment necessitates a nomadic and socially interdependent life with little opportunity to accumulate worldly goods. But the Wape are neither momads nor dependent upon hunting and gathering for their food. They are essentially gardeners, albeit not particularly dedicated ones, who regularly plant sago, taro, sweet potatoes, bananas, and other foods on which they subsist. Living within a comparatively lush environment and having a sedentary residence pattern, it is possible for the Wape—if they wished—to compete in the production and possession of both perishable and nonperishable goods. In this sense the Wape, like most New Guineans, live in an ecological niche that encourages the emergence of wealth differences among men and the establishment of at least a rudimentary hierarchical political system.

Yet I only knew one man among the Wape who was able to break the status-leveling ties of reciprocity among relatives and become a true Melanesian 'bikman.' A forceful and ambitious man from the village of Lumi, he was able to become a man of wealth and power through his close relationships with the government and mission personnel who established their compounds on Lumi land after World War II. Makain was very much in sympathy with the Australians' plans for the economic advancement of the Wape area and with the help of his family raised taro for sale as a cash crop at the station. In 1962, in recognition of his cooperation with the government, he was granted one of the first indigenous shotgun licenses. But his big chance to break loose from Wape egalitarianism came after his election in 1964 to the House of Assembly—Papua New Guinea's national legislature— as the area's first elected representative. With the salary from his legislative position he was able to purchase a Fordson tractor, which he rented to the Lumi government; he also began a cattle-raising project, established a successful trade store to compete with those run by the missions and private enterprise, and built a Western-style house. He also was the president of the Lumi Local Government Council. Before Makain, no Wape man had attained such economic and political eminence.

At first, Makain gave much of his new wealth to his relatives, but his distributions did not keep up with his income. His ostentatious wealth was considered inappropriate for a Wape, and I sometimes heard mutterings against his wealth and power. He also was relentless in pushing the Wape people toward economic progress and, like some of the government and mission people, considered the Wape penchant for ceremonial festivals a waste of energy and time. Once when I was attending a Spirit Fish festival in the village of Otemgi at the end of the Lumi airstrip, he verbally abused a large group of celebrants, including many of his fellow Lumi villagers. Angrily bounding down the narrow path to the river where many *faf* had just completed an important ceremonial washing of their *lulem,* Makain loudly proclaimed the celebrants' laziness and unconcern for progress. It was the kind of self-righteous bullying one encounters on the Sepik River and in the highlands (and among the white colonialists, for that matter), but it was quite out of place as a way for one Wape man to address another.

When the 1972 House of Assembly elections were held, Makain was thoroughly repudiated by the Wape, being defeated by an overwhelming majority. He became ill with pneumonia. Aware that the ancestors and spirits were angry with him, he distributed some of his wealth, and a number of healing rituals were performed by his fellow villagers. He also received Western medical treatment, but he did not regain his health. When I last saw him just before I left Wapeland, he was a sick and depressed man. Not long afterward, I learned of his death by heart failure.

Why do the Wape so strongly resist the development of hierarchical differences among themselves and concentrate instead on the cultural elaboration of status-leveling mechanisms? I do not know and probably never will. At present there is no archaeological record of the Wape to help solve the problems of their cultural history. But anthropologists do know a great deal about the cultural dynamics of similar "egalitarian" societies. To maintain equality or status equivalency among men, an egalitarian society must have an effective system of reciprocal exchange to consistently distribute community wealth. A rigorous exchange system—and the Wape system is certainly rigorous—will prevent the emergence of rich men with real power or extensive authority over others.

If we take our clues from contemporary Wape society to reconstruct their past—often a dangerous procedure but we have no alternative—Wape excitement about hunting and boredom with gardening indicates that they probably are a hunting and gathering people who moved, or were pushed, into their mountain homeland, bringing their swamp-growing sago with them. Gradually, as the population grew, they added other plants to increase food production. As the Wapes' ecological adaptation as sedentary gardeners became more complete, they also elaborated and intensified their ancient reciprocal exchange system to assure that wealth maintained its fluidity and that men remained economic and political equals. Perhaps this is how the Wape became the people I knew, but it is only a guess.

Regardless, by elevating two men to be my main and best-paid assistants, I was setting myself against some formidable historical and cultural odds. The organizational thrust of Wape society is to maintain economic and political equality among men, and I was in flagrant violation of a historic tradition. The men of Taute were confused and angry that I would behave toward them in this high-handed fashion. It was one thing for a white man to be the boss of his private coastal plantation, but quite another to set himself up as a boss in the middle of their own village. And it made no difference to the Tautes that it was my personal household I was trying to organize or that it was my money I was spending. These were irrelevant details. I was living in their midst, and the only fair thing for me to do was to rotate the houseman jobs among *all* the village men!

At first I was just as confused and angry about their attempts to boss me. There was no way humanly possible to comply with their demand to rotate the houseman jobs and, at the same time, do effective work and maintain the health of my family. Egalitarian society or not, I felt it was sheer madness for them to think that I could. The houseman job was a complex one, demanding superior intelligence, physical adroitness, a compatible personality, impeccable character, and excellent health and hygiene. And the Taute men, like any such group, varied enormously. It was impossible to place each of them in intimate interaction with the children and our food even if Joyce and I had the time and patience—which we didn't—to train them serially in the jobs' multiple tasks. Both tuberculosis and leprosy were local health problems; we were already risking the children's health simply by living in a village.

But my rational explanations to the men why I could not rotate the houseman jobs were to no avail, nor were the several compromises already initiated. When I first hired Kumoi and Kuruwai as housemen, I naïvely believed that the other men would be satisfied if they each had an opportunity to occasionally earn some money. I set up two carrier's jobs on a two-week rotating basis that entailed going into Lumi several times a week to meet the mail and supply planes. But the men let me know that this was hardly an equitable arrangement. So, among other compromises, I eliminated the water-carrying job from the housemen tasks to rotate it also among the men. But it only gave me temporary respite from their lobbying. Then for a while the men's preoccupation with the shotgun cult distracted them from my hiring practices. Now, suddenly it seemed, the men were mobilized in an all-out effort to shape me up once and for all. What followed was a series of confrontations between us that irrevocably modified our relations.

On Easter Sunday morning we had pancakes with Vermont

maple syrup—a gift from Joyce's aunt—and a jelly-bean hunt for the children. Later in the day I interviewed Auwe on the demons that inhabit his clan's land. Auwe's clan was almost extinct, and the village he originally came from, Yingowam, was ordered abandoned by the government after the dysentery epidemic during the war virtually exterminated the inhabitants. The few remaining families scattered; Moala and Wamala came to live in nearby Kafiere as did the orphaned Auwe, who was brought here by his *faf*, old Tongol. Gradually the Tautes had appropriated some of the extensive Yingowam lands, a fact that rankled the survivors, who could only acquiesce.

In the afternoon I noticed a number of Mifu men in the hamlet. As the day wore on, they and the Kafiere men were joined by others, and I felt certain my obstinate behavior was about to be the subject of another public meeting. And I was not in the mood. Didn't they know this was Easter Sunday? Of course they did but it made little difference to them. Even the baptized Tautes were only nominal Catholics, not practicing ones. As far as the day Christ arose from the dead being significant to their lives, it simply wasn't. They had, however, adopted the use of the Western calendar. Before European contact, Wape days flowed one into the other, unnamed and unmarked except by memorable local events. Now it was convenient to segment time into days of the weeks, months, and years, but this did not necessarily mean adopting religious holidays as well. Only Sunday made sense to them. It was good to have a day of rest in the village or to visit nearby relatives to consummate some phase of their continual reciprocal exchanges. I wasn't a relative, but as the biggest spender in the local exchange system it was only appropriate they choose this day, Sunday, to visit.

Finally Kumoi came over to explain what the men wanted. He got right to the point. Now that they each had completed a turn of carrying supplies from Lumi, they wanted a pay raise for the second time around. Already I paid more for carrying than other Westerners in the area, including the government. If I got too far out of line, it would annoy the Westerners on whom we

also were dependent for many favors and privileges by inflating
local wages.

"All right," I said to Kumoi, "we can discuss it." After all,
that was the way things were decided here. No unilateral decisions; everything was worked out by consensus. "But I'm making
no promises about a possible raise." I was annoyed that they were
hitting me up again for an increase, but, at the same time I
couldn't blame them. "Nothing ventured, nothing gained" is our
American folk expression; in Pidgin it was 'Mi traim tasol.'

One of the problems regarding monetary transactions with
the Tautes was their exquisite sense of economic proportion and
balance; it was far more sensitive than mine. Any change in my
economic dealings with them was quickly and widely publicized,
necessitating changes in all my dealings as they perceived the old
relationships in terms of new ratios. This was interesting—even
entertaining—when I was first learning about Wape reciprocity
and economic balance, but I *knew* the point from all angles and
was quite frankly sick of it. Why couldn't they be as thorough in
teaching me about their seemingly endless food taboos, a topic I
never seemed to get on top of?

And so we had another meeting. Witauwa, the 'bosboi' for
building the house, was the chief protagonist. Our relationship
had been strained since I terminated his job shortly after the
house was finished because he did not meet my standards for a
dependable assistant.

Witauwa began by saying the men wanted twice as much as
I was now paying them, adding that it was a new "law," inferring
that the government had decreed a minimum wage for carrying.
That was both patently untrue and absurd, and I said as much.
The new salary they were demanding for part-time work would
almost be equal to the housemen's wages. So that was their strategy! If I wouldn't rotate the housemen jobs, they would raise the
carrier wages to the housemen's level. A great feeling of depres-
sion and hopelessness overcame me. Of all the cultures in the
world where talk about money is considered shameful, why did I
have to pick the Wape, where it wasn't?

Several of the men then brought up an old argument—I had heard it many times—that they were not paid for some of the trees cut down to make room for our house. Yet I had been very clear that the men's housebuilding salaries were to include all the expenses for the building. Yes, that's true, they agreed, but not every man had trees cut to make room for the house. It was unfair that they weren't given special compensation.

Every time I settled one of these claims on me, there was always another to take its place. Nothing I did regarding money with the Tautes, no matter how clear and concise I thought I was being, could ever cover all the contingencies. There were always new ways for having me pay them. Some of the men were quite frank in telling me that I was their "business," their only ready source for making money. I deeply resented—although I could intellectually understand—being treated like a tipped cornucopia tumbling out shillings instead of like a fellow human being.

When I did not readily comply with their demands, Witauwa, impatient and angry, laid down the ultimate sanction.

"Bill," he said coldly, "if you don't raise our wages, we will make you leave Taute!"

For months I had expected, and dreaded, to hear those words. They were keenly aware of my investment of time and money in the village and of my great dependency upon them. Then came a final threat. If they did force me to leave, Witauwa added, they would not even carry my cargo out to Lumi.

I knew if I complied with their demands I would be completely at their mercy; there would be no end to the demands upon me. Our relationship had now entered the arena of naked power politics. They knew that I, like any one of them, would not easily bear the stigmatization of being expelled from the village. But they were playing a dangerous game. If I did leave, there would be no money at all!

I looked around at the men. None of the older men was at the meeting; only the younger married men—the "young Turks" of Taute—were there. And Witauwa was an acknowledged "hothead," a rare type of Wape personality. He was the kind of vio-

lent man, others had told me, that in the old days would have in-
stigated murderous raids against neighboring villages. And he
was violent. Several months later I dressed a bloody gash in his
young daughter's head that he had inflicted.

As I looked at the men, I had the feeling that Witauwa had
gone too far with his threats toward me and that the men were
embarrassed and anxious. I finally said that it was impossible to
double their pay. If they felt they no longer wanted to help me,
then it was true that I would have to leave Taute. Just then I
would have happily walked out of the village forever.

But my statement had opened the situation for compromise,
and Kumoi made a proposition. He suggested that I give the men
another job to rotate among themselves similar to the carrying of
supplies and water. Couldn't the men bring in the firewood too?
Kumoi, the consummate politician! Bringing in wood was part of
the housemen's job and one he disliked. What more judicious
and worthwhile way to be rid of it? If I gave the men the firewood
job, he reasoned gravely, then they would have three kinds of
work—carrying the cargo, water, and firewood—and the housemen would have three kinds of work—cooking, cutting the grass
near the house, and helping me with my research. It *sounded* equitable but the men looked a bit confused; wasn't it equal pay they
wanted?

I thought a break would do us all good. I had managed to
keep my cool, but I was raging inside at the blackmail tactics. So
I suggested that we resume our parley after I had eaten. In the
house Kumoi and I went into a huddle and decided on an amount
to offer for the firewood job, and he assured me they would be
pleased with the offer.

When I rejoined the men, I was in a good mood and so were
they. We squatted on the path near the house, and I made the
offer exactly as Kumoi had suggested it to me. They undoubtedly
already knew all about it, and none of us needed any more surprises. The men smilingly accepted the new job—there was no
more talk about a raise—and I shook hands with each man as we
assured each other that we bore no grudges. This was an impor-

tant part of the decision-making process and not simply good manners. If one of us departed from the meeting angry, his ancestors might inflict sickness on the others. None of us wanted that to happen. That night I sat in my tent and philosophically typed up my notes:

And another crisis is settled. But I am happy that my time here is drawing to an end. This kind of bitchy "pulling" is irritating; it makes me feel like I'm being taken, that I'm not really their friend after all. Such a tragedy. Perhaps it is inevitable when the very rich and the very poor attempt to live together in intimate proximity. . . . . Yet I learn a lot about the culture when I am pushed by the people. It's worth it.

It might have seemed "worth it" on Easter Sunday night but on the following Tuesday, two more money problems surfaced. I shook my head. Was there to be no respite at all? Were the rest of my days in Taute to be spent wrangling over money?

Kumoi had cut some saplings in the forest near the hamlet to repair the fence he had placed around the cook house after he had missed some money. As he had carried them homeward, he was accosted by Weti, who said Kumoi had cut them from his land and that I would have to pay for them. Kumoi was insulted and angered because saplings were considered of no value. Then the old issue of the trees cut to make room for the house was brought up again. Money, money, money!

All right! ALL RIGHT! I told Kumoi we would call a meeting tomorrow, and everyone who had a money complaint against me must present it or forever hold his peace. Then Kumoi and Walos, the new houseman who replaced Kuruwai after villagers had temporarily pressured him from the job, and Ewum, who was now doing the washing, met to decide on our strategy. Kumoi said that if each of them as my principal assistant contributed a dollar to the total payment for the cut trees it would help to end the gossip and demands. That was fine with me; I could always return the dollar to each of them when I left the village. But no sooner had I received Kumoi's dollar than he said that he had "bought" his job, and was entitled to name his replacement when he took his "vacation." Even Kumoi could no longer withstand the village pressure against him and was relinquishing his job temporarily to give another man an opportunity for his salary. Annoyed, I told Kumoi that he, of all men, knew that Joyce and I reserved the right to hire who worked within the household.

The men could plainly see that I was being pushed beyond my tolerance. There was not a good-natured bone left in my body. They were conciliatory, insisting that I must stay in Taute forever and that once we had this meeting we would, in effect, all live happily ever after. But I knew the culture too well now. There would always be dissension as long as I remained in the village. The Tautes could not tolerate any kind of hierarchical structure within their midst. The wealth must be equally shared, and that was that! If there were a windfall, whether it was a wild pig or a domesticated anthropologist, he should be cut up equally for all. Each person should get a fair share. Well, I was not going around in enough equal pieces. Some were getting big pieces and the rest just the waste. Again, I could appreciate their point of view, but it was hell to try and pick my way through it all and keep my own equanimity, especially at crisis time.

That night old Moala came to my tent alone while I was typing, and his voice shook with emotion. He and his family had been at their garden house the past few days, and he had just learned of the Sunday meeting and the one proposed for tomorrow. He was majestically disdainful of the greed of the young Taute men. He ticked off my monetary contributions to the village, including my large contribution to the shotgun. What particularly enraged him was that the land Weti and his patrilineage now claimed as theirs and where Kumoi had cut the saplings was actually his, for it had belonged to his native village of Yingowam. 'Ol i hangamap nating' he repeated over and over; Weti and his kin were squatters.

Earlier that day I had learned what was actually behind the Easter Sunday wage demands. There had been a big 'satu' game Saturday night, and Kumoi had belittled—and infuriated—the

Taute men by arrogantly exclaiming that none of them had large amounts of money to gamble; he was bored with rolling the dice for one or two shillings! Then Ewum's wife had bragged to the other women about her husband's income now that he was working for me. So it was my very own people who had undone me. The village men, stung by these status insults, had mobilized their hostility and turned it on me. It didn't resolve anything to know this, but I did feel better knowing it wasn't exclusively my behavior that had precipitated the meeting and the men's overt antagonism.

Early Wednesday I asked Witauwa to blow his conch shell to bring all the villagers together who had a money grievance with me. For me it was to be the Meeting to End All Meetings; we would settle once and for all these irritating monetary claims so that I could begin again to think positively about the people and their culture. My present attitude could only be described as lousy and not conducive to the best field work.

It was a typical Taute village meeting. I opened the meeting by announcing that we—Kumoi, Ewum, Walos, and I—would pay for the trees cut to make room for my house. But, I added, if there was any further gossiping about my household and those who worked in it, or any more ganging up on me about money matters, I would demand my money back for the two shotguns. I ended saying that only those men who are my friends can work for me; men who gossip about my household behind my back will have to go elsewhere to find their money.

That was my opening and what a flood of discourse it turned loose. Some of the items were directly related to my household, but it was also a time for other submerged interpersonal irritations among the villagers to be expressed. Although some of the items at first seemed completely irrelevant to my problems with the Taute people, so tightly intermeshed had our lives become that it was actually true that everything was interrelated to everything else. It was impossible to make any precise boundaries regarding relevance.

The tension that preceded the meeting was gradually eased

as each person stated his grievances, gave an interpretation of facts, or an issue was settled. I said very little. After an hour and a half of constant discussion there was no more to be said, at least not just then. So the meeting ended with my paying the claimants for the cut trees and settling with Weti for his saplings.

It was a satisfying catharsis for all of us, and the group dispersed, as always, in a smiling and joking mood. Was it actually a Meeting to End All Meetings as far as I was concerned? Not exactly. But never again would it be necessary for me to initiate a confrontation with the villagers. As the hamlet emptied I went over to my office tent and again began to type:

WM NOTES
14.4.71 Wed.

THE MEETING TO END ALL MEETINGS!

Thank God it's over. And it is quiet for now. I think it will last until I leave the village the end of July. Although I wouldn't mind getting out sooner, I won't. It's just my attitude for the day. . . . What have I learned?

1. If one works in a fiercely egalitarian culture, expect trouble with the distribution of one's largesse.

2. If one lives in a poor culture and one is rich, expect hostility toward oneself and one's helpers as you are the "haves," the others the "have nots." And it makes no difference if you are a good guy or a bastard; you'll get the hostility either way. . . .

3. When one arrives in a new village to live, make the following clear in a public speech before settling down:

a) Only you may choose the men who work for you.

b) Find the rightful owners of everything used within your household and see that they are reimbursed on the spot. Don't expect or accept any favors. Pay for everything!

4. As much as possible try to disperse the work among the different clans and families. It is, of course, impossible to do.

5. Village squabbles in which one is directly involved are even more important ethnographically than I had been led to believe.

So we will see what happens. And how fascinating it will be to see how life shapes up in the second village I will live in. And how will the Tautes take it when I finally leave them? That is going to be less difficult, I think, because of the present confrontation. They know that I have been pushed too far. But I must tread carefully because my actual leaving may really make them angry. After all, I am their "business" and what businessman wants to loose business?

While the Tautes and I were undergoing our personal ordeals of disillusionment with each other, they already had begun preparations for a confrontation with another benefactor. But he was no mere mortal like myself who could be summarily dismissed without ceremony or ritual. Both his personality and powers were of cosmic proportions, and, accordingly, he was wheedled and cajoled in ritually precise ways. Right now his stone-hard heart lay in the ceremonial house bathed in the blood of recent pig kills and warmed by the bodies of sleeping men.

The villagers' relationship with *mani,* as with me, was conflicted. He was both their adversary and benefactor. A demon of frightful capriciousness, he took diabolical pleasure in smiting them down with boils, sickness, and death. It was *mani* who had thrown my neighbor Walmaiya to the ground with a shaking fit and whose wrath recently had paralyzed the hind quarters of a village piglet. Day after day I watched it drag itself around the hamlet until a dog mercifully killed it. But *mani,* if treated with attentive respect, also had the awesome power to bring to the villagers the one thing they valued over all others: meat.

Kafiere had begun the rituals to stage a major *mani* hunting festival. Some of the men already were sleeping in the ceremonial house, and *mani* had shown his appreciation by directing a wild sow to Auwe's gun that he quickly dispatched. As a bonus, two of her piglets were captured alive. This was a sure sign that *mani* was pleased with the men's attentions and would send them many wild pigs if they produced a festival in his honor.

In the forest, a half-hour walk from the hamlet and near the abandoned village of Yingowam, the men built a temporary shelter to construct the great conical mask that symbolized *mani*. Each step of the process was surrounded with ritual. The mask frame must be cut from a special kind of tree during a successful pig hunt. After it is assembled it must be smeared with pig blood from other hunts and hung with magical leaves. Then the frame, so long it stretched the length of the shelter, was covered with smooth sheets of sago spathe.

With the men's permission, I had set up my camera to film the painting of the mask or, as the men expressed it, the painting of *mani*'s skin. After the Wilkili *mani* sent the earthquake as retribution for my earlier filming intrusion, I was taking no chances. But the Taute men only laughed. The Taute *mani* couldn't be angry with my filming, they said. I was a man of Taute, not a stranger to the village.

The Wilkili *mani* had been painted an ominous black, but the traditional color for the Taute *mani* was a fiery red covered with many colorful designs outlined in black. There was no *mani*, the Taute men asserted, as handsome as theirs. I watched as the men carefully painted on the black designs with the tips of feathers and small sticks. Before Western contact the black paint was made from the black ash of burned sago palm stems; now it was made by mixing water with flashlight battery cores. The other traditional colors used in Wape painting were white, yellow, and red. White was made from light ashes or a local white clay, yellow from crushed stones, and red—a beautiful, bright red—from the mashed seeds of the *sinali yali* tree. But manufacturing enough paint for a giant mask like *mani* was slow, tedious work. The men were pleased that they had some light blue paint, bought on the coast by a returned plantation worker and saved for this special occasion. It would be used in painting some of the designs.

The painting of the mask took two days. Witauwa seemed to be the expert on the appropriate *mani* designs, but, as usual, there was no boss. Each man and teenage boy painted when and what he wanted to. With so many casual artists, at first I was dubious about the results. But the painters seemed to have shared an overall image of the mask—as they must have also for our house—for the result was a resplendent work of forest art.

Mani was scheduled to make his grand entrance from the forest into the village on Friday afternoon, and the entire village was in a state of joyous preparation. Women were bringing in extra loads of firewood and large quantities of sago to feed relatives who would be visiting them during the festivities. The festival would last at least a week and, if many pigs were being killed, would continue even longer.

As I ate my breakfast on our veranda, I looked out at the plaza where several young men were building a semicircular enclosure extending in front of the ceremonial house. Even the boys and girls were helping by bringing the men palm leaves that, once fastened to the framework, would shield *mani* and his priests from view. But the toddlers were having the most fun. Their brown, naked bodies sprawled and rolled in a pile of bouncing palm leaves as they laughed the open laughter of those still free from community responsibilities. Inside the enclosure one man was making a small thronelike frame on which *mani* would rest, enabling a priest to slip inside to shoulder the majestic form and dance around the plaza to an admiring audience.

At *mani*'s forest shelter the finishing decorations were being prepared for his auspicious debut in the village. Miembel, the teenage boy on whose lands *mani* lived, was making a skirt of long green leaves to encircle the mask, and I sat down to help him as he explained how it was assembled. Auwe and Kuruwai had just returned from a long but unsuccessful early-morning hunt. They did not see a single pig track. Although they dare not say it aloud, I knew they were thinking that *mani* should have sent them a pig on this important day. There were speculations, as usual, of what had gone wrong, and I heard them mention various forest demons who may have been responsible. Biai, sitting nearby, was making a pair of long bark-cloth leggings to hide the legs of the priests who would take turns in dancing with the mask. Pounding laboriously on the bark, I wondered how he possibly could finish them for *mani*'s entrance today. Witauwa and Bilu were working on some spectacular feather decorations, and Mehti, a Wabuf village man who recently had come to live in Taute, his wife's village, after a quarrel with his older brother, was doing some last-minute painting on the mask itself. It could not have been a more relaxed group of men. Only I was anxious. I was anxious because I wanted to know when and where the mask would enter the village so I could record the event on film.

As usual, I could not get a precise or even an approximate time. It was silly for me to press for a time—I knew that. There was no manager of *mani*'s debut, and many tasks had yet to be completed by voluntary helpers before *mani* could make his grand entrance. The most help they could give me was that it would not be before 'belo bek' or one o'clock. So I returned to the hamlet to be with the children, since Joyce was in Lumi, and to supervise the preparation of lunch.

By noon the enclosure was completed, and several visitors arrived from Talbipi village, located on the ridge across the Sibi. I could hear hand drums beating from the ceremonial house. Then the hamlet began to empty of men as they went out to the *mani* shelter to eat a special ritual meal before escorting *mani* into the village. After lunch I began setting up the filming and re-cording equipment by a large red Hibiscus near my office tent. I knew the path that *mani* would enter on even if I didn't know the exact time. So I placed the camera in order to get some sweeping shots. It was nice to be filming in my own village because I didn't have to guess what would be happening where. Only when.

By two o'clock I had tested the equipment a number of times and was ready to begin filming. This was always the most difficult time of field work for me—waiting for the long antici-pated event to begin. I walked up to the plaza and watched two young girls sweep it free of debris then poked my head into the *mani* enclosure. No one was there. The little girls, their work fin-ished, went into their houses to be with their mothers. Women, girls, and babies must stay inside when the dangerous *mani* parades through the village to the ceremonial house. I had ex-plained this custom to Ned and Elizabeth, telling them they must remain at the house together while I was filming and if Elizabeth did watch, as I knew she would, to do it discreetly.

Shortly after three I could hear the men whooping it up in the forest as they carried *mani* toward the village, for this was no longer just a mask. Before leaving the shelter the spirit of *mani* himself had entered into it. I was already tape recording the approaching celebration when Kapul, a friendly young man who was frequently helpful to me, came running up to report that *mani* was coming by another path. He would not be entering the village by my tent but a path far below it.

Not even in my own village could I depend upon anything happening as planned. Each time I set up my filming equipment far in advance and was confident and relaxed, something like this happened. Once I had set up my equipment in the Gwenif River to film the ritual washing of Otemgi village children by their *faf*. All afternoon I waited in the sweltering sun for the men and children to arrive, and when they finally did, they arrived out of sight downstream. With only two little Otemgi boys to help me, I had to dismantle the sync-sound filming equipment and lug it over slippery rocks and rushing water to the newly chosen ritual site. With no time to properly check out the equipment after reassembling it, it was only by luck that I secured some superb footage.

But this time I had no time to take the equipment apart and move it to the lower part of the village where *mani* would come prancing out of the forest into the village. That visual scene would be lost forever. With Kapul's help we moved the equipment to the other side of the Hibiscus where at least I could get a shot of *mani* as he paraded up the path by our house on his way to the plaza.

Mani, a pageant unto himself, came prancing into view just below Bilu's house. His sudden appearance in the humble village was dazzling. His gloriously colored skin glistened in the orange afternoon sun, and his crown of lofty black cassowary plumes swayed grandly twenty feet above the sandy path. *Mani,* one of the most exalted of the Taute forest demons, was deigning to come and live for a while in the village. The vibrant beat of drums bit into my ears as *mani*'s escort of chanting men dropped their voices down a mournful chromatic scale.

Thrilled with his astonishing presence, I began to film. Just as *mani* passed in front of me, there was an odd click in the camera. Then it stopped.

The procession continued to the plaza while I dismounted the film magazine and took it to my tent, where I opened it in the black film-changing bag to discover what was wrong. I assumed that the film had broken, but it hadn't. For inexplicable reasons it had simply jammed. I wondered to myself if the Taute *mani* was as hospitable to filming as the men believed him to be. I continued to be plagued with various difficulties every time I attempted to film the *mani* festivities. Eventually I had to send the camera's tape recorder to Australia for unknown repairs.

Once *mani* had entered the plaza, the women and girls joined the men and boys to watch his vigorous prancing as the slit gongs boomed out the *mani* signal. When the males began to congregate inside the ceremonial enclosure, the girls brought them large leaves filled with sago pudding and garnished with smoked pig. Inside the enclosure the food was laid in rows; it was the biggest display of feast foods I had seen in Taute. There was much questioning about which women had prepared what food, because in the *mani* feast Kafiere hamlet must exchange food with Mifu and Obuenga hamlets. It was one of several instances I discovered where the Tautes treated their village as a "moiety" or dual type of organization.

Toward the end of the feasting it began to rain, but there was no dampening of the good humor pervading the ceremonial house. *Mani* was brought inside to protect his finery, almost filling the house, the men's bodies pressed against one another in holiday camaraderie. *Mani* must have been overjoyed by the human warmth generated in his honor that night. After dark the men began to sing the beautiful songs composed by their ancestors to celebrate the *mani* festival. Each clan had its own songs commemorating significant events in its history. There were songs about murder, witchcraft, goring by a wild pig, an elopement, the felling of a mammoth tree, a marital dispute, a bird hunt, food gifts from a *faf,* a fall into a large hole, and on and on and on.

Each of the songs was a brief poem that, if one was familiar with the event it symbolized, projected a rich imagery evocative of the story itself. "A bird flies down to the Sibi sand and tosses it into the air" was one. But no one could remember the story it epitomized. The content of the tale was lost; only its poetic symbol survived. Night after night the men sang their ancestral songs as *mani* danced in darkness on the plaza. I recorded as many of the songs as I could. In another generation or less the poems themselves may be lost. Already the *winar* songs for the *wenil* curing festival were forgotten, obliterated by the deaths of the two old men who still remembered them.

Each morning at daybreak after the singing had ceased and the sun flashed its warmth across the damp plaza, *mani* would lead the armed hunters to the edge of the forest. As they disappeared into the dark foliage, he would return to the plaza to dance. Sometimes he would be joined by a group of young girls skipping gaily after him. The priest that carried *mani*'s dancing form had a small peephole to prevent him from running into spectators or prancing over the cliffside. But if the visibility was poor, as it sometimes was, he would veer off course as spectators yelled until someone showed him the right way. Then a boy might whisper to me the name of the priest who had made *mani* appear so foolish.

The *mani* priests, except when carrying the mask, were confined to the enclosure for the duration of the festival. While in such intimate contact with *mani,* they were physically avoided even by the men who joined them in the enclosure. I once started to sit down on the spot from which one of the priests had just stood up. "No," I was warned, "the heat of his body is still there; wait until it has cooled." The priest was immune to *mani*'s dangers, but I was not. And if I became contaminated I might touch others, especially my wife or children, bringing misfortune to them as well.

One day I was amused to see the majestic *mani* walking from house to house like a door-to-door salesman, soliciting tobacco and newsprint from the villagers to give to his faithful priests. Black fingers extended from a single bark-cloth-covered arm to receive the presents. Ned and Elizabeth were as amused and surprised at his begging behavior as I, and they jumped down the house steps to greet him and carefully presented our contribution.

Friday, Saturday, Sunday, and Monday *mani* danced as the men hunted unsuccessfully. Then on Tuesday *mani* finally rewarded the village with a wild pig, and we all celebrated. The rest of the week visitors continued to come and go in the village. Lyn arranged a visit to coincide with her village clinic for mothers and babies, and on Thursday the village was jammed with men who came to gamble while enjoying the *mani* festivities. Over the weekend more visitors arrived to help with the singing, but the men's hunting continued in vain. Some of them began to grumble that *mani* was exploiting them. A single pig was scant reward for the strenuous efforts they had expended to honor him. The hunters, weary from the long and futile chase, and the priests, whose shoulders, in spite of some foam rubber I had given them, were blistered and sore from carrying *mani,* were deeply disillusioned. "This *mani,*" one man said to me derisively, "he is making fools of us all!"

On Monday, men from Kamnum, Kafiere's old enemy, came to sell smoked pig. They had heard the festival was a failure and knew that if we wanted to eat pig, we must buy it. It was humiliating, but I bought some and sent it to the ceremonial house to be divided among the cloistered priests. That night the men sang long into the night, still hopeful that *mani* would reciprocate. From my tent I made a long-distance recording of the mournful *mani* songs while the night insects and birds sang a forest obbligato. It is one of my favorite Wape tapes and one of the last I was to make of the festival.

The next morning when I met Wamala, he said bitterly, "Today we will send *mani* back to the forest." I knew everyone in the village was angry with *mani*'s duplicity. For weeks they had dedicated their efforts to make this a great festival worthy of his powers. I felt sadness for the men and women of Taute. They had treated *mani* as a resplendent, honored guest, but he had chosen to ignore them.

Late in the afternoon the once gay and graceful *mani* lumbered awkwardly from his enclosure. Slowly he walked around the plaza stopping at each house and, reaching into a bag with his single, strange arm, threw ashes over his handsome body and feathered finery. He would miss the close companionship of Taute's dutiful men and women and attentive children. Stained with the ashes of sorrow he quietly walked out of the village and into the forest.

I followed with the men and boys to the edge of the cliff near the shelter where they had labored to create *mani*'s magnificent image. As *mani* lay on his side Auwe plunged a knife into his bright skin and, ripping several large gashes, he pulled back the skin so *mani*'s spirit could return to its place in the forest. Then lifting *mani* for one last time, the men hurled him over the cliff. Spinning in the late afternoon sun, he crashed and disappeared into the jungle below.

12

▼△▼△▼△▼△▼△▼△▼△▼

THE NIGHT OF
THE SEVEN DAYS

It was graduation day. Ned had successfully completed his kindergarten correspondence course from Australia, and we were going to celebrate. The course was an excellent one. He had mastered basic mathematical concepts and, most exciting of all, had learned to read. While Elizabeth and I made him a mortar-board cap from my typing paper with a prestigious purple tassel purloined from a Japanese fan, Joyce prepared diplomas for both children. Elizabeth was graduating from my "nursery school," where she practiced drawing and printing in my screen tent while Joyce and Ned worked on his lessons.

Lunch was a party. As the balloons tossed in the breeze, Joyce presented the diplomas to the children and I gave them their graduation gifts. Ned fastened his new hunting knife to his belt and, as we proudly listened, read aloud to us—the valedictorian of his class.

Then Joyce and the children were gone. Within weeks they moved to their new house in Lumi, and I was alone in the field for the first time. Several of the men chided me for permitting Ned to leave at all, reminding me that it is a man's sons who look out for him in old age. If Ned were to remain close to me, they said, he must visit me often.

I wanted to leave Taute in July to begin my second study, but events were conspiring against me. For one, the Mifu men who were away as laborers on a copra plantation near Madang suddenly appeared in the village toward the end of June. Although I did not know it at the time, they had quit their jobs to return to the relative safety of the mountains, frightened by tales that a great earthquake and darkness was to overtake the land as a tidal wave swept in from the sea.

The stories were related to a cargo cult that was sweeping the East Sepik District. In earlier years it might have been confined to that area, but Radio Wewak's Pidgin broadcasts and the Territory's Pidgin newspapers quickly spread the sensational news. Even the English-language paper I received from Port Moresby was filled with reports of the cult and the predictions of the strange events to come.

A principal belief of the cult was that a cement marker placed atop Mount Turu near Wewak in 1962 by U.S. Army surveyors was preventing cash crops from flourishing and, more importantly, obstructing the delivery of material wealth or 'kago' to the people by their ancestors. Some stories said that money and valuable goods would be found under the marker; others that a flight of American planes would bring the 'kago' to the people. The press also reported that Yaliwan, the 'bembi' or leader of the cult, had offered himself as a human sacrifice. Regardless of the stories—they varied from week to week, with numerous versions of each one—the only unchanging piece of information was the climax date for the cult. Whatever was eventually to happen would happen on the seventh day of the seventh month. That would be July 7th, the same day that Joyce's younger brother John was to arrive in Lumi from his teaching post in Holland for a month's visit.

As the stories of the cult grew and spread, Yaliwan gained

many followers, some of whom went to the Mount Turu area to await the great occasion so they could share in the wealth. All of Yaliwan's serious disciples contributed money to the cult; one newspaper reported he had received at least twenty-five thousand dollars.

But no one mentioned the cult in Taute. Surely they must know about it, I thought. Joyce recently had told me that Don McGregor changed his sermon on a visit to Yebil village west of Lumi because the people were frightened about a "Doomsday," when everything was to go dark. But when I asked Kumoi if the word "Doomsday" was a Pidgin word, he said he had never heard of it. I did not inquire further, thinking the concern might be more related to the influence of the mission than the cult stories. I began to doubt if the Tautes knew much about the cult at all or, if they did, were simply ignoring it because Mount Turu was so far away. Even the return of the Mifu laborers did not tip me off. I was told the men returned because they were tired of the work. They were scheduled to return to Taute in October at the completion of their contracts, but the village had such a bad reputation with Ron Kitson, the Lumi labor contractor, as contract breakers, I thought no more about it. The only reason the hamlet of Kafiere was filled with active young men was because Kit refused to sign them on again because of their poor record with him.

So if the Tautes didn't want to talk about the cult, I wouldn't either. My active interest in the cult, I reasoned, might seemingly justify the reality of the stories they were hearing. But it was a bad decision. With hindsight, I think that my silence probably only intensified their anxiety and deepened the cult's mysteries.

About a week before the day Yaliwan and his diciples were to remove the marker from the mountain and obtain the 'kago,' I went into Lumi to observe a sorcery court trial involving several of the Lujere people who live in the swamps of the lower Yellow River (in Wapeland we called it the Sibi River) emptying into the Sepik River. I had tentatively selected the Lujere as the culture I would study after I left the Wape. I was attracted to them for many reasons. For one, their ecological niche was very different. Also, unlike the Wape, they were reportedly obsessed with beliefs and practices focusing on witchcraft and sorcery. If I did go to live with them, the upcoming court case might be my only data on a sorcery trial.

On the afternoon of the trial, Ann Chowning, a fellow American anthropologist who taught at the University of Papua New Guinea and a friend of ours, arrived in Lumi for a short visit with us. The next day Ann, Ned, and I trekked to Taute in a terrific downpour. The people of Kafiere were delighted that Ned had returned to visit them. They lined up to shake Ann's hand, and Waiape embarrassed me by openly expressing effusive admiration for her strong legs. Then Kuruwai and I went into the pantry to prepare some dinner. But Kuruwai had something else on his mind. He stopped, then looking at me very intently, spoke softly.

"Bill," he said seriously, "you and I have always spoken frankly with each other. I want to ask you a question."

It was unlike Kuruwai to be so intense. What could be troubling him? Perhaps it was related to the recent sickness of Kino, his younger brother.

"Yes," I replied, "we have always spoken the truth to each other. What is it?"

"Is it true that Makain and the whites at Lumi are leaving for Mount Turu to remove a marker?" There were other stories, he said, that the mountain was filled with 'kago.' I told Kuruwai that I had heard similar stories about the Mount Turu 'bembi' but assured him that the Lumi white men had no intention of going to Mount Turu, and I was quite sure that Makain did not either. What the 'bembi's' people intended to do about the marker was another matter.

As Kuruwai and I discussed the 'kago' stories, I obtained my first understanding of the villagers' interpretation of the cult's activities. The Tautes were unclear as to whether the 'kago' would be extended to them or not. No one in the village was a disciple of the 'bembi' or had contributed money to the cult; some felt they probably were too far away from the source of the 'kago' to benefit even if it did appear. Still, if the ancestors intended the 'kago' for the black New Guineans . . .

But 'kago' or not, the stories said that the day before the marker was to be removed, everyone must harvest some of their taro and bring in firewood because the next morning, July 7, the sun would not rise and the land would be in total darkness for seven days. When the sun reappeared, the 'kago' would be visible.

Kuruwai said they first heard the 'kago' stories about two months ago.

"Why," I asked impatiently, "has no one mentioned the stories to me until now?"

"Because we were afraid that you would report us to the 'kiap.'"

And before I could check myself I became angrily indignant, reminding Kuruwai that I knew of numerous illegal activities and customs of the Tautes that could land a large group in jail if I wanted to report them.

"But I haven't reported them and I wouldn't. You know that!" Then it dawned on me that this was something very different; something that divided the blacks against the whites, something that placed me irrevocably in the enemy camp.

There had been cargo cults in the past, not as far away as Mount Turu, but in the Lumi Sub-District itself, and the Tautes never had known a white man to take a neutral position toward 'bembi' talk. Cult leaders and their followers were damned and threatened by the missionaries and 'kiaps,' and, inevitably, a group of men went to jail. Only now, as the cult neared its climax, did the villagers decide it was worth the risk to approach me. They did not know which of the many conflicting stories circulating to believe and, in their confusion and fear, had designated Kuruwai to sound me out.

I knew my conversation with Kuruwai would be reported

throughout the village, so the next morning, when I stopped to visit with Kumoi at the cook house, there was no need to preface my remarks about the 'kago' stories. Raba came in to sell me some tomatoes, and together they reported the latest stories. One story said that at Mount Turu a man's head is to be cut off by his younger brother. When the head falls to the ground, the people will try to pick it up. If the Americans and the New Guinea Army pick it up, there won't be a fight. But if the Australian Army picks up the head first, there will be a battle between the two factions. The beheading will be followed by an earthquake, accompanied by rain, thunder, and lightening. At the end of the storm, the head will reveal all of its possessions.

That was but one of the two "head" stories Kumoi and Raba had heard. The other was about a head lost on Mount Kabori, a large mountain located to the west of the Kabori mission station, where Seiforu and I had begun our trek back to Lumi many months before. In this story all of the villages in the vicinity of Lumi were to harvest taro for a large group of men going from Lumi to Mount Kabori to search for the head of the 'tumbuna papa bipor yet'—the original ancestor of the blacks, whites, and Chinese. He has light skin and once owned all of the wealth until his head was lost. Now it is buried somewhere on the mountain, and although the rest of his body is only bones, his head is still intact. The searchers will use binoculars to locate where the head is buried, and when it is found, the 'kago' will appear. The Lumi 'kiaps' and Makain will go with the Wapes to search for the head.

The Mount Kabori story, I decided, must be a local version of the Mount Turu story. Then I had a flash of insight; I was certain I knew what part of the tale was about. It was a mixture of traditional 'kago' thinking that provided a plausible explanation for something unusual that, just then, was happening in Lumi.

The Territory of Papua New Guinea was being censused, and Lumi was filled with 'kiaps' and young educated New Guinea men who would mount the census patrols throughout the Sub-District. The "head count" somehow had become a "head hunt" for the 'tumbuna papa bipor yet!' The unusual build-up of men in Lumi and half-understood bits of information about the census was transformed into something sensible by relating it to the Mount Turu cult activities. Census patrols already were leaving Lumi, and one directed by Ray Lanaghan, the 'kiap' at the Yellow River station, was to census the population west to Mount Kabori.

I had, repeatedly, recorded similar misinterpretations about what the Lumi whites were doing. Planes zoomed in out of the airstrip, boxes with unknown contents were unloaded and loaded, and people arrived and departed on secret missions. And the missions and government were forever sending out unpublicized patrols into the countryside and initiating new projects. It was impossible for a Wape to know exactly what was going on. Now the stories emanating from the Mount Turu cargo cult were imposing another form of distortion.

What Lumi needed was a big sheltered bulletin board at the market place where the 'kiaps,' missionaries, and the Lumi Local Council could fasten short, clear statements in Pidgin about their activities and special projects. It would go a long way to dispel the distorting rumors that constantly circulated as the people tried to interpret what the whites were doing just then or planning to do next. As things were, there was no way to find out what was really happening unless one could find a white man to ask. And that wasn't easy to do. So the bits and pieces of fact, in themselves often true, were woven into comprehensive explanations that attempted to make sense of the incomprehensible details. But their imaginative creations were failures. They triumphed only as dramatic testimony to the compelling urge, shared by all humans, to make sense of the multiple unknowns that surround our lives.

Sunday was the Fourth of July and our wedding anniversary. I went up to the plaza and squatted down on the sand with Moala and Suwe as we warmed our backs in the early morning sun. They were worried about the 'bembi' talk concerning the predicted earthquake and seven days of darkness. But it was not a day of rest for Taute's women. Far down in the valley I could hear the resounding blows of women cutting out the pith of sago palms. They were preparing their food for the siege of darkness. And some of the Mifu people already had moved their valuable shell possessions to relatives' houses in Obuenga hamlet, where the land was believed to be safer from an earthquake.

Saturday night Mifu had hosted a big 'satu' game, and the men of Kafiere had returned with more of the latest 'bembi' tales. The president of the United States has given one hundred dollars or two hundred dollars to the Mount Turu 'bembi.' The Australian Army wants to behead the 'bembi,' who has told them they must wait. The 'bembi' has discovered how to make money, so he isn't looking for the 'kago.' When the earthquake comes, all of the witches and sorcerers will be buried alive; only the good people will survive. When the great darkness comes, fire will not burn—not even a match will light. The Lumi 'kiap' announced at the market that the 'bembi' talk is lies, but the people think it is the 'kiap' who lies.

Poor Peter! Someone had asked him at the market if the 'bembi' talk was true, and he, judiciously, replied he had heard similar talk when stationed in the Highlands but nothing ever came of it. Yet anything a white person said against the stories, however mild, was interpreted as verifying the truth of the stories. The people knew the whites already possessed both wealth and power and discredited the 'bembi' stories simply to maintain their superior position.

Perhaps my own comments, guarded as they were, also were misunderstood. When the men asked me about the stories, I replied that if I was worried about an earthquake or a long time of darkness I would have sent my family away by now. As to the other 'bembi' stories, I said that I simply didn't know. Hardly adequate, but it was the best I could do. I had made the mistake of trying to explain to Wamala my interpretation of the Mount Kabori 'bembi' story in terms of the census patrols only to end with a tale as bizarre to him as the original was to me.

In the early afternoon Kumoi stopped by on his way to Tal-bipi, his wife's village. He was going to claim his portion of a pig they had slaughtered and was sorry he could not cook for me that night.

I already had decided I would stay in Taute until after the cargo cult climaxed on the seventh. Not only did I want to get as much data on what Ann had called "fallout" from the Mount Turu cargo cult, but I also felt that my presence in the village might be reassuring. If I went to Lumi on the sixth to greet John's plane the next morning, I knew the villagers would read other meanings into my departure. I would be "running away" because the tales of impending disaster and darkness were indeed true. But this was only the fourth, and, with Kumoi gone for the evening, I changed my plans and decided to surprise Joyce by going to Lumi. I knew that she would not believe that I had taken time out from my research at this critical time to spend it with her.

Joyce's surprise was complete! The next morning, as I passed the Catholic mission buildings on my way back to Taute, I learned that Father Gerald and Brother Steve had gone to Aitape to attend a long-arranged meeting with other Franciscan men. That should start some stories, I thought.

When I arrived in Taute one of the first stories I heard was that all of the Wape priests had run away to safety. No one knew where, but they were seen boarding the mission plane. By Tuesday, July 6, five Taute pigs were killed and the village was filled with people, food, and firewood. It was the day the earthquake was expected, and everyone stayed home. But the earth never moved; there was not the slightest tremor.

Even before darkness fell, the villagers quietly went into their houses and fastened the doors. Not even a pig or a dog was to be seen. From the houses the sound of low talking melded into a hoarse, unsettling rumble. As I walked back to my house from the empty plaza, an eerie sensation overcame me. I did not belong here. For the first time since moving to Taute over a year before, I felt insecure and vaguely threatened. I read until late then slept fitfully.

On July 7—our first day of darkness—the sun rose as usual over the Talbipi ridge, throwing slender shadows from the coconut palms across the sandy plaza. The comforting smell of cooking fires drifted through the hamlet on gentle winds that barely stirred the Poinsettia leaves outside my window. I watched Aif's children run laughing down the path. Taute was in a holiday mood. No one would go to bed hungry tonight. Even Taute's *moli* or white man would eat pork on this special day. Aif and Moala both brought me pieces of fresh pig, apparently some kind of "thank you," for it was the first meat I had received not killed by the gun.

At noon I listened to the English news and announced to the waiting men that the Mount Turu 'bembi' and his followers had removed the cement marker and carried it down the mountain to the Yangoru Patrol Post. No 'kago' had appeared. For once, the government had not interfered in a cargo cult and let the people—there were six thousand of them on the mountain that day—do as they wish. There was no violence, and no one was sent to jail. Times were changing in New Guinea. This was still colonialism but tempered with experience and some appreciation for the values of the local culture.

In the evening Kumoi and I listened together to the Pidgin news broadcast from Wewak. Kumoi was very impressed. The report was similar to what I had told the men at noon, but this time Kumoi heard it from a New Guinea man like himself. There was no 'kago.'

"The 'bembi' tried to trick us," he said dryly, then fell silent. A short while later I passed the pantry window that looked into the cook house, where Kumoi was cleaning up after dinner.

"Bill," he called, "this Mount Turu 'bembi' is *kilfene*'s child!" and smiled derisively before continuing. "If you sit down by a pool in the forest and say you are hungry, the demon *kilfene* will give you food. Then he will kill you! That's why we never say we are hungry when we are in the forest; we just think it."

Kumoi had made the logical connection between the *kilfene* demon and the 'bembi,' who both offer you valuables that are meaningless.

"And according to the Catholic priests," he added, "it is the same with Satan."

There was no other man in Taute whose mind worked so interestingly with complex material. Kumoi was an intellectual; his restless mind was forever playing over experience, seeking the continuities, the analogies, and patterning that give it coherence. Then he began to lecture himself—and me—on the importance of education, this man of the forest who himself had received no formal education.

"The government, the Protestant and Catholic missionaries," he said with emphasis, "all have important things to teach the people. While we are learning these new ways, we must trust the whites and do as they do."Kumoi paused, then spoke slowly. "The whites understand about everything!" Then scornfully, "We blacks of the forest are ignorant!"

I often had heard this litany, not only from Kumoi but from other young men as well. Like Kumoi, they were trying to find a way into the modern world that the whites already had mastered and controlled. It wasn't just material goods they desired, they wanted to *know!* Yet it always distressed me to hear one of the men speak like this. I knew the modern world. It wasn't so great. The blacks of Los Angeles had burned their city for the same reasons the Tautes were dreaming of magical riches. Both groups were cut off from access to power and wealth; what they did about it was simply the accidents of culture and history.

Kumoi ended his discourse with a final injunction.

"If this 'bembi' talk comes up again, we must ignore it. We can't be afraid again!"

13

▼▲▼▲▼▲▼▲▼▲▼▲▼

EMBERS AND ASHES

If Joyce found village life stultifying, her reaction to patrolling was just the opposite. Hiking through the rugged forest, stopping in a village to relax and visit with the people, and then moving on was an exhilarating experience. She occasionally joined Lyn on a brief medical patrol from Lumi but longed to go on an extended bush patrol, sleeping in a different village each night. I could appreciate her enthusiasm for trekking; exploring strange country and meeting new and truly exotic people is high adventure. So Joyce and I planned a patrol to the Lujere or Yellow River people in the Sepik swamps in hopes of locating a village suitable for my next field station. John had volunteered to look after Ned and Elizabeth so we could be gone almost a week.

I was packing my backpack for the trip when Kit, the Lumi labor recruiter, came up to Joyce's door. He had received a rush order for laborers and was going to send the Tautes since he had no time to bring in other men. Kit wanted to make sure he did not recruit someone who had a steady job with me. Since he provided the only access for the majority of Wape men to make money, he felt a responsibility to recruit only those who did not have local jobs.

"If you want to talk some of the others out of going," he added genially, "I don't mind."

The Mifu men had just returned from plantation work, and I knew they would not sign on again this quickly. Besides, they had begun preparations for a Spirit Fish curing festival, a major community undertaking. Already the new *niyl* priests for the festival had undergone several initiation rites. No, I thought, it's not the Mifus who will go; it will be the men of Kafiere hamlet, the men with whom I live and am the closest.

Their leaving would mean the end of an active and complete hamlet life; the young men who animated the life of Kafiere with their pig hunts, meetings, and ceremonials would all be gone. Yet I was lucky they had stayed as long as they had. Without Kit's work injunction against them, they would have departed for the plantations immediately after their first disenchantment with me.

"It's okay with me if they want to sign on," I said. "They are free men. Anyway, I won't be in Taute much longer to give them jobs. Joyce and I are flying down to Magaleri this afternoon to patrol the Yellow River villages. I want to begin working down there in a month or so."

My field work with the Tautes was coming to an end; the people and I were slipping away from each other as we redirected our lives and thoughts to other tasks in other places. Within hours I would say good-by to some of the men who had taught me how to see and feel the texture of their lives and their enveloping culture. With their cooperation Joyce and I had collected a rich corpus of cultural materials about a unique way of life. We had typed hundreds of pages of notes and written even more in our notebooks. We had taken thousands of photographs, filmed hours of their everyday and ceremonial life, and recorded almost 100,000 feet of tape with their conversation and music.

Eventually we would write articles and books from these

data stamped with our personal interpretations of what we had seen and heard. But someday—perhaps long after I was dead— men and women of Wape descent who were professional social scientists like myself, would study these same materials for insights into how their culture had changed since my family and I had lived among their ancestors. Examining our field materials in detail, they would judge the strengths and weaknesses of the data in terms of our guiding theoretical approach and research methodology. Undoubtedly they would challenge some of our findings and offer some new interpretations of the data as well. But as long as the recorded data existed, they would stand as a rough record, available to the scrutiny of others, of Wape culture as expressed in one village, at one point in time, and as seen and understood by one American man and woman.

Joyce and I took our gear up to the Lumi airstrip to wait for the mission plane that would fly us down to the Sepik swamps. After our patrol I would return to Taute and stay until the Spirit Fish festival was completed. Then, like the Kafiere men, I too would be gone. Gone to study the witch-ridden Lujere, awash in their malarial swamps. And, with luck, I would learn yet another way to think and to feel, a new way to organize the life of a family and community—a new way to interpret the universal cultural problems of human morality and mortality, the difference between right and wrong, and how to change what is bad to good.

At the airstrip we placed our backpacks at the plane's loading bay and walked over to Kit's office to say good-by to our Kafiere friends. Kuruwai, Auwe, Witauwa, Weti—fourteen of our neighbors—stood waiting in the sun, anxious and silent, for Kit to arrive and give them their final instructions. They had completed their physicals, signed their contracts; they needed only to know the day they would be flown out to the coast.

This would be the first time I had seen the men since learning of their departure. They had known about their leaving for several days but had kept it a secret. Their trust in me, a white man, could never be complete. That was a cold fact in our relationship, yet it continued to hurt and disturb me.

I hated to say good-by to them there. When the Tautes were out of the village, and especially when in Lumi, they spoke in whispers and treated me, and each other, like a stranger. But there was no choice. In a few days, Kafiere would be a hamlet of women, children, and old men.

I reached out to grab each man's strong hand, looking into empty eyes for some reflection of the intimacy we had shared. These were the men I had hunted with, sat with, had joked and argued with. They pumped my hand mechanically and glanced away. Then someone spotted Kit walking down the path toward his office.

" 'Masta Kit i kam!' " With my outstretched hand in the air, they broke abruptly away and fell into rigid formation. Then I remembered—so long ago—how they had lined themselves this same rigid way when I came out of the house in Taute to pay them for carrying our trunks to the village.

Now, like West Point plebes, they stood at grotesque attention, a caricature of the white man's unbending discipline they so disliked. They had a new 'masta,' and no one was going to spoil this fresh chance to fulfill their thwarted wishes and dreams. We were of their past—not their future—so for the moment, best forgotten.

This was a terrible way to say good-by. Embarrassed, we turned toward the airstrip and walked slowly away.

EPILOGUE

In 1982 – ten years after we said good-by – I returned to Papua New Guinea alone. Although I was anxious to learn what had happened in Taute during my absence, this visit would not be the open-ended field work adventure of before. I "knew" the Wape and the Wape "knew" me. Even though important aspects of our lives might have changed, we could never be strangers again.

It would be a short stay as my visa was only for a month. One week would be taken for entering and leaving the country and checking out changes in the coastal towns and another week was budgeted to visit the Lujere people on the Yellow River with whom I had lived after leaving the Wape. That left me only two weeks to be in Taute village.

The Tautes welcomed me warmly. A couple of the men kidded me about my thinning hair then smilingly pointed to their own balding pates. Everyone was concerned that I had returned without Joyce, Ned and Elizabeth. When I showed them pictures of the children, they were pleased to see how big they had grown, then, as I wandered through the village, pointed out to me their own teenage children whom I had known as toddlers. Just as before, small children unfamiliar with whitemen crowded around me to gently touch my bare blond legs and arms.

During my first visit to Taute, I infrequently entered a Taute home and never had eaten in one. Dining was private and the home a bastion to be shared only with close relatives. But this time, perhaps because I was a returning friend and alone, both Kuruwai and Weitauwa invited me to eat with their families. Weitauwa's wife had died and he had married Pauwis who, after Epilo's death, I had assumed would never marry. She greeted me with a shy smile and I was pleased to know how wrong I had been.

Returning to Taute was not easy for me. I am not the kind of person who derives a special pleasure in going back to situations that I have closed and left; I tend to relish the present and future. Also, during that year and a half in Taute, neither the villagers nor I had always had an easy time. It had been a deeply moving experience with much joy but also considerable pathos and sadness. Now, just walking through the village filled me with an uneasy nostalgia so I threw myself into work assessing the changes and trying to fill the gaps, often monumental ones, in my original data.

The village seemed quieter and the Western shorts and skirts of the villagers fresher looking than I had remembered. But in most ways the look and feel of the village was very much as before. The tempo of events, the style of interaction, the aroma of smoking fires, the houses, gardens, and muddy paths were completely familiar. Still, it was *not* the same village. The children I had known not only had grown but, during my absence, twenty-one of the villagers had died. All of the older men and women were dead as were a number of the younger people like Auwe and Weti with whom I had been close.

That was one of the strangest and most unsettling aspects of my returning; not to know before I arrived who would be alive or dead. During the intervening years, I had rarely received any news from the village. The missionaries who knew the village and with whom I still kept in touch, had long ago returned home or moved to other posts. The villagers themselves had no extra money for stamps and stationary and the few times I did hear, it was a request of some kind with no appended village news.

After completing a new village census I discovered that Taute's population was slightly smaller than before. This was not so much because of the intervening deaths — babies also had been born — but because several of the families had moved out of Wapeland to find work on the coast. During my first field work, there already was serious depopulation in some of the villages north of Lumi in longer and closer contact with the missions and government. Now it was beginning to happen in Taute.

Because of the many deaths believed to be caused by Taute ghosts and demons, some of the men in Mifu hamlet had moved their families to two new small hamlets along the ridge where they thought they might be safer. Kumoi, however, remained in Mifu and was now an important senior man. He was as enthusiastic and conversant as ever but during my stay became very ill. So Kuruwai, strong, soft spoken and always helpful, was my main informant.

As Mifu hamlet had shrunk in size, Obuenga had grown, but Kafiere, where we had lived, looked much the same except that our house had been dismantled and its beams and posts used in the building of others. After a cold, damp night, people still came to the plaza on sunny mornings to sit with their backs to the warming rays and, in the late afternoon, the mournful call of an impatient baby-sitting husband still echoed through the forest to his wife working sago by the river. There were, however, several small structures in the village with padlocks on their doors that I did not recognize. These, I was told, were 'kantins' or stores owned by individual men who stocked a few commodities like rice and matches. Although the stores usually were open only on request and often out of supplies, they were a definite innovation marking the beginning of modern commerce within the village itself.

'Satu' remained an important diversion for the men and still functioned to rapidly redistribute money that found its way into Wapeland. The indigenous ceremonial exchange system also was still strongly in force and I heard the same complaints about stingy men who tried to hold on to their wealth and the bemoaning of others who owed gifts to their *fafs*. Taute village and the Wape generally were still an egalitarian society and, just as before, aside from the police and government officials – now all Papua New Guineans – no man could command another except on the basis of an acknowledged kinship tie.

Although some of the villagers like Kumoi had a clearer understanding of Catholic dogma than before, their own religious beliefs were as important as ever. The first local diagnosis Kumoi gave me for his illness was that he probably had been attacked by the ghost of a friend's dead twin son when he recently had eaten at his friend's house. When the illness persisted, Kumoi invited two men from distant Kwieftim village who were visiting Lumi to come and treat him. They magically mended broken bones in his chest but his condition only worsened. At the time I left Taute, Kumoi, still very sick, suggested it might be *wene*, one of the local 'masalai,' causing his illness.

Another time when I was with Kuruwai, Maiane and his wife came with their very sick baby to be exorcised because they believed one of Kuruwai's ancestors had caused the illness. Kuruwai exhorted his ancestor to leave the baby, then Maiane and his wife continued to Lumi where the baby also would be treated at the hospital. The villagers' attitude toward modern medical treatment and etiology seemed unchanged. While modern medicine might be utilized, it was still witches and malevolent spirits who were blamed for most illnesses and any effective cure must center upon them. This meant that the staging of curing festivals was still a major concern and that the descent and kinship systems around which these were organized, were intact. During my brief stay there was a large *niyl* festival in nearby Yebil village that a number of Tautes and I attended.

Just as some of the men had a deeper appreciation of Catholicism, I also noticed a deeper understanding and concern about the government. Before, the Tautes had little interest or knowledge about the governmental forces that at times acted upon them so decisively. Now, however, most villagers clearly appreciated that Papua New Guinea had become an independent country. Their knowledge did not just stop at Lumi, but extended to the provincial government in Vanimo and the national government in Port Moresby.

The villagers were proud that Papua New Guineans ran the government, but some regretted the departure of the majority of whites and wished that they would return with new opportunities for lucrative jobs. The Tautes, like most Wape, remained subsistence farmers with few opportunities to earn money for the packaged foods, radios, and other commodities sold in Lumi and the coastal towns. Heavy beer drinking, a scourge in some New Guinea areas, was a luxury they could not afford. Lumi store prices, as in 1972, were high because there was no dependable truck transportation from the coast and plane transport was expensive. While the road was improved, some of the tribal groups over whose lands the road crossed were angry about the lack of governmental compensation and frequently threatened the drivers with road blocks and verbal abuse.

In almost every way, Taute village seemed fundamentally unchanged. Time had not stood still, but there were no major technological changes like a road or electric lines running through the village with the power to transform village life. Taute, like many other villages of the West Sepik Province, remained physically separate from most of the world and approachable only on foot.

There was, however, a significant new institution on the ridge a short walk from the village that may, if it endures, eventually have a transforming impact on the life of the villagers. Taute now has a school. During my absence, the villages of Taute, Wilkili, Lau'um and Boru'um with the backing of the Catholic mission convinced the government that they should have their own elementary school; that it was too much to ask of their children to be sent to Lumi as boarding students. Neither the children nor the parents liked it. That was why only one Taute child had attended during my first visit.

The new community school consisted of several classrooms and teacher's houses made mostly of bush materials, and was situated on the path to Lau'um. Of the seventy-five students in grades one through five, the majority — fifty-nine percent — were from Taute and that explained why the village was so quiet during the day. The children who would have been playing on the plaza or hanging around my 'ofis' were now in school studying. Because the school was the most interesting new facet of Taute life, I decided to live there, especially after John and Kim Smith, a young American Peace Corps couple stationed at the school on an agricultural project, arranged for me to stay in an unused teacher's house. Kuruwai helped me settle in and, except for the low pole beams that cracked my head almost daily the two weeks I was there, I was comfortable enough.

Job, one of the teachers and a Wape, had delighted me saying he had read *The Bamboo Fire*. Another day when I was walking into Lumi alone, a very alert young school boy from a village near Lumi stopped and asked in English who I was. To my astonishment he replied with a grin, "I've read your book!" While technological advances in Wapeland remained almost nonexistent, there was no question that modern education was having an impact. Learning to read, write and speak English was opening up vast new intellectual and occupational opportunities for the more successful students.

It was not, however, necessarily perceived as education for the sheer joy of knowing. Most parents were quick to see the economic advantages of modern schooling. One father explained to me that parents work hard to find the money to pay the school tuition because when the child eventually gets a good job, money will be sent home. Sometimes even a child's *fafs* contributed to the tuition guaranteeing themselves a later return on their investment.

Modern education, however, like almost everything else new in Wapeland, had been co-opted into the traditional exchange system. For this reason, as Job explained to me, Wape teachers generally prefer to teach in other parts of the country. When far away, relatives have fewer opportunities to deplete a teacher's resources.

Taute did have a school but, like others similarly isolated, it was beset by many problems. Teachers' housing was inadequate and some teachers were frequently absent from the classroom. There was no provision for substitutes so Kim and John often found themselves teaching classes just because they were there and cared. Students too were sometimes capricious about attendance and school supplies were woefully inadequate. Also there was the glaring question of what was this education for? Did it make the students into more productive slash and burn cultivators? Would it really prepare them for satisfying and well-paying jobs? What was its purpose?

As transient Peace Corps volunteers, John and Kim were assiduously addressing the first question with their demonstration school garden while the more ambitious students were motivated in their class work by the chance to find a job with a decent income. Yet few would have that opportunity. In 1982, the school had not yet produced a graduating class but when it did, the tuition costs at the Lumi High School would preclude many from attending. Without advanced training their formal education would be an economic dead end.

While not yet a concern in Taute, the problem of "school-leavers" was troubling communities throughout Papua New Guinea. There was no way to bring modern education to the local populations without raising aspirations, yet the developing economy of the new nation could not provide sufficient jobs to those "school-leavers" whose level of education was inadequate. In all parts of the country there were male students who had dropped out and others who had flunked out. Those dissatisfied with village life then moved to the rapidly expanding towns in hope of finding work. Organized into groups, some of these young men roamed the towns at night breaking into prosperous homes, stoning automobiles, robbing passers-by and raping women. They were derisively referred to by the locals as "rascals" and, as their attacks were against both blacks and whites, the problem was recognized as one of class differences, not race.

During my 1970-72 field work, many Port Moresby homes had heavy wire screens over their windows to retard break-ins, but the downtown streets were still safe. This had changed when I returned to the capitol in 1982. When an old friend invited me to dinner at a restaurant a short walk from my hotel, I offered to meet him there, but he insisted on picking me up in his car. "You don't understand," he said, "It's the rascals. Port Moresby has changed."

Even in provincial Wewak I was warned not to walk alone at night. After a new community center was opened at Lumi station, its large tin roof was pelted repeatedly with rocks by local young men protesting that the movie being shown, in spite of a nominal admission price, was not free. After they repeated their protest, the movie program was dropped and the building was generally unused. It appeared that one was only truly safe in the villages.

Events were changing rapidly in many sectors of Papua New Guinea. It would, however, be disingenuous to over-emphasize the nation's "law and order" problem, at the expense of not acknowledging the country's tremendous educational and economic advancement in such a short time. "School-leavers" are a serious concern for the nation, but there are thousands of other students who have finished high school. Many young people also graduate each year from the national university and some continue graduate studies abroad. During my stay I met them in banks, schools, stores and offices where, a few years before, most of the important jobs were held by whites. These were the men and women who were creating and shaping the new nation.

Regardless of how far Taute village might be from the center of political and economic power and how unclear its future, one thing was certain: there was a spirit in the village that I had not discerned before. The people felt connected to a unity bigger than the village, bigger than Wapeland itself. The era of colonialism was over. Papua New Guinea was a sovereign power with its ambassadors scattered around the world.

My visit to Taute had ended and I walked through the village stopping at each house to say my goodbyes. My work was not finished – it never would be – and perhaps I might be able to return again. In Kafiere hamlet, Namgeti and Kuruwai's wife, Youki, cried as I shook their hands. Nevertheless, it was a much happier farewell than my first. The villagers were pleased that I had returned from so far and I was glad that I had come. Then Yinge, one of Ned's and Elizabeth's favorite playmates and now a young man, gallantly escorted me to the edge of the hamlet as children circled us shouting and laughing. I was fine until I stopped down the trail and turned toward the village for a final look. Gripped by a sudden poignancy, I waved one last good-bye.

What is it, then, that motivates an anthropologist to do ethnographic field work, to leave the comforts of one's own society and friends to live for months or years among strangers? Can he or she really discover the "truth" about a society that may be fundamentally different from one's own? Even if one should succeed, of what value are the published findings to others including the people themselves?

These are not simple questions and there is no unanimity among anthropologists as to how they should be answered. I can, however, suggest some partial replies. Although there is a small minority of anthropologists who have never done any field work, it is partly the fact that field work *is* expected of anthropologists that draws creative and energetic young men and women into the profession. Ethnographic field work, as I have tried to show in this book, is an intellectual and physical adventure with risks and excitement of a very special type that is not for everyone. As any traveler knows, it is one thing to discover excitement in the exotic landscapes and cultures of other societies, but it would be quite something else to settle down in one of them and figure out what is really going on. After almost unconsciously learning one's own culture as a growing child, the field situation demands that the anthropologist learn through studious and protracted labor the ideas and ways of a society that, most likely, is completely foreign to her or him. Knowledge about the society's language, groups, technology and belief systems, is just the beginning of what must be mastered. So the field working anthropologist needs to be someone who is intellectually challenged by moving into a strange society and digging into the surrounding complexity. It takes personal tact, grace under pressure, considerable patience and, because cultural knowledge comes slowly and in bits and pieces, an extraordinary tolerance for ambiguity.

What about the scholarly products that result from these excursions into the field? With so many uncontrolled variables in the field work situation, can the anthropologist really get at the "truth" about a society? Is this book, for example, a truthful presentation of what occurred while I was in New Guinea or only an abstracted fiction? Do we really understand the nature of the relationship between the field work experience itself and the emergent published products? These kinds of searching epistemological questions about ethnographic research are a serious concern in contemporary anthropology.

The field work experience in and of itself, of course, is non-reproducible. A by-gone reality cannot be resurrected *in toto*; its presence as a past phenomenon, as historians have long known, can only be indicated. Even a film of a two-minute exorcism rite is highly selective in what it records as the field worker is restricted, for example, by the angle, width, height and direction of the lens.

The problem becomes infinitely more complex when the anthropologist writes a report or book based on an analysis of her or his research corpus of, for example, field notes, tape recordings, photographs, films, and memories, often accumulated over a period of years. These "raw" data or "first level abstractions" of the actual experience are then reviewed and "shaped" through various conscious and unconscious mediums including the anthropologist's particular theoretical stance and publishing objectives, his or her creative imagination and intellect, discussions with others, and situationally by the time and place where the analysis and writing is carried out. As a "secondary level abstraction," the published book is obviously a highly mediated product far removed from the actual field work experience. It is not, however, a "fictional invention," as some current theorists about the production of ethnographic accounts might have it, but consists of "interpretations" and "findings" rooted in a corpus of richly detailed field work data. In this sense, even though an account may contain errors of fact or interpretation, it is an authentic version of what happened and, therefore, *truthful* if not the "truth." No ethnographic account can ever be more than that. When considered in a broader context, the account itself is an artifact or product of a culturally circumscribed theory of knowledge that disallows final truths and our society calls "scientific."

What is the worth of these ethnographic accounts? Do they have any value over and above that of a version of what someone thought some people were doing and thinking at a particular place and time in history? What do they tell us about humanity, about ourselves?

One important thing ethnographic accounts have taught us is about the tremendous behavioral and cognitive plasticity and variability of our species, *Homo sapiens*. By documenting a multitude of arrangements for living, ethnographic accounts have had a liberalizing effect on modern society. Once one has delved into a series of ethnographies and shared the field worker's intimate understanding of what is going on, it is difficult to persist in viewing other societies with the blindness of the ethnocentric zealot. While we may still prefer our own culture, other societies no longer look "crazy;" there is a demonstrable internal organization and rationale about how and why people behave as they do. Similarly, the ethnographic accounts of anthropologists also have had an impact on the behavioral sciences and humanities. Instead of. scholars being locked into their own ethnocentrism, anthropology's rich crosscultural record has opened other disciplines to thinking and generalizing about humanity in terms of its complex cultural heterogeneity.

But I have said nothing about the people in these field work ventures, i.e., the people into whose lives we interject ourselves. Do they receive any tangible benefits from our benevolent intrusions? What's in it for them?

Certainly some people appreciate, for example, the money and gifts we bring with us, our attempts at first aid in those areas without modern medicine, and even the novelty of our presence in an otherwise predictable day. But these attributes hardly compensate for the intrusive nuisance the field worker sometimes becomes. There are, however, more lasting benefits resulting from the encounter with the field worker. Many anthropologists have intervened on behalf of the people with whom they worked, sometimes years after their field work was completed. Their expert knowledge of the society and its culture as well as familiarity with the external governing powers, puts them in an excellent position to facilitate the people's requests or disputes vis-a-vis governmental agencies and other organizations.

Lastly, there is the contribution of the published books, articles, films, recordings and other field work products that become part of a peoples historical legacy. As societies evolve or drastically change through time, these may be the only record about how things used to be. More than one American Indian community radically transformed by the government's military conquest of their lands and the resulting decimation and forced migration of their ancestors, has gratefully turned to the old reports of long dead anthropologists to gain some understanding and appreciation of how their forefathers and mothers once lived.

As the vestiges of 19th century colonial empires continue to fade away, the Third World — where much of ethnographic field work has been done — is continuing its often painful transformation from a group of exploited colonial dependencies into independent nations, each with its own intellectual, economic and political base. The so-called "primitive" peoples — those people rich in culture but devoid of writing — are almost gone from the face of the earth. But cultural anthropology always has been more than simply the study of "exotic" peoples in faraway places. It's domain is humanity itself in all of its cultural manifestations. Today one may find ethnographic field workers in our own society studying, for example, an urban ethnic community, a factory, a hospital ward, or a retirement home. As long as people exist on earth in an open society that values scientific knowledge, there probably always will be those curious "others" — the anthropologist — wondering how the people over the next hill live, then going to stay with them to discover how and why they do what they do.

SELECTED BIBLIOGRAPHY

Anthropological Field Work and Ethnography

Berreman, Gerald
  1962   *Behind Many Masks: Ethnography and Impression Management in a Himalayan Village.* Ithaca: Society for Applied Anthropology Monograph No. 4.
Casagrande, Joseph, ed.
  1960   *In the Company of Man: Twenty Portraits of Anthropological Informants.* New York: Harper and Brothers.
Clifford, James and George E. Marcus, eds.
  1986   *Writing Culture: The Poetics and Politics of Ethnography.* Berkeley: University of California Press.
Crane, Julia G. and Michael V. Angrosino
  1984   *Field Projects in Anthropology: A Student Handbook, Second Edition.* Prospect Heights: Waveland Press.
Marcus, George E. and Michael M.J. Fischer
  1986   "Ethnography and Interpretive Anthropology." Chapter Two in *Anthropology as Cultural Critique.* Chicago: University of Chicago Press.
Malinowski, Bronislaw
  1967   *A Diary in the Strict Sense of the Term.* London: Routledge and Kegan Paul.
Mead, Margaret
  1977   *Letters from the Field 1925-1975.* New York: Harper and Row.

Mitchell, William E.
 i.p. "A Goy in the Ghetto: Gentile-Jewish Communication in Field Work Research." In *Between Two Worlds: Essays on the Ethnography of American Jewry*, ed. Jack Kugelmass. Ithaca: Cornell University Press.
Naroll, Raoul and Ronald Cohen, eds.
 1973 *A Handbook of Method in Cultural Anthropology*. New York: Columbia University Press.
Pelto, Pertti J. and Gretel H. Pelto
 1973 "Ethnography: The Fieldwork Enterprise." In *Handbook of Social and Cultural Anthropology*, ed. John J. Honigmann. Chicago: Rand McNally.
Rabinow, Paul
 1977 *Reflections on Fieldwork in Morocco*. Berkeley: University of California Press.
Read, Kenneth E.
 1965 *The High Valley*. New York: Charles Scribner's Sons.
Ruby, Jay, ed.
 1982 *A Crack in the Mirror: Reflexive Perspectives in Anthropology*. Philadelphia: University of Pennsylvania Press.
Rynkiewich, Michael A. and James P. Spradley
 1976 *Ethics and Anthropology: Dilemmas in Fieldwork*. New York: John Wiley & Sons.
Stocking, George W., Jr., ed.
 1983 *Observers Observed: Essays on Ethnographic Fieldwork*. Madison: University of Wisconsin Press.

The Wape of Papua New Guinea

Bau., G.P.
 1956 *I Kanaka di Wapi: Usi Costume e Religione*. Padova: Missioni Francescane.
Gillam, Elizabeth A.
 1973 "Beliefs of the Wape People about Conception, Childbirth and Early Child Care." *Tropical Doctor* 3:85-87.
McGregor, Donald E.
 1982 *The Fish and the Cross*. Goroko: The Melanesian Institute.
McGregor, Donald E. and Aileen R.F. McGregor
 1982 *Olo Language Materials*. Canberra: Australian National University (Pacific Linguistics, Series D, No. 42).

Mitchell, Joyce S.
    1973   "Life and Birth in New Guinea." *Ms. Magazine* 1:20-23.
Mitchell, William E.
    1973   "A New Weapon Stirs up Old Ghosts." *Natural History* 82:74-84.
    1978   *The Living, Dead and Dying: Music of the New Guinea Wape.* Folkways Record Album No. FE 4269 (with notes).
    1979   "On Keeping Equal: Polity and Reciprocity among the New Guinea Wape." *Anthropological Quarterly* 51:5-15.
    i.p.   "The Intrinsic and Extrinsic Therapeutic Systems of the Taute Wape." In *Sepik Heritage: Tradition and Change in Papua New Guinea,* eds. N. Lutkehaus et al. Durham: Carolina Academic Press.
Wark, Lynette and L.A. Malcolm
    1969   "Growth and Development of the Lumi Child in the Sepik District of New Guinea." *Medical Journal of Australia* 2:129-136.